Analysis of Algorithms: An Active Learning Approach

Jeffrey J. McConnell
Canisius College

JONES AND BARTLETT PUBLISHERS
Sudbury, Massachusetts
BOSTON   TORONTO   LONDON   SINGAPORE

World Headquarters
Jones and Bartlett Publishers
40 Tall Pine Drive
Sudbury, MA 01776
978-443-5000
info@jbpub.com
www.jbpub.com

Jones and Bartlett Publishers
Canada
2406 Nikanna Road
Mississauga, ON L5C 2W6
CANADA

Jones and Bartlett Publishers
International
Barb House, Barb Mews
London W6 7PA
UK

ISBN: 0-7637-1634-0

Production Credits

Chief Executive Officer: Clayton Jones
Chief Operating Officer: Don W. Jones, Jr.
Executive Vice President and Publisher: Tom Manning
V.P., Managing Editor: Judith H. Hauck
V.P., Design and Production: Anne Spencer
V.P., Manufacturing and Inventory Control: Therese Bräuer
Senior Acquisitions Editor: Michael Stranz
Development and Product Manager: Amy Rose
Production Assistant: Tara McCormick
Assistant Marketing Manager: Nathan Schultz
Composition: Northeast Compositors, Inc.
Production Coordination: Trillium Project Management
Text Design: Mary McKeon
Cover Design: ko Design Studio
Printing and Binding: Courier Westford
Cover printing: John Pow Company

Library of Congress Cataloging-in-Publication Data

McConnell, Jeffrey J.
    The analysis of algorithms: an active learning approach / Jeffrey J. McConnell.
      p. cm.
    Includes bibliographical references and index.
    ISBN 0-7637-1634-0
      1. Computer algorithms. I. Title.
  QA76.9.A43 M38 2001
  005.1—dc21   00-067853

This book was typeset in FrameMaker 5.5 on a Macintosh G4. The font families used were Bembo, Helvetica Neue, Trajan, and Courier. The first printing was printed on 50# Decision 94 Opaque.

Printed in the United States of America
05 04 03 02 01   10 9 8 7 6 5 4 3 2 1

To Fred and Barney

The two major goals of this book are to raise awareness of the impact that algorithms can have on the efficiency of a program and to develop the skills necessary to analyze any algorithms that are used in programs. In looking at many commercial products today, it appears that some software designers are unconcerned about space and time efficiency. If a program takes too much space, they expect that the user will buy more memory. If a program takes too long, they expect that the user will buy a faster computer.

There are limits, however, on how fast computers can ever become because there are limits on how fast electrons can travel down "wires," how fast light can travel along fiber optic cables, and how fast the circuits that do the calculations can switch. There are other limits on computation that go beyond the speed of the computer and are directly related to the complexity of the problems being solved. There are some problems for which the fastest algorithm known will not complete execution in our lifetime. Since these are important problems, algorithms are needed that provide approximate answers.

In the early 1980s, computer architecture severely limited the amount of speed and space on a computer. Some computers of that time frequently limited programs and their data to 64K of memory, where today's personal computers regularly come equipped with more than 1,000 times that amount. Though today's software is much more complex than that in the 1980s and today's computers are much more capable, these changes do not mean we can ignore efficiency in our program design. Some project specifications will include time and space limitations on the final software that may force programmers to look for places to save memory and increase speed. The compact size of personal digital assistants (PDAs) also limits the size and speed of software.

Pedagogy

What I hear, I forget.
What I see, I remember.
What I do, I understand.
—*Confucius*

The material in this book is presented with the expectation that it can be read independently or used as part of a course that incorporates an active and cooperative learning methodology. To accomplish this, the chapters are clear and complete so as to be easy to understand and to encourage readers to prepare by reading before group meetings. All chapters include study suggestions. Many include additional data sets that the reader can use to hand-execute the algorithms for increased understanding of them. The results of the algorithms applied to this additional data are presented in Appendix C. Each section has a number of exercises that include simple tracing of the algorithm to more complex proof-based exercises. The reader should be able to work the exercises in each chapter. They can, in connection with a course, be assigned as homework or can be used as in-class assignments for students to work individually or in small groups. An instructor's manual that provides background on how to teach this material using active and cooperative learning as well as giving exercise solutions is available. Chapters 2, 3, 5, 6, and 9 include programming exercises. These programming projects encourage readers to implement and test the algorithms from the chapter, and then compare actual algorithm results with the theoretical analysis in the book.

Active learning is based on the premise that people learn better and retain information longer when they are participants in the learning process. To achieve that, students must be given the opportunity to do more that just listen to the professor during class. This can best be accomplished in an analysis of algorithms course by the professor giving a short introductory lecture on the material, and then having students work problems while the instructor circulates around the room answering questions that this application of the material raises.

Cooperative work gives students an opportunity to answer simple questions that others in their group have and allows the professor to deal with bigger questions that have stumped an entire group. In this way, students have a greater opportunity to ask questions and have their concerns addressed in a timely manner. It is important that the professor observe group work to make sure that group-wide misconceptions are not reinforced. An additional way for the professor to identify and correct misunderstandings is to have groups regularly submit exercise answers for comments or grading.

To support student preparation and learning, each chapter includes the prerequisites needed, and the goals or skills that students should have on completion, as well as suggestions for studying the material.

Algorithms

Since the analysis of algorithms is independent of the computer or programming language used, algorithms are given in pseudo-code. These algorithms are readily understandable by anyone who knows the concepts of conditional statements (for example, IF and CASE/SWITCH), loops (for example, FOR and WHILE), and recursion.

Course Use

One way that this material could be covered in a one-semester course is by using the following approximate schedule:

Chapter 1	2 weeks
Chapter 2	1 week
Chapter 3	2 weeks
Chapter 4	1 week
Chapter 5	1 week
Chapter 6	2 weeks
Chapter 7	2 weeks
Chapter 8	1 week
Chapter 9	2 weeks

Chapters 2, 4, and 5 are not likely to need a full week, which will provide time for an introduction to the course, an explanation of the active and cooperative learning pedagogy, and hour examinations. Depending on the background of the students, Chapter 1 may be covered more quickly as well.

Acknowledgements

I would like to acknowledge all those who helped in the development of this book. First, I would like to thank the students in my "Automata and Algorithms" course (Spring 1997, Spring 1998, Spring 1999, Spring 2000, and Fall 2000) for all of their comments on earlier versions of this material.

The reviews that Jones and Bartlett Publishers obtained about the manuscript were most helpful and produced some good additions and clarifications. I would like to thank Douglas Campbell (Brigham Young University), Nancy Kinnersley (University of Kansas), and Kirk Pruhs (University of Pittsburgh) for their reviews.

At Jones and Bartlett, I would like to thank my editors Amy Rose and Michael Stranz, and production assistant Tara McCormick for their support of this book. I am especially grateful to Amy for remembering a brief conversation about this project from a few years ago. Her memory and efforts are appreciated very much. I would also like to thank Nancy Young for her copyediting and Brooke Albright for her proofreading. Any errors that remain are solely the author's responsibility.

Lastly, I am grateful to Fred Dansereau for his support and suggestions during the many stages of this book, and to Barney for the wonderful diversions that only a dog can provide.

CONTENTS

Chapter 7   Parallel Algorithms   177

CHAPTER 1

Analysis Basics

PREREQUISITES

Before beginning this chapter, you should be able to

- Read and create algorithms
- Read and create recursive algorithms
- Identify comparison and arithmetic operations
- Use basic algebra

GOALS

At the end of this chapter you should be able to

- Describe how to analyze an algorithm
- Explain how to choose the operations that are counted and why others are not
- Explain how to do a best-case, worst-case, and average-case analysis
- Work with logarithms, probabilities, and summations
- Describe $\theta(f), \Omega(f), O(f)$, growth rate, and algorithm order
- Use a decision tree to determine a lower bound on complexity
- Convert a simple recurrence relation into its closed form

STUDY SUGGESTIONS

As you are working through the chapter, you should rework the examples to make sure you understand them. Additionally, you should try to answer any questions before reading on. A hint or the answer to the question is in the sentences following it.

There are many algorithms that can solve a given problem. They will have different characteristics that will determine how efficiently each will operate. When we analyze an algorithm, we first have to show that the algorithm does properly solve the problem because if it doesn't, its efficiency is not important. Next, we look at how efficiently it solves the problem. This chapter sets the groundwork for the analysis and comparison of more complex algorithms.

Analyzing an algorithm determines the amount of "time" that algorithm takes to execute. This is not really a number of seconds or any other clock measurement but rather an approximation of the number of operations that an algorithm performs. The number of operations is related to the execution time, so we will sometimes use the word *time* to describe an algorithm's computational complexity. The actual number of seconds it takes an algorithm to execute on a computer is not useful in our analysis because we are concerned with the relative efficiency of algorithms that solve a particular problem. You should also see that the actual execution time is not a good measure of algorithm efficiency because an algorithm does not get "better" just because we move it to a faster computer or "worse" because we move it to a slower one.

The actual number of operations done for some specific size of input data set is not very interesting nor does it tell us very much. Instead, our analysis will determine an equation that relates the number of operations that a particular algorithm does to the size of the input. We can then compare two algorithms by comparing the rate at which their equations grow. The growth rate is critical because there are instances where algorithm A may take fewer operations than algorithm B when the input size is small, but many more when the input size gets large.

In a very general sense, algorithms can be classified as either repetitive or recursive. Repetitive algorithms have loops and conditional statements as their basis, and so their analysis will entail determining the work done in the loop and how many times the loop executes. Recursive algorithms solve a large problem by breaking it into pieces and then applying the algorithm to each of the pieces. These are sometimes called divide and conquer algorithms and provide a great deal of power in solving problems. The process of solving a large problem by breaking it up into smaller pieces can produce an algorithm that is small, straightforward, and simple to understand. Analyzing a recursive algorithm will entail determining the amount of work done to produce the smaller pieces and then putting their individual solutions together to get the solution to the whole problem. Combining this information with the number of the smaller pieces and their sizes, we can produce a recurrence relation for the algorithm. This recurrence relation can then be converted into a closed form that can be compared with other equations.

We begin this chapter by describing what analysis is and why we do it. We then look at what operations will be considered and what categories of analysis we will do. Because mathematics is critical to our analysis, the next few sections explore the important mathematical concepts and properties used to analyze iterative and recursive algorithms.

1.1   WHAT IS ANALYSIS?

The analysis of an algorithm provides background information that gives us a general idea of how long an algorithm will take for a given problem set. For each algorithm considered, we will come up with an estimate of how long it will take to solve a problem that has a set of N input values. So, for example, we might determine how many comparisons a sorting algorithm does to put a list of N values into ascending order, or we might determine how many arithmetic operations it takes to multiply two matrices of size $N \times N$.

There are a number of algorithms that will solve a problem. Studying the analysis of algorithms gives us the tools to choose between algorithms. For example, consider the following two algorithms to find the largest of four values:

```
largest = a
if b > largest then
    largest = b
end if
if c > largest then
    largest = c
end if
if d > largest then
    largest = d
end if
return largest
```

```
if a > b then
   if a > c then
      if a > d then
         return a
      else
         return d
      end if
   else
      if c > d then
         return c
      else
         return d
      end if
   end if
else
   if b > c then
      if b > d then
         return b
      else
         return d
      end if
   else
      if c > d then
         return c
      else
         return d
      end if
   end if
end if
```

If you examine these two algorithms, you will see that each one will do exactly three comparisons to find the answer. Even though the first is easier for us to read and understand, they are both of the same level of complexity for a computer to execute. In terms of time, these two algorithms are the same, but in terms of space, the first needs more because of the temporary variable called largest. This extra space is not significant if we are comparing numbers or characters, but it may be with other types of data. In many modern programming languages, we can define comparison operators for large and complex objects or records. For those cases, the amount of space needed for the temporary variable could be quite significant. When we are interested in the efficiency of algorithms, we will primarily be concerned with time issues, but when space may be an issue, it will also be discussed.

The purpose of determining these values is to then use them to compare how efficiently two different algorithms solve a problem. For this reason, we will never compare a sorting algorithm with a matrix multiplication algorithm, but rather we will compare two different sorting algorithms to each other.

The purpose of analysis of algorithms is not to give a formula that will tell us exactly how many seconds or computer cycles a particular algorithm will take. This is not useful information because we would then need to talk about the type of computer, whether it has one or many users at a time, what processor it has, how fast its clock is, whether it has a complex or reduced instruction set processor chip, and how well the compiler optimizes the executable code. All of those will have an impact on how fast a program for an algorithm will run. To talk about analysis in those terms would mean that by moving a program to a faster computer, the algorithm would become better because it now completes its job faster. That's not true, so, we do our analysis without regard to any specific computer.

In the case of a small or simple routine it might be possible to count the exact number of operations performed as a function of N. Most of the time, however, this will not be useful. In fact, we will see in Section 1.4 that the difference between an algorithm that does $N + 5$ operations and one that does $N + 250$ operations becomes meaningless as N gets very large. As an introduction to analysis of algorithms, however, we will count the exact number of operations for this first section.

Another reason we do not try to count every operation that is performed by an algorithm is that we could fine-tune an algorithm extensively but not really make much of a difference in its overall performance. For instance, let's say that we have an algorithm that counts the number of different characters in a file. An algorithm for that might look like the following:

```
for all 256 characters do
   assign zero to the counter
end for
while there are more characters in the file do
   get the next character
   increment the counter for this character by one
end while
```

When we look at this algorithm, we see that there are 256 passes for the initialization loop. If there are N characters in the input file, there are N passes for the second loop. So the question becomes What do we count? In a `for` loop, we have the initialization of the loop variable and then for each pass of the loop, a check that the loop variable is within the bounds, the execution of the loop, and the increment of the loop variable. This means that the initialization loop does a set of 257 assignments (1 for the loop variable and 256 for the counters), 256 increments of the loop variable, and 257 checks that this variable is within the loop bounds (the extra one is when the loop stops). For the second loop, we will need to do a check of the condition $N + 1$ times (the $+ 1$ is for the last check when the file is empty), and we will increment N counters. The total number of operations is

Increments	$N + 256$
Assignments	257
Conditional checks	$N + 258$

So, if we have 500 characters in the file, the algorithm will do a total of 1771 operations, of which 770 are associated with the initialization (43%). Now consider what happens as the value of N gets large. If we have a file with 50,000 characters, the algorithm will do a total of 100,771 operations, of which there are still only 770 associated with the initialization (less than 1% of the total work). The number of initialization operations has not changed, but they become a much smaller percentage of the total as N increases.

Let's look at this another way. Computer organization information shows that copying large blocks of data is as quick as an assignment. We could initialize the first 16 counters to zero and then copy this block 15 times to fill in the rest of the counters. This would mean a reduction in the initialization pass down to 33 conditional checks, 33 assignments, and 31 increments. This reduces the initialization operations to 97 from 770, a saving of 87%. When we consider this relative to the work of processing the file of 50,000 characters, we have saved less than 0.7% (100,098 vs. 100,771). Notice we could save even more time if we did all of these initializations without loops, because only 31 pure assignments would be needed, but this would only save an additional 0.07%. It's not worth the effort.

We see that the importance of the initialization is small relative to the overall execution of this algorithm. In analysis terms, the cost of the initialization becomes meaningless as the number of input values increases.

The earliest work in analysis of algorithms determined the computability of an algorithm on a Turing machine. The analysis would count the number of times that the transition function needed to be applied to solve the problem. An analysis of the space needs of an algorithm would count how many cells of a Turing machine tape would be needed to solve the problem. This sort of analysis is a valid determination of the relative speed of two algorithms, but it is also time consuming and difficult. To do this sort of analysis, you would first need to determine the process used by the transition functions of the Turing machine that carries out the algorithm. Then you would need to determine how long it executes—a very tedious process.

An equally valid way to analyze an algorithm, and the one we will use, is to consider the algorithm as it is written in a higher-level language. This language can be Pascal, C, C++, Java, or a general pseudocode. The specifics don't really matter as long as the language can express the major control structures common to algorithms. This means that any language that has a looping mechanism, like a for or while, and a selection mechanism, like an if, case, or switch, will serve our needs. Because we will be concerned with just one algorithm at a time, we will rarely write more than a single function or code fragment, and so the power of many of the languages mentioned will not even come into play. For this reason, a generic pseudocode will be used in this book.

Some languages use short-circuit evaluation when determining the value of a Boolean expression. This means that in the expression A and B, the term B will only be evaluated if A is true, because if A is false, the result will be false no matter what B is. Likewise, for A or B, B will not be evaluated if A is true. As we will see, counting a compound expression as one or two comparisons will not be significant. So, once we are past the basics in this chapter, we will not worry about short-circuited evaluations.

■ 1.1.1 Input Classes

Input plays an important role in analyzing algorithms because it is the input that determines what the path of execution through an algorithm will be. For example, if we are interested in finding the largest value in a list of N numbers, we can use the following algorithm:

```
largest = list[1]
for i = 2 to N do
   if (list[i] > largest) then
      largest = list[i]
   end if
end for
```

We can see that if the list is in decreasing order, there will only be one assignment done before the loop starts. If the list is in increasing order, however, there will be N assignments (one before the loop starts and $N - 1$ inside the loop). Our analysis must consider more than one possible set of input, because if we only look at one set of input, it may be the set that is solved the fastest (or slowest). This will give us a false impression of the algorithm. Instead we consider all types of input sets.

When looking at the input, we will try to break up all the different input sets into classes based on how the algorithm behaves on each set. This helps to reduce the number of possibilities that we will need to consider. For example, if we use our largest-element algorithm with a list of 10 distinct numbers, there are 10!, or 3,628,800, different ways that those numbers could be arranged. We saw that if the largest is first, there is only one assignment done, so we can take the 362,880 input sets that have the largest value first and put them into one class. If the largest value is second, the algorithm will do exactly two assignments. There are another 362,880 inputs sets with the largest value second, and they can all be put into another class. When looking at this algorithm, we can see that there will be between one and N assignments. We would, therefore, create N different classes for the input sets based on the number of assignments done. As you will see, we will not necessarily care about listing or describing all of the input sets in each class, but we will need to know how many classes there are and how much work is done for each.

The number of possible inputs can get very large as N increases. For instance, if we are interested in a list of 10 distinct numbers, there are 3,628,800 different orderings of these 10 numbers. It would be impossible to look at all of these different possibilities. We instead break these possible lists into classes based on what the algorithm is going to do. For the above algorithm, the breakdown could be based on where the largest value is stored and would result in 10 different classes. For a different algorithm, for example, one that finds the largest and smallest values, our breakdown could be based on where the largest and smallest are stored and would result in 90 different classes. Once we have identified the classes, we can look at how an algorithm would behave on one input from each of the classes. If the classes are properly chosen, all input sets in the class will have the same number of operations, and all of the classes are likely to have different results.

■ 1.1.2 Space Complexity

Most of what we will be discussing is going to be how efficient various algorithms are in terms of time, but some forms of analysis could be done based on how much space an algorithm needs to complete its task. This space complexity analysis was critical in the early days of computing when storage space on a computer (both internal and external) was limited. When considering space complexity, algorithms are divided into those that need extra space to do their work and those that work in place. It was not unusual for programmers to choose an algorithm that was slower just because it worked in place, because there was not enough extra memory for a faster algorithm.

Computer memory was at a premium, so another form of space analysis would examine all of the data being stored to see if there were more efficient ways to store it. For example, suppose we are storing a real number that has only one place of precision after the decimal point and ranges between -10 and $+10$. If we store this as a real number, most computers will use between 4 and 8 bytes of memory, but if we first multiply the value by 10, we can then store this as an integer between -100 and $+100$. This needs only 1 byte, a savings of 3 to 7 bytes. A program that stores 1000 of these values can save 3000 to 7000 bytes. When you consider that computers as recently as the early 1980s might have only had 65,536 bytes of memory, these savings are significant. It is this need to save space on these computers along with the longevity of working computer programs that lead to all of the Y2K bug problems. When you have a program that works with a lot of dates, you use half the space for the year by storing it as 99 instead of 1999. Also, people writing programs in the 1980s and earlier never really expected their programs to still be in use in 2000.

Looking at software that is on the market today, it is easy to see that space analysis is not being done. Programs, even simple ones, regularly quote space needs in a number of megabytes. Software companies seem to feel that making their software space efficient is not a consideration because customers who don't have enough computer memory can just go out and buy another 32 megabytes (or more) of memory to run the program or a bigger hard disk to store it. This attitude drives computers into obsolescence long before they really are obsolete.

A recent change to this is the popularity of personal digital assistants (PDAs). These small handheld devices typically have between 2 and 8 megabytes for both their data and software. In this case, developing small programs that store data compactly is not only important, it is critical.

■ 1.1.3 EXERCISES

1. Write an algorithm in pseudocode to count the number of capital letters in a file of text. How many comparisons does it do? What is the fewest number of increments it might do? What is the largest number? (Use N for the number of characters in the file when writing your answer.)

2. There is a set of numbers stored in a file, but we don't know how many it contains. Write an algorithm in pseudocode to calculate the average of the numbers stored in this file. What type of operations does your algorithm do? How many of each of these operations does your algorithm do?

3. Write an algorithm, without using compound conditional expressions, that takes in three integers and determines if they are all distinct. On average, how many comparisons does your algorithm do? Remember to examine all input classes.

4. Write an algorithm that takes in three distinct integers and determines the largest of the three. What are the possible input classes that would have to be considered when analyzing this algorithm? Which one causes your algorithm to do the most comparisons? Which one causes the least? (If there is no difference between the most and least, rewrite the algorithm with simple conditionals and without using temporary variables so that the best case gets done faster than the worst case.)

5. Write an algorithm to find the second largest element in a list of N values. How many comparisons does your algorithm do in the worst case? (Later, we will see an algorithm that will do this with about N comparisons.)

1.2   WHAT TO COUNT AND CONSIDER

Deciding what to count involves two steps. The first is choosing the significant operation or operations, and the second is deciding which of those operations are integral to the algorithm and which are overhead or bookkeeping.

There are two classes of operations that are typically chosen for the significant operation: comparison or arithmetic. The comparison operators are all considered equivalent and are counted in algorithms such as searching and sorting. In these algorithms, the important task being done is the comparison of two values to determine, when searching, if the value is the one we are looking for or, when sorting, if the values are out of order. Comparison operations include equal, not equal, less than, greater than, less than or equal, and greater than or equal.

We will count arithmetic operators in two groups: additive and multiplicative. Additive operators (usually called *additions* for short) include addition, subtraction, increment, and decrement. Multiplicative operators (usually called *multiplications* for short) include multiplication, division, and modulus. These two groups are counted separately because multiplications are considered to take longer than additions. In fact, some algorithms are viewed more favorably if they reduce the number of multiplications even if that means a similar increase in the number of additions. In algorithms beyond the scope of this book, logarithms and geometric functions that are used in algorithms would be another group even more time consuming than multiplications because those are frequently calculated by a computer through a power series.

A special case is integer multiplication or division by a power of 2. This operation can be reduced to a shift operation, which is considered as fast as an addition. There will, however, be very few cases when this will be significant, because multiplication or division by 2 is commonly found in divide and conquer algorithms that frequently have comparison as their significant operation.

■ 1.2.1 Cases to Consider

Choosing what input to consider when analyzing an algorithm can have a significant impact on how an algorithm will perform. If the input list is already sorted, some sorting algorithms will perform very well, but other sorting algorithms may perform very poorly. The opposite may be true if the list is randomly arranged instead of sorted. Because of this, we will not consider just one input set when we analyze an algorithm. In fact, we will actually look for those input sets that allow an algorithm to perform the most quickly and the most slowly. We will also consider an overall average performance of the algorithm as well.

Best Case

As its name indicates, the best case for an algorithm is the input that requires the algorithm to take the shortest time. This input is the combination of values that causes the algorithm to do the least amount of work. If we are looking at a searching algorithm, the best case would be if the value we are searching for (commonly called the target or key) was the value stored in the first location that the search algorithm would check. This would then require only one comparison no matter how complex the algorithm is. Notice that for searching through a list of values, no matter how large, the best case will result in a constant time of 1. Because the best case for an algorithm will usually be a very small and frequently constant value, we will not do a best-case analysis very frequently.

Worst Case

Worst case is an important analysis because it gives us an idea of the most time an algorithm will ever take. Worst-case analysis requires that we identify the input values that cause an algorithm to do the most work. For searching algorithms, the worst case is one where the value is in the last place we check or is not in the list. This could involve comparing the key to each list value for a total of N comparisons. The worst case gives us an upper bound on how slowly parts of our programs may work based on our algorithm choices.

Average Case

Average-case analysis is the toughest to do because there are a lot of details involved. The basic process begins by determining the number of different groups into which all possible input sets can be divided. The second step is to determine the probability that the input will come from each of these groups. The third step is to determine how long the algorithm will run for each of these groups. All of the input in each group should take the same amount of time, and if they do not, the group must be split into two separate groups. When all of this has been done, the average case time is given by the following formula:

$$A(n) = \sum_{i=1}^{m} p_i * t_i \tag{1.1}$$

where n is the size of the input, m is the number of groups, p_i is the probability that the input will be from group i, and t_i is the time that the algorithm takes for input from group i.

In some cases, we will consider that each of the input groups has equal probabilities. In other words, if there are five input groups, the chance the input will be in group 1 is the same as the chance for group 2, and so on. This would mean that for these five groups all probabilities would be 0.2. We could calculate the average case by the above formula, or we could note that the following simplified formula is equivalent in the case where all groups are equally probable:

$$A(n) \; = \; \frac{1}{m} \sum_{i=1}^{m} t_i \qquad\qquad (1.2)$$

■ 1.2.2 EXERCISES

1. Write an algorithm that finds the middle, or median, value of three distinct integers. The input for this algorithm falls into six groups; describe them. What is the best case for your algorithm? What is the worst case? What is the average case? (If the best and worst cases are the same, rewrite your algorithm with simple conditionals and without temporary variables so the best case is better than the worst case.)

2. Write an algorithm that determines if four integers are distinct. Depending on your viewpoint, the input for this algorithm can be divided into classes based on the structure of your algorithm or the structure of the problem. Describe how one of these two class divisions would be set up. Using your classes, what is the best case for your algorithm? What is the worst case? What is the average case? (If the best and worst cases are the same, rewrite your algorithm with simple conditionals and without temporary variables so the best case is better than the worst case.)

3. Write an algorithm that determines, given a list of numbers and the average or mean of those numbers, if there are more numbers above the average than below. Describe the groups that the input would fall into for this algorithm. What is the best case for your algorithm? What is the worst case? What is the average case? (If the best and worst cases are the same, rewrite your algorithm so it stops as soon as it knows the answer, making the best case better than the worst case.)

1.3   MATHEMATICAL BACKGROUND

There are a few mathematical concepts that will be used through out this book. The first of these are the floor and ceiling of a number. We say that the floor of X (written $\lfloor X \rfloor$) is the largest integer that is less than or equal to X. So, $\lfloor 2.5 \rfloor$ would be 2 and $\lfloor -7.3 \rfloor$ would be -8. We say that the ceiling of X (written $\lceil X \rceil$) is the smallest integer that is greater than or equal to X. So, $\lceil 2.5 \rceil$ would be 3 and $\lceil -7.3 \rceil$ would be -7. Because we will be using just positive numbers, you can think of the floor as truncation and the ceiling as rounding up. For negative numbers, the effect is reversed.

The floor and ceiling will be used when we need to determine how many times something is done, and the value depends on some fraction of the items it is done to. For example, if we compare a set of N values in pairs, where the first value is compared to the second, the third to the fourth, and so on, the number of comparisons will be $\lfloor N / 2 \rfloor$. If N is 10, we will do five comparisons of pairs and $\lfloor 10 / 2 \rfloor = \lfloor 5 \rfloor = 5$. If N is 11, we will still do five comparisons of pairs and $\lfloor 11 / 2 \rfloor = \lfloor 5.5 \rfloor = 5$.

The factorial of the number N, written $N!$, is the product of all of the numbers between 1 and N. For example, 3! is $3 * 2 * 1$, or 6, and 6! is $6 * 5 * 4 * 3 * 2 * 1$, or 720. You can see that the factorial gets large very quickly. We will look at this more closely in Section 1.4.

■ 1.3.1 Logarithms

Because logarithms will play an important role in our analysis, there are a few properties that must be discussed. The logarithm base y of a number x is the power of y that will produce the number x. So, the $\log_{10} 45$ is about 1.653 because $10^{1.653}$ is 45. The base of a logarithm can be any number, but we will typically use either base 10 or base 2 in our analysis. We will use log as shorthand for $\log_{10}$ and lg as shorthand for $\log_2$.

Logarithms are a strictly increasing function. This means that given two numbers X and Y, if $X > Y$, $\log_B X > \log_B Y$ for all bases B. Logarithms are one-to-one functions. This means that if $\log_B X = \log_B Y$, $X = Y$. Other properties that are important for you to know are

$$\log_B 1 = 0 \tag{1.3}$$

$$\log_B B = 1 \tag{1.4}$$

$$\log_B(X * Y) = \log_B X + \log_B Y \tag{1.5}$$

$$\log_B X^Y = Y * \log_B X \tag{1.6}$$

$$\log_A X = \frac{(\log_B X)}{(\log_B A)} \tag{1.7}$$

These properties can be combined to help simplify a function. Equation 1.7 is a good fact to know for base conversion. Most calculators do $\log_{10}$ and natural logs, but let's say you need to know $\log_{42} 75$. Equation 1.7 would help you find the answer of 1.155.

■ 1.3.2 Binary Trees

A binary tree is a structure in which each node in the tree is said to have at most two nodes as its children, and each node has exactly one parent node. The top node in the tree is the only one without a parent node and is called the root of the tree. A binary tree that has N nodes has at least $\lfloor \lg N \rfloor + 1$ levels to the tree if the nodes are packed as tightly as possible. For example, a full binary tree with 15 nodes has one root, two nodes on the second level, four nodes on the third level, eight nodes on the fourth level, and our equation gives $\lfloor \lg 15 \rfloor + 1 = \lfloor 3.9 \rfloor + 1 = 4$. Notice, if we add one more node to this tree, it has to start a new level and now $\lfloor \lg 16 \rfloor + 1 = \lfloor 4 \rfloor + 1 = 5$. The largest binary tree that has N nodes will have N levels if each node has exactly one child (in which case the tree is actually a list).

If we number the levels of the tree, considering the root to be on level 1, there are 2^{K-1} nodes on level K. A complete binary tree with J levels (numbered from 1 to J) is one where all of the leaves in the tree are on level J, and all nodes on levels 1 to $J - 1$ have exactly two children. A complete binary tree with J levels has $2^J - 1$ nodes. This information will be useful in a number of the analyses we will do. To better understand these formulas, you might want to draw some binary trees and compare your count of the nodes with the results of these formulas.

■ 1.3.3 Probabilities

Because we will analyze algorithms relative to their input, we may at times need to consider the likelihood of a certain set of input. This means that we will need to work with the probability that the input will meet some condition. The probability that something will occur is given as a number in the range of 0 to 1, where 0 means it will never occur and 1 means it will always occur. If we know that there are exactly 10 different possible inputs, we can say that the probability of each of these is between 0 and 1 and that the total of all of the individual probabilities is 1, because one of these must happen. If there is an equal chance that any of these can occur, each will have a probability of 0.1 (one out of 10, or 1/10).

For most of our analyses, we will first determine how many possible situations there are and then assume that all are equally likely. If we determine that there are N possible situations, this results in a probability of $1 / N$ for each of these situations.

■ 1.3.4 Summations

We will be adding up sets of values as we analyze our algorithms. Let's say we have an algorithm with a loop. We notice that when the loop variable is 5, we do 5 steps and when it is 20, we do 20 steps. We determine in general that when the loop variable is M, we do M steps. Overall, the loop variable will take on all values from 1 to N, so the total steps is the sum of the values from 1 through N. To easily express this, we use the equation $\sum_{i=1}^{N} i$. The expression below the Σ represents the initial value for the summation variable, and the value above the Σ represents the ending value. You should see how this expression corresponds to the sum we are looking for.

Once we have expressed some solution in terms of this summation notation, we will want to simplify this so that we can make comparisons with other formulas. Deciding whether $\sum_{i=11}^{N} i^2 - i$ or $\sum_{i=0}^{N} i^2 - 20i$ is greater would be difficult to do by inspection, so we use the following set of standard summation formulas to determine the actual values these summations represent.

$$\sum_{i=1}^{N} C * i = C * \sum_{i=1}^{N} i \text{, with } C \text{ a constant expression not dependent on } i \qquad \textbf{(1.8)}$$

$$\sum_{i=C}^{N} i = \sum_{i=0}^{N-C} (i + C) \qquad \textbf{(1.9)}$$

$$\sum_{i=C}^{N} i = \sum_{i=0}^{N} i - \sum_{i=0}^{C-1} i \qquad \textbf{(1.10)}$$

$$\sum_{i=1}^{N} (A + B) = \sum_{i=1}^{N} A + \sum_{i=1}^{N} B \qquad \textbf{(1.11)}$$

$$\sum_{i=0}^{N} (N - i) = \sum_{i=0}^{N} i \qquad \textbf{(1.12)}$$

Equation 1.12 just shows that adding the numbers from N down to 0 is the same as adding the numbers from 0 up to N. In some cases, it will be easier to solve equations if we can apply Equation 1.12.

$$\sum_{i=1}^{N} 1 = N \tag{1.13}$$

$$\sum_{i=1}^{N} C = C * N \tag{1.14}$$

$$\sum_{i=1}^{N} i = \frac{N(N+1)}{2} \tag{1.15}$$

Equation 1.15 is easy to remember if you consider pairing up the values. Matching the first and last, second and second last, and so on gives you a set of values that are all $N + 1$. How many of these $N + 1$ totals do you get? Well, you get half of the number of values you started with before you paired them, or $N / 2$. So, the result is

$$\frac{N}{2}(N+1) = \frac{N(N+1)}{2}$$

$$\sum_{i=1}^{N} i^2 = \frac{N(N+1)(2N+1)}{6} = \frac{2N^3 + 3N^2 + N}{6} \tag{1.16}$$

$$\sum_{i=0}^{N} 2^i = 2^{N+1} - 1 \tag{1.17}$$

Equation 1.17 is easy to remember if you consider binary numbers. When you add the powers of 2 from 0 to 10, this is the same as the binary number 11111111111. If we add 1 to this number, we get 100000000000, which is 2^{11}. But because we added 1 to it, it is 1 larger than the sum of the powers of 2 from 0 to 10, so the sum must be $2^{11} - 1$. If we now substitute N for 10, we get Equation 1.17.

$$\sum_{i=1}^{N} A^i = \frac{A^{N+1} - 1}{A - 1}, \quad \text{for some number } A \tag{1.18}$$

$$\sum_{i=1}^{N} i 2^i = (N-1)2^{N+1} + 2 \tag{1.19}$$

$$\sum_{i=1}^{N} \frac{1}{i} = \ln N \tag{1.20}$$

$$\sum_{i=1}^{N} \lg i \approx N \lg N - 1.5 \tag{1.21}$$

When we are trying to simplify a summation equation, we can apply Equations 1.8 through 1.12 to break down the equation into simpler parts and then apply the rest to get an equation without summations.

■ 1.3.5 EXERCISES

1. Typical calculators have the ability to calculate natural logs (to the base e) and logs base 10. How would you use a calculator with just these capabilities to calculate $\log_{27} 59$?

2. Assume that we have a fair five-sided die with the numbers 1 through 5 on its sides. What is the probability that each of the numbers 1 through 5 will be rolled? If we roll two of these dice, what is the range of possible totals of the values showing on the two dice? What is the chance that each of these totals will be rolled?

3. Assume we have a fair eight-sided die with the numbers 1, 2, 3, 3, 4, 5, 5, 5 on its sides. What is the probability that each of the numbers 1 through 5 will be rolled? If we roll two of these dice, what is the range of possible totals of the values showing on the two dice? What is the chance that each of the numbers in this range will be rolled?

4. You are given four dice that have numbers on their faces according to the following lists:

   d_1: 1, 2, 3, 9, 10, 11
   d_2: 0, 1, 7, 8, 8, 9
   d_3: 5, 5, 6, 6, 7, 7
   d_4: 3, 4, 4, 5, 11, 12

   For each pair of dice, compute the probability that the first die will have a higher value showing than the second will, and vice versa. You can easily show your results in a 4 × 4 matrix where the row represents one die and the column represents another. (Because we assume that you will toss two different dice, the diagonal of this matrix should be left blank because it represents matching a die against itself.) These dice have an interesting property—can you determine it?

5. There are five coins on the table. You choose one at random and flip it. For each of the four cases below, what is the chance that the majority of coins will be tails when you are done?

    a. Two heads and three tails   c. Four heads and one tail

    b. Three heads and two tails   d. One head and four tails

6. There are five coins on the table. Each coin is flipped exactly once. For each of the four cases below, what is the chance that the majority of coins will be tails when you are done?

    a. Two heads and three tails   c. Four heads and one tail

    b. Three heads and two tails   d. One head and four tails

7. For the following summations, give an equivalent equation without the summation:

    a. $\displaystyle\sum_{i=1}^{N} (3i + 7)$

    b. $\displaystyle\sum_{i=1}^{N} (i^2 - 2i)$

    c. $\displaystyle\sum_{i=7}^{N} i$

    d. $\displaystyle\sum_{i=5}^{N} (2i^2 + 1)$

    e. $\displaystyle\sum_{i=1}^{N} 6^i$

    f. $\displaystyle\sum_{i=7}^{N} 4^i$

1.4 RATES OF GROWTH

In analysis of algorithms, it is not important to know exactly how many operations an algorithm does. Of greater concern is the rate of increase in operations for an algorithm to solve a problem as the size of the problem increases. This is referred to as the rate of growth of the algorithm. What happens with small sets of input data is not as interesting as what happens when the data set gets large.

Because we are interested in general behavior, we just look at the overall growth rate of algorithms, not at the details. If we look closely at the graph in Fig. 1.1, we will see some trends. The function based on x^2 increases slowly at first, but as the problem size gets larger, it begins to grow at a rapid rate. The functions that are based on x both grow at a steady rate for the entire length of the graph. The function based on $\log x$ seems to not grow at all, but this is because it is actually growing at a very slow rate. The relative height of the functions is also different when we have small values versus large ones. Consider the value of the functions when x is 2. At that point, the function with

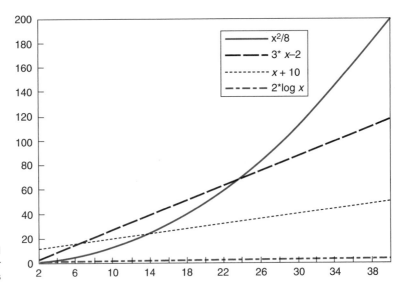

■ FIGURE 1.1
Graph of four
functions

	lg n	n	n lg n	n^2	n^3	2^n
1	0.0	1.0	0.0	1.0	1.0	2.0
2	1.0	2.0	2.0	4.0	8.0	4.0
5	2.3	5.0	11.6	25.0	125.0	32.0
10	3.3	10.0	33.2	100.0	1000.0	1024.0
15	3.9	15.0	58.6	225.0	3375.0	32768.0
20	4.3	20.0	86.4	400.0	8000.0	1048576.0
30	4.9	30.0	147.2	900.0	27000.0	1073741824.0
40	5.3	40.0	212.9	1600.0	64000.0	1099511627776.0
50	5.6	50.0	282.2	2500.0	125000.0	1125899906842620.0
60	5.9	60.0	354.4	3600.0	216000.0	1152921504606850000.0
70	6.1	70.0	429.0	4900.0	343000.0	1180591620717410000000.0
80	6.3	80.0	505.8	6400.0	512000.0	1208925819614630000000000.0
90	6.5	90.0	584.3	8100.0	729000.0	1237940039285380000000000000.0
100	6.6	100.0	664.4	10000.0	1000000.0	1267650600228230000000000000000.0

■ FIGURE 1.2
Common algorithm
classes

the smallest value is $x^2 / 8$ and the one with the largest value is $x + 10$. We can see, however, that as the value of x gets large, $x^2 / 8$ becomes and stays the function with the largest value.

Putting all of this together means that as we analyze algorithms, we will be interested in which rate of growth class an algorithm falls into rather than trying to find out exactly how many of each operation are done by the algorithm. When we consider the relative "size" of a function, we will do so for large values of x, not small ones.

Some of the common classes of algorithms can be seen in the chart in Fig. 1.2. In this chart, we show the value for these classes over a wide range of input sizes. You can see that when the input is small, there is not a significant difference in the values, but once the input value gets large, there is a big difference. This reinforces what we saw in the graph in Fig. 1.1. Because of this, we will always consider what happens when the size of the input is large, because small input sets can hide rather dramatic differences.

The data in Figs. 1.1 and 1.2 illustrate a second point. Because the faster-growing functions increase at such a significant rate, they quickly dominate the slower-growing functions. This means that if we determine that an algorithm's complexity is a combination of two of these classes, we will frequently ignore all but the fastest growing of these terms. For example, if we analyze an algorithm and find that it does $x^3 - 30x$ comparisons, we will just refer to this algorithm as growing at the rate of x^3. This is because even at an input size of just 100 the difference between x^3 and $x^3 - 30x$ is only 0.3%. This idea is formalized in the next section.

■ 1.4.1 Classification of Growth

Because the rate of growth of an algorithm is important, and we have seen that the rate of growth is dominated by the largest term in an equation, we will discard the terms that grow more slowly. When we strip all of these things away, we are left with what we call the *order* of the function or related algorithm. We can then group algorithms together based on their order. We group them in three categories—those that grow at least as fast as some function, those that grow at the same rate, and those that grow no faster.

Big Omega

We use $\Omega(f)$, called *big omega,* to represent the class of functions that grow at least as fast as the function f. This means that for all values of n greater than some threshold n_0, all of the functions in $\Omega(f)$ have values that are at least as large as f. You can view $\Omega(f)$ as setting a lower bound on a function, because all the functions in this class will grow as fast as f or even faster. Formally, this means that if $g(x) \in \Omega(f), g(n) \geq cf(n)$ for all $n \geq n_0$ (where c is a positive constant).

Because we are interested in efficiency, $\Omega(f)$ will not be of much interest to us because $\Omega(n^2)$, for example, includes all functions that grow faster than n^2 including n^3 and 2^n.

Big Oh

At the other end of the spectrum, we have $O(f)$, called *big oh,* which represents the class of functions that grow no faster than f. This means that for all values of n greater than some threshold n_0, all of the functions in $O(f)$ have values that are no greater than f. The class $O(f)$ has f as an upper bound, so none of the functions in this class grow faster than f. Formally this means that if $g(x) \in O(f), g(n) \leq cf(n)$ for all $n \geq n_0$ (where c is a positive constant).

This is the class that will be of the greatest interest to us. Considering two algorithms, we will want to know if the function categorizing the behavior of the first is in big oh of the second. If so, we know that the second algorithm does no better than the first in solving the problem.

Big Theta

We use $\theta(f)$, called *big theta*, to represent the class of functions that grow at the same rate as the function f. This means that for all values of n greater than some threshold n_0, all of the functions in $\theta(f)$ have values that are about the same as f. Formally, this class of functions is defined as the place where big omega and big oh overlap, so $\theta(f) = \Omega(f) \cap O(f)$.

When we consider algorithms, we will be interested in finding algorithms that might do better than the one we are considering. So, finding one that is in big theta (in other words, is of the same complexity) is not very interesting. We will not refer to this class very often.

Finding Big Oh

We can find if a function is in $O(f)$, by using the formal description above or by using the following alternative description:

$$g \in O(f) \quad \text{if} \quad \lim_{n \to \infty} \frac{g(n)}{f(n)} = c, \quad \text{for some} \quad c \in R^{\star} \tag{1.22}$$

This means that if the limit of $g(n) / f(n)$ is some real number less than ∞, g is in $O(f)$. With some functions, it might not be obvious that this is the case. We can then take the derivative of f and g and apply this same limit.

Notation

Because $\theta(f), \Omega(f)$, and $O(f)$ are sets, it is proper to say that a function g is an element of these sets. The analysis literature, however, accepts that a function g is equal to these sets as being equivalent to being a member of the set. So, when you see $g = O(f)$, this really means that $g \in O(f)$.

■ 1.4.2 EXERCISES

1. List the following functions from highest to lowest order. If any are of the same order, circle them on your list.

2^n	$\lg \lg n$	$n^3 + \lg n$
$\lg n$	$n - n^2 + 5n^3$	2^{n-1}
n^2	n^3	$n \lg n$
$(\lg n)^2$	$\sqrt{n}$	6
$n!$	n	$(3/2)^n$

2. For each of the following pairs of functions $f(n)$ and $g(n)$, either $f(n)=O(g(n))$ or $g(n)=O(f(n))$, but not both. Determine which is the case.

   a. $f(n) = (n^2 - n)/2$, $g(n) = 6n$

   b. $f(n) = n + 2\sqrt{n}$, $g(n) = n^2$

   c. $f(n) = n + n\log n$, $g(n) = n\sqrt{n}$

   d. $f(n) = n^2 + 3n + 4$, $g(n) = n^3$

   e. $f(n) = n\log n$, $g(n) = n\sqrt{n}/2$

   f. $f(n) = n + \log n$, $g(n) = \sqrt{n}$

   g. $f(n) = 2(\log n)^2$, $g(n) = \log n + 1$

   h. $f(n) = 4n\log n + n$, $g(n) = (n^2 - n)/2$

1.5 DIVIDE AND CONQUER ALGORITHMS

As the introduction indicated, divide and conquer algorithms can provide a small and powerful means to solve a problem; this section is not about how to write such an algorithm but rather how to analyze one. When we count comparisons that occur in loops, we only need to determine how many comparisons there are inside the loop and how many times the loop is executed. This is made more complex when a value of the outer loop influences the number of passes of an inner loop.

When we look at divide and conquer algorithms, it is not clear how many times a task will be done because it depends on the recursive calls and perhaps on some preparatory and concluding work. It is usually not obvious how many times the function will be called recursively. As an example of this, consider the following generic divide and conquer algorithm:

```
DivideAndConquer( data, N, solution )
data      a set of input values
N         the number of values in the set
solution  the solution to this problem

if (N ≤ SizeLimit) then
   DirectSolution( data, N, solution )
else
   DivideInput( data, N, smallerSets, smallerSizes, numberSmaller )
```

```
   for i = 1 to numberSmaller do
      DivideAndConquer(smallerSets[i], smallerSizes[i], smallSolution[i])
   end for
   CombineSolutions(smallSolution, numberSmaller, solution)
end if
```

This algorithm will first check to see if the problem size is small enough to determine a solution by some simple nonrecursive algorithm (called `Direct-Solution` above) and, if so, will do that. If the problem is too large, it will first call the routine `DivideInput`, which will partition the input in some fashion into a number (`numberSmaller`) of smaller sets of input values. These smaller sets may be all of the same size or they may have radically different sizes. The elements in the original input set will all be put into at least one of the smaller sets, but values can be put in more than one. Each of these smaller sets will have fewer elements than the original input set. The `Divide-AndConquer` algorithm is then called recursively for each of these smaller input sets, and the results from those calls are put together by the `Combine-Solutions` function.

The factorial of a number can easily be calculated by a loop, but for the purpose of this example, we consider a recursive version. You can see that the factorial of the number N is just the number N times the factorial of the number $N - 1$. This leads to the following algorithm:

```
Factorial( N )
N          is the number we want the factorial for
Factorial returns an integer

If (N = 1) then
   return 1
else
   smaller = N - 1
   answer = Factorial( smaller )
   return (N * answer)
end if
```

This algorithm is written in simple detailed steps so that we can match things up with the standard algorithm above. Even though earlier in this chapter we discussed how multiplications are more complex than additions and are, therefore, counted separately, to simplify this example we are going to count them together.

In matching up the two algorithms, we see that the size limit in this case is 1, and our direct solution is to return the answer of 1, which takes no mathematical operations. In all other cases, we use the `else` clause. The first step in the general algorithm is to "divide the input" into smaller sizes, and in the factorial function that is the calculation of `smaller`, which takes one subtraction. The next step in the general algorithm is to make the recursive calls with these smaller problems, and in the factorial function there is one recursive call with a problem size that is 1 smaller than the original. The last step in the general algorithm is to combine the solutions, and in the factorial function that is the multiplication in the last return statement.

Recursive Algorithm Efficiency

How efficient is a recursive algorithm? Would it make it any easier if you knew that the direct solution is quadratic, the division of the input is logarithmic, and the combination of the solutions is linear,[1] all with respect to the size of the input, and that the input set is broken up into eight pieces all one-quarter of the original? This is probably not a problem for which you can quickly find an answer or for that matter are even sure where to start. It turns out, however, that the process of analyzing any divide and conquer algorithm is very straightforward if you can map the steps of your algorithm into the four steps shown in the generic algorithm above: a direct solution, division of the input, number of recursive calls, and combination of the solutions. Once you know how each piece relates to the others, and you know how complex each piece is, you can use the following formula to determine the complexity of the divide and conquer algorithm:

$$
DAC(N) = \begin{cases} DIR(N) & \text{for } N \le \text{SizeLimit} \\ DIV(N) + \displaystyle\sum_{i=1}^{\text{numberSmaller}} DAC(\text{smallerSizes}[i]) + COM(N) & \text{for } N > \text{SizeLimit} \end{cases}
$$

where DAC is the complexity of DivideAndConquer
       DIR is the complexity of DirectSolution
       DIV is the complexity of DivideInput
       COM is the complexity of CombineSolutions

---

[1] To say that an algorithm is linear is the same as saying its complexity is in $O(N)$. If it's quadratic, it is in $O(N^2)$, and logarithmic is in $O(\lg N)$.

Now that we have this generic formula, the answer to the question posed at the start of the last paragraph is quite easy. All we need to do is to plug in the complexities for each piece given into the previous general equation. This gives the following result:

$$DAC(N) = \begin{cases} N^2 & \text{for } N \le \text{SizeLimit} \\ \lg N + \sum_{i=1}^{8} DAC(N/4) + N & \text{for } N > \text{SizeLimit} \end{cases}$$

or a bit more simply, because all smaller sets are the same size,

$$DAC(N) = \begin{cases} N^2 & \text{for } N \le \text{SizeLimit} \\ \lg N + 8\ DAC(N/4) + N & \text{for } N > \text{SizeLimit} \end{cases}$$

This form of equation is called a recurrence relation because the value of the function is based on itself. We prefer to have our equations in a form that is dependent only on N and not other function calls. The process that is used to remove the recursion in this equation will be covered in Section 1.6, which covers recurrence relations.

Let's return to our factorial example. We identified all of the elements in the factorial algorithm relative to the generic `DivideAndConquer`. We now use that identification to decide what values get put into the general equation above. For the `Factorial` function, we said that the direct solution does no calculations, the input division and result combination steps do one calculation each, and the recursive call works with a problem size that is one smaller than the original. This results in the following recurrence relation for the number of calculations in the `Factorial` function:

$$Calc(N) = \begin{cases} 0 & \text{for } N = 1 \\ 1 + Calc(N-1) + 1 & \text{for } N > 1 \end{cases}$$

■ 1.5.1 Tournament Method

The tournament method is based on recursion and can be used to solve a number of different problems where information from a first pass through the data can help to make later passes more efficient. If we use it to find the largest value, this method involves building a binary tree with all of the elements in the leaves. At each level, two elements are paired and the larger of the two gets copied into the parent node. This process continues until the root node is reached. Figure 1.3 shows a complete tournament tree for a given set of data.

In Exercise 5 of Section 1.1.3, it was mentioned that we would develop an algorithm to find the second largest element in a list using about N comparisons. The tournament method helps us do this. Every comparison produces one "winner" and one "loser." The losers are eliminated and only the winners move up in the tree. Each element, except for the largest, must "lose" one comparison. Therefore, building the tournament tree will take $N - 1$ comparisons.

The second largest element could only have lost to the largest element. We go down the tree and get the set of elements that lost to the largest one. We know that there can be at most $\lceil \lg N \rceil$ of these elements because of our tree formulas in Section 1.3.2. There will be $\lceil \lg N \rceil$ comparisons to find these elements in the tree and $\lceil \lg N \rceil - 1$ comparisons to find the largest in this collection. The entire process takes $N + 2 \lceil \lg N \rceil - 2$ comparisons, which is $O(N)$.

The tournament method could also be used to sort a list of values. In Chapter 3, we will see a method called heapsort that is based on the tournament method.

■ 1.5.2 Lower Bounds

An algorithm is optimal when there is no algorithm that will work more quickly. How do we know when have we found an algorithm that is optimal or when is an algorithm not optimal, but good enough? To answer these ques-

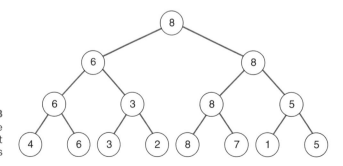

■ FIGURE 1.3
Tournament tree
for a set of eight
values

tions, we need to know the absolute smallest number of operations needed to solve a particular problem. This must be determined by looking at the problem itself and not any particular algorithm to solve it. This lower bound tells us the amount of work that is necessary to solve the problem and shows that any algorithm that claims to be able to solve the problem more quickly must fail in some cases.

We can again use a binary tree to help us analyze the process of sorting a list of three numbers. We can construct a binary tree for the sorting process by labeling each internal node with the two elements of the list that would be compared. The ordering of the elements that would be necessary to move from the root to that leaf would be in the leaves of the tree. The tree for a list of three elements is shown in Fig. 1.4. Trees of this form are called decision trees.

Each sort algorithm produces a different decision tree based on the elements that it compares. Within a decision tree, the longest path from the root to a

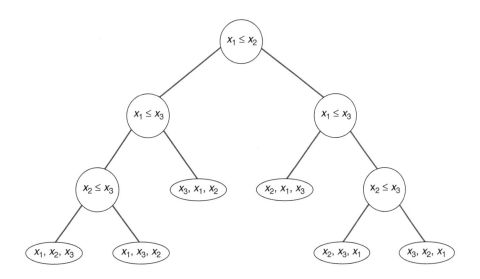

■ FIGURE 1.4
The decision tree for sorting a three-element list

leaf represents the worst case. The best case is the shortest path. The average case is the total number of edges in the decision tree divided by the number of leaves in the tree. As simple as it would seem to be able to determine these numbers by drawing decision trees and counting, think about what the decision tree would look like for a sort of 10 numbers. As was said before, there are 3,628,800 different ways these can be ordered. A decision tree would need at least 3,628,800 different leaves, because there may be more than one way to get to the same order. This tree would then need at least 22 levels.

So, how can decision trees be used to give us an idea of the bounds on an algorithm? We know that a correct sorting algorithm must properly order all of the elements no matter what order in which they begin. There must be at least one leaf for every possible permutation of input values, which means that there must be at least $N!$ leaves in the decision tree. A truly efficient algorithm would have each permutation appear only once. How many levels does a tree with $N!$ leaves have? We have already seen that each new level of the tree will have twice as many nodes as the previous level. Because there are 2^{K-1} nodes on level K, our decision tree will have L levels, where L is the smallest integer with $N! \le 2^{L-1}$. Applying algebraic transformations to this formula we get

$$\lg N! \le L - 1$$

Because we are trying to find out the smallest value for L, is there anyway to simplify this equation further to get rid of the factorial? Let's see what we can observe about the factorial of a number. Consider the following:

$$\lg N! = \lg(N * (N-1) * (N-2) * \ldots * 1)$$

By Equation 1.5, we get

$$\lg(N * (N-1) * (N-2) * \ldots * 1) = \lg(N) + \lg(N-1) + \lg(N-2) + \ldots + \lg(1)$$

$$\lg(N) + \lg(N-1) + \lg(N-2) + \ldots + \lg(1) = \sum_{i=1}^{N} \lg i$$

By Equation 1.21, we get

$$\sum_{i=1}^{N} \lg i \approx N \lg N - 1.5$$

$$\lg N! \approx N \lg N$$

This means that L, the minimum depth of the decision tree for sorting problems, is of order $O(N \lg N)$. We now know that any sort that is of order $O(N \lg N)$ is the best we will be able to do, and it can be considered optimal. We also know that any sort algorithm that runs faster than $O(N \lg N)$ must not work.

This analysis for the lower bound for a sorting algorithm assumed that it does its work through the comparison of pairs of values from the list. In Chapter 3, we will see a sorting algorithm (radix sort) that will run in linear time. That algorithm doesn't compare key values but rather separates them into "buckets" to accomplish its work.

■ 1.5.3 EXERCISES

1. Fibonacci numbers can be calculated with the algorithm that follows. What is the recurrence relation for the number of "additions" done by this algorithm? Be sure to clearly indicate in your answer what you think the direct solution, division of the input, and combination of the solutions are.

```
int Fibonacci( N )
N   the Nth Fibonacci number should be returned
if (N = 1) or (N = 2) then
   return 1
else
   return Fibonacci( N-1 ) + Fibonacci( N-2 )
end if
```

2. The greatest common divisor (GCD) of two integers M and N is the largest integer that divides evenly into both M and N. For example, the GCD of 9 and 15 is 3, and the GCD of 51 and 34 is 17. The following algorithm will calculate the greatest common divisor of two numbers:

```
GCD(M, N)
M, N are the two integers of interest
GCD  returns the integer greatest common divisor
if ( M < N ) then
   swap M and N
end if
if ( N = 0) then
   return M
else
   quotient = M / N    //NOTE: integer division
```

```
      remainder = M mod N
      return GCD( N, remainder )
   end if
```

Give the recurrence relation for the number of multiplications (in this case, the division and mod) that are done in this function.

3. We have a problem that can be solved by a direct (nonrecursive) algorithm that operates in N^2 time. We also have a recursive algorithm for this problem that takes $N \lg N$ operations to divide the input into two equal pieces and $\lg N$ operations to combine the two solutions together. Show whether the direct or recursive version is more efficient.

4. Draw the tournament tree for the following values: 13, 1, 7, 3, 9, 5, 2, 11, 10, 8, 6, 4, 12. What values would be looked at in stage 2 of finding the second largest value in the list?

5. What is the lower bound on the number of comparisons needed to do a search through a list with N elements? Think about what the decision tree might look like for this problem in developing your answer. (*Hint:* The nodes would be labeled with the location where the key is found.) If you packed nodes into this tree as tightly as possible, what does that tell you about the number of comparisons needed to search?

1.6 RECURRENCE RELATIONS

Recurrence relations can be directly derived from a recursive algorithm, but they are in a form that does not allow us to quickly determine how efficient the algorithm is. To do that we need to convert the set of recursive equations into what is called closed form by removing the recursive nature of the equations. This is done by a series of repeated substitutions until we can see the pattern that develops. The easiest way to see this process is by a series of examples.

A recurrence relation can be expressed in two ways. The first is used if there are just a few simple cases for the formula:

$$T(n) \;=\; 2\,T(n-2) - 15$$
$$T(2) \;=\; 40$$
$$T(1) \;=\; 40$$

The second is used if the direct solution is applied for a larger number of cases:

$$T(n) = \begin{cases} 4 & \text{if } n \le 4 \\ 4\,T(n/2) - 1 & \text{otherwise} \end{cases}$$

These forms are equivalent. We can convert from the second form to the first by just listing those values for which we have the direct answer. This means that the second recurrence relation above could also be given as

$$T(n) = 4\,T(n/2) - 1$$
$$T(4) = 4$$
$$T(3) = 4$$
$$T(2) = 4$$
$$T(1) = 4$$

Consider the following recurrence relation:

$$T(n) = 2\,T(n-2) - 15$$
$$T(2) = 40$$
$$T(1) = 40$$

We will want to substitute an equivalent value for $T(n-2)$ back into the first equation. To do so, we replace every n in the first equation with $n-2$, giving:

$$T(n-2) = 2\,T(n-2-2) - 15$$
$$= 2\,T(n-4) - 15$$

But now we can see when this substitution is done, we will still have $T(n-4)$ to eliminate. If you think ahead, you will realize that there will be a series of these values that we will need. As a first step, we create a set of these equations for successively smaller values:

$$T(n-2) = 2\,T(n-4) - 15$$
$$T(n-4) = 2\,T(n-6) - 15$$
$$T(n-6) = 2\,T(n-8) - 15$$
$$T(n-8) = 2\,T(n-10) - 15$$
$$T(n-10) = 2\,T(n-12) - 15$$

Now we begin to substitute back into the original equation. We will be careful not to simplify the resulting equation too much because that will make the pattern more difficult to see. Doing the substitution gives us

$$T(n) = 2T(n-2) - 15 = 2(2T(n-4) - 15) - 15$$
$$T(n) = 4T(n-4) - 2*15 - 15$$

$$T(n) = 4(2T(n-6) - 15) - 2*15 - 15$$
$$T(n) = 8T(n-6) - 4*15 - 2*15 - 15$$

$$T(n) = 8(2T(n-8) - 15) - 4*15 - 2*15 - 15$$
$$T(n) = 16T(n-8) - 8*15 - 4*15 - 2*15 - 15$$

$$T(n) = 16(2T(n-10) - 15) - 8*15 - 4*15 - 2*15 - 15$$
$$T(n) = 32T(n-10) - 16*15 - 8*15 - 4*15 - 2*15 - 15$$

$$T(n) = 32(2T(n-12) - 15) - 16*15 - 8*15 - 4*15 - 2*15 - 15$$
$$T(n) = 64T(n-12) - 32*15 - 16*15 - 8*15 - 4*15 - 2*15 - 15$$

You are probably beginning to see a pattern develop here. First, we notice that each new term at the end of the equation is -15 multiplied by the next higher power of 2. Second, we notice that the coefficient of the recursive call to T is going through a series of powers of 2. Third, we notice that the value that we are calling T with keeps going down by 2 each time. Now, you might wonder When does this process end? If we look back at the original equation, you will see that we have a fixed value for $T(1)$ and $T(2)$. How many times would we have to substitute back into this equation to get to either of these values? We can see that $2 = n - (n - 2)$ if n is even. This seems to indicate that we would substitute back into this equation $[(n - 2) / 2] - 1$ times giving $n / 2 - 1$ terms based on -15 in the equation, and the power of the coefficient of T will be $n / 2 - 1$. To see this, consider what we would have if the value of n was 14. In this case, the previous sentence indicates that we would have substituted five times, would have six terms based on -15, and would have 2^6 for the coefficient of $T(2)$. If you look closely at the last equation and substitute 14 in for n, you will see that this is exactly what we have.

What if n is an odd number? Will these formulas still work? Let's consider an n value of 13. In the above equation, the only thing that would change is that T would have a value of 1 instead of 2, but by our equations, $n / 2 - 1$ is 5 (not 6) when n is 13. For odd n, we will use $n / 2$ instead of $n / 2 - 1$. We will have two cases in our answer.

$$T(n) = 2^{(n/2)-1}T(2) - 15 \sum_{i=0}^{(n/2)-1} 2^i \quad \text{if } n \text{ is even} \qquad T(n) = 2^{n/2}T(1) - 15 \sum_{i=0}^{n/2} 2^i \quad \text{if } n \text{ is odd}$$

$$T(n) = 2^{(n/2)-1} * 40 - 15 \sum_{i=0}^{(n/2)-1} 2^i \quad \text{if } n \text{ is even} \qquad T(n) = 2^{n/2} * 40 - 15 \sum_{i=0}^{n/2} 2^i \quad \text{if } n \text{ is odd}$$

Now, applying Equation 1.17, for an even value of n we get

$$\begin{aligned} T(n) &= 2^{(n/2)-1} * 40 - 15 * (2^{n/2} - 1) \\ &= 2^{n/2} * 20 - 2^{n/2} * 15 + 15 \\ &= 2^{n/2}(20 - 15) + 15 \\ &= 2^{n/2} * 5 + 15 \end{aligned}$$

and, if n is odd, we get

$$\begin{aligned} T(n) &= 2^{n/2} * 40 - 15 * (2^{(n/2)+1} - 1) \\ &= 2^{n/2} * 40 - 2^{n/2} * 30 + 15 \\ &= 2^{n/2}(40 - 30) + 15 \\ &= 2^{n/2} * 10 + 15 \end{aligned}$$

Consider another recurrence relation:

$$T(n) = \begin{cases} 5 & \text{if } n \leq 4 \\ 4\,T(n/2) - 1 & \text{otherwise} \end{cases}$$

We will proceed in the same way as we did in the previous example. We first substitute in a set of values for n, only in this case, because n is being divided by 2, each of the subsequent equations will have half the value. This gives us the equations

$$T(n/2) = 4T(n/4) - 1$$
$$T(n/4) = 4T(n/8) - 1$$
$$T(n/8) = 4T(n/16) - 1$$
$$T(n/16) = 4T(n/32) - 1$$
$$T(n/32) = 4T(n/64) - 1$$

Now, we again substitute back into the original giving the following series of equations:

$$T(n) = 4T(n/2) - 1 = 4(4T(n/4) - 1) - 1$$
$$T(n) = 16T(n/4) - 4 * 1 - 1$$

$$T(n) = 16(4T(n/8) - 1) - 4 * 1 - 1$$
$$T(n) = 64T(n/8) - 16 * 1 - 4 * 1 - 1$$

$$T(n) = 64(4T(n/16) - 1) - 16 * 1 - 4 * 1 - 1$$
$$T(n) = 256T(n/16) - 64 * 1 - 16 * 1 - 4 * 1 - 1$$

$$T(n) = 256(4T(n/32) - 1) - 64 * 1 - 16 * 1 - 4 * 1 - 1$$
$$T(n) = 1024T(n/32) - 256 * 1 - 64 * 1 - 16 * 1 - 4 * 1 - 1$$

$$T(n) = 1024(4T(n/64) - 1) - 256 * 1 - 64 * 1 - 16 * 1 - 4 * 1 - 1$$
$$T(n) = 4096T(n/64) - 1024 * 1 - 256 * 1 - 64 * 1 - 16 * 1 - 4 * 1 - 1$$

We notice that the coefficient of -1 increases by a power of 4 each time we substitute, and it is the case that the power of 2 that we divide n by is 1 greater than the largest power of 4 for this coefficient. Also, we notice that the coefficient of T is the same power of 4 as the power of 2 that we divide n by. When we have $T(n/2^i)$, its coefficient will be 4^i and we will have terms from $-(4^{i-1})$ to -1. Now, for what value of i can we stop the substitution? Well, because we have the direct case specified for $n \le 4$, we can stop when we get to $T(4) = T(n/2^{\lg n - 2})$. Putting this together we get

$$T(n) = 4^{\lg n - 2} T(4) - \sum_{i=0}^{\lg n - 3} 4^i$$

Using the value for the direct case, and Equation 1.18, we get

$$T(n) = 4^{\lg n - 2} * 5 - \frac{4^{\lg n - 2} - 1}{4 - 1}$$

$$T(n) = 4^{\lg n - 2} * 5 - \frac{4^{\lg n - 2} - 1}{3}$$

$$T(n) = \frac{15 * 4^{\lg n - 2} - 4^{\lg n - 2} + 1}{3}$$

$$T(n) = \frac{4^{\lg n - 2}(15 - 1) + 1}{3}$$

$$T(n) = \frac{4^{\lg n - 2} * 14 + 1}{3}$$

As you can see, the closed form of a recurrence relation may not be simple or neat, however, it does eliminate the recursive "call" so that we can quickly compare equations and determine their order.

■ 1.6.1 EXERCISES

Put the following recurrence relations into closed form.

1. $\begin{cases} T(n) = 3T(n-1) - 15 \\ \quad\quad T(1) = 8 \end{cases}$

2. $\begin{cases} T(n) = T(n-1) + n - 1 \\ \quad\quad T(1) = 3 \end{cases}$

3. $\begin{cases} T(n) = 6T(n/6) + 2n + 3 \\ \quad\quad T(1) = 1 \end{cases}$ for n a power of 6

4. $\begin{cases} T(n) = 4T(n/3) + 2n - 1 \\ \quad\quad T(1) = 2 \end{cases}$ for n a power of 3

1.7 ANALYZING PROGRAMS

Let's say that we have a large, complex program that takes longer to run than we want. How can we identify parts of this program that with fine-tuning could improve the overall speed?

We could look at the program and find the subprograms (sometimes called subroutines, procedures, or functions) that have many calculations or loops and work on improving those. After a lot of effort to do this, we might not see an impact because the subprograms we worked on may not be used very much.

A better technique would be to first identify the subprograms that are used a lot and then improve those. One way to do this would be to create a set of global counters, one for each subprogram. They are initialized to zero at the start of the program. Every subprogram is then altered to increment one of those counters as its new first statement. Each time that subprogram is entered, it will now increase its counter by 1, so at the end of the program, our set of counters will tell us how many times each subprogram was called. We can now see which are called many times and which are called just a few.

Suppose we have a program where one simple subprogram is called 50,000 times and a bunch of complex subprograms are called just once each. We would have to reduce the complex subprograms by 50,000 operations to have the same effect as reducing the simple subprogram by just one operation. You should see that finding a simple improvement in one subprogram is much easier than finding 50,000 in a group of subprograms.

The technique of using counters can be applied at the subprogram level as well. In this case, we create a set of global counters, one for each of the significant points we want to know about. Suppose we wanted to know how many times the then and else parts of an if statement are executed. We could create two counters and increment the first inside the then part and increment the other inside the else part. At the end of the program, these two counters would tell us the information we are interested in. Other significant points we might want to test would be inside loops and just before conditional statements. More generally, we would place increment statements at any place where control can be transferred.

At the end of a program, these counters would tell us how many times each of the blocks of code in a subprogram was executed. We can then look at those parts where the most work is done for improvements.

This process is important, and many computers and software development systems have program profiling tools that will produce this information for you automatically.

Searching and Selection Algorithms

Before beginning this chapter, you should be able to

- Read and create algorithms
- Use summations and probabilities presented in Chapter 1

At the end of this chapter, you should be able to

- Explain the sequential search algorithm
- Explain the worst-case analysis of the sequential search algorithm
- Explain the average-case analysis of the sequential search algorithm
- Explain the binary search algorithm
- Explain the worst-case analysis of the binary search algorithm
- Explain the average-case analysis of the binary search algorithm
- Explain the selection algorithms and their analysis

STUDY SUGGESTIONS

As you are working through the chapter, you should rework the examples to be sure you understand them. For example, you should create a list of 5 to 8 elements and then use it to trace the sequential search and selection algorithms. You should do the same thing with an ordered list of 7 and 15 elements and binary search. Additionally, you should try to answer any questions before reading on. A hint or the answer is in the sentences following the question.

The act of searching for a piece of information in a list is one of the fundamental algorithms in computer science. In discussing searching, we assume that there is a list that contains records of information, which in practice is stored using an array in a program. The records, or items, are assumed to be in adjacent locations in the list, with no gaps or blank records in the middle. The list locations will be indexed from 1 to N, which represents the number of records in the list. Each record can be separated into fields, but we will only be interested in one of these fields, which we will call the key. Lists will be either unsorted or sorted based on their key value. Records are in a random order in an unsorted list and are in order by increasing key value in a sorted list.

When a list is unsorted, we only have one search option and that is to sequentially look through the list for the item we want. This is the simplest of the searching algorithms. We will see that this algorithm is not very efficient but will successfully search in any list.

When a list of elements is sorted, the options for searching are expanded to include binary search. Binary search takes advantage of the ordered nature of the list to eliminate more than one element of the list with each comparison. This results in a more efficient search.

A problem related to searching for a particular value is the selection problem, where we are interested in finding the element that meets some criterion. It might be that we are looking for the fifth largest value, seventh smallest value, or the median value in the list. We will look at two techniques that can be used to solve this problem.

2.1   SEQUENTIAL SEARCH

In search algorithms, we are concerned with the process of looking through a list to find a particular element, called the target. Although not required, we usually consider the list to be unsorted when doing a sequential search, because there are other algorithms that perform better on sorted lists. Search algorithms are not just interested in whether the target is in the list but are usually part of a larger process that needs the data associated with that key. For example, the key value might be an employee number, a serial number, or other unique identifier. When the proper key is found, the program might change some of the data stored for that key or might simply output the record. In any case, the important task for a search algorithm is to identify the location of the key. For this reason, search algorithms return the index of where the record with the key is located. If the target value is not found, it is typical for the algorithm to return an index value that is outside the range of the list of elements. For our purposes, we will assume that the elements of the list are located in positions 1 to N in the list. This allows us to return a value of zero if the target is not in the list. For the sake of simplicity, we will assume that the key values are unique for all of the elements in the list.

Sequential search looks at elements, one at a time, from the first in the list until a match for the target is found. It should be obvious that the further down the list a particular key value is, the longer it will take to find that key value. This is an important fact to remember when we begin to analyze sequential search.

The complete algorithm for sequential search is

```
SequentialSearch( list, target, N )
list      the elements to be searched
target    the value being searched for
N         the number of elements in the list

for i = 1 to N do
   if (target = list[i])
      return i
   end if
end for
return 0
```

■ 2.1.1 Worst-Case Analysis

There are two worst cases for the sequential search algorithm. The first is if the target matches the last element in the list. The second is if the target is not in the list. For both of these cases, let's look at how many comparisons are done. We have said that all of the list keys will be unique, and so if the match is in the last location, that means that all of the other locations are different from the target. The algorithm will, therefore, compare the target with each of these values until it finds the match in the last location. This will take N comparisons, where N is the number of elements in the list.

We will have to compare the target to all of the elements in the list to determine that the target is not there. If we skip any of the elements, we will not know if the target is not present or is present in one of the locations we skipped. This means that we need to do N comparisons to see that none of the elements match the target.

In both cases, whether the target is in the last location or not in the list, this algorithm takes N comparisons. You should see that this is the upper bound for any search algorithm, because to do more than N comparisons would mean that the algorithm compared at least one element with the target at least twice, which is unnecessary work, so the algorithm could be improved.

There is a difference between the concept of an upper bound and a worst case. The upper bound is a concept based on the problem to be solved, and the worst case is based on the way a particular algorithm solves that problem. For this algorithm, the worst case is also the upper bound for the problem. We will see in Section 2.2 another search algorithm that has a worst case that is less than this upper bound of N.

■ 2.1.2 Average-Case Analysis

There are two average-case analyses that can be done for a search algorithm. The first assumes that the search is always successful and the other assumes that the target will sometimes not be found.

If the target is in the list, there are N places where that target can be located. It could be in the first, second, third, fourth, and so on, locations in the list. We will assume that all of these possibilities are equally likely, giving a probability of $1/N$ for each potential location.

Take a moment to answer the following questions before reading on:

• How many comparisons are done if the match is in the first location?
• What about the second location?

- What about the third?
- What about the last or N^{th} location?

If you looked at the algorithm carefully, you should have determined that the answers to these questions are 1, 2, 3, and N, respectively. This means that for each of our N cases, the number of comparisons is the same as the location where the match occurs. This gives the following equation for this average case:[1]

$$A(N) = \frac{1}{N}\sum_{i=1}^{N} i$$

$$A(N) = \frac{1}{N} * \frac{N(N+1)}{2} \qquad \text{by Equation 1.15}$$

$$A(N) = \frac{N+1}{2}$$

If we include the possibility that the target is not in the list, we will find that there are now $N + 1$ possibilities. As we have seen, the case where the target is not in the list will take N comparisons. If we assume that all $N + 1$ possibilities are equally likely, we wind up with the following:

$$A(N) = \left(\frac{1}{N+1}\right) * \left[\left(\sum_{i=1}^{N} i\right) + N\right]$$

$$A(N) = \left(\frac{1}{N+1}\sum_{i=1}^{N} i\right) + \left(\frac{1}{N+1} * N\right)$$

$$A(N) = \left(\frac{1}{N+1} * \frac{N(N+1)}{2}\right) + \frac{N}{N+1}$$

$$A(N) = \frac{N}{2} + \frac{N}{N+1} = \frac{N}{2} + 1 - \frac{1}{N+1}$$

$$A(N) \approx \frac{N+2}{2} \qquad \text{(As } N \text{ gets very large, } \frac{1}{N+1} \text{ becomes almost 0.)}$$

We see that including the possibility of the target not being in the list only increases the average case by 1/2. When we consider this amount relative to the size of the list, which could be very large, this 1/2 is not significant.

---

[1] See Section 1.2.1 on average case if this first equation looks unfamiliar.

■ 2.1.3 EXERCISES

1. Sequential search can also be used for a sorted list. Write an algorithm called `SortedSequentialSearch` that will return the same results as the algorithm above but will run more quickly because it can stop with a failure the minute it finds that the target is smaller than the current list value. When you write your algorithm, use the Compare(x, y) function defined as

$$\text{Compare}(x, y) = \begin{cases} -1 & \text{if } x < y \\ 0 & \text{if } x = y \\ 1 & \text{if } x > y \end{cases}$$

The Compare function should be counted as one comparison and can best be used in a switch. Do an analysis of the worst case, average case with the target found, and average with the target not found. (*Note:* This last analysis has many possibilities because of all of the additional early exits when the target is smaller than the current value.)

2. What is the average complexity of sequential search if there is a 0.25 chance that the target will not be found in the list and there is a 0.75 chance that when the target is in the list, it will be found in the first half of the list?

2.2   BINARY SEARCH

If we compare the target with the element that is in the middle of a sorted list, we have three possible results: the target matches, the target is less than the element, or the target is greater than the element. In the first and best case, we are done. In the other two cases, we learn that half of the list can be eliminated from consideration.

When the target is less than the middle element, we know that if the target is in this ordered list, it must be in the list before the middle element. When the target is greater than the middle element, we know that if the target is in this ordered list, it must be in the list after the middle element. These facts allow this one comparison to eliminate one-half of the list from consideration. As the process continues, we will eliminate from consideration one-half of what is left of the list with each comparison. This results in the following algorithm:[2]

```
BinarySearch( list, target, N )
list      the elements to be searched
target    the value being searched for
N         the number of elements in the list

start = 1
end = N
while start ≤ end do
   middle = (start + end) / 2
   select (Compare(list[middle], target)) from
      case -1:start = middle + 1
      case  0:return middle
      case  1:end = middle - 1
   end select
end while
return 0
```

In this algorithm, start gets reset to 1 larger than the middle when we know that the target is larger than the element at the middle location. End gets reset to 1 smaller than the middle when we know that the target is smaller than the element at the middle location. These are shifted by 1 because we know by the three-way comparison that the middle value is not equal and so can be eliminated from consideration.

Does this loop always stop? If we find the target, the answer is obviously Yes, because of the return. If we don't find a match, each pass through the loop will either increase the value of start or decrease the value of end. This means that they will continue to get closer to each other. Eventually, they will become equal to each other, and the loop will be done one more time, with start = end = middle. After this pass (assuming that this is not the element we are looking for), either start will be 1 greater than middle and end, or end will be 1 less than middle and start. In both of these cases, the while

---

[2] The function Compare(x,y) is defined in Exercise 1 of Section 2.1.3. As was mentioned in that exercise, this function will return -1, 0, or 1, depending on whether x is less than, equal to, or greater than y, respectively. When analyzing an algorithm that uses Compare, it is counted as just one comparison.

loop's conditional will become false, and the loop will stop. Therefore, the loop does always stop.

Does this algorithm return the correct answer? If we find the target, the answer is obviously Yes because of the return. If the middle element doesn't match, each pass through the loop eliminates from consideration one-half of the remaining elements because they are all either too large or too small. As was discussed in the previous paragraph, we will eventually get down to just one element that must be examined.[3] If this is the key we are looking for, the value of `middle` will be returned. If it is not the key we are looking for, `start` will become greater than `end` or `end` will become less than `start`. This means that if the target was in the list, it would be above or below the middle value, respectively. But, based on the values of `start` and `end`, we know that previous comparisons eliminated all of the other values, so the target is not in the list. The loop will stop, and the function will indicate a failed search by returning zero. So, the algorithm does return the correct answer.

Because of the halving nature of this algorithm, we will assume for our analysis that $N = 2^k - 1$ for some value of k. If this is the case, how many elements will be left for the second pass? What about the third pass? In general, you should see that if on some pass of the loop we have $2^j - 1$ elements under consideration, there are $2^{j-1} - 1$ elements in the first half, 1 element in the middle, and $2^{j-1} - 1$ in the second half. Therefore, the next pass will have $2^{j-1} - 1$ elements left (for $1 \leq j \leq k$). This assumption will make the following analysis easier to do, but this assumption is not necessary, as you will see in the exercises.

■ 2.2.1 Worst-Case Analysis

In paragraph above, we showed that the power of 2 is decreased by one each pass of the loop. It was also shown that the last pass of the loop occurs when the list has a size of 1, which occurs when j is 1 ($2^1 - 1 = 1$). This means that there are at most k passes when $N = 2^k - 1$. Solving this equation tells us that the worst case is $k = \lg(N + 1)$.

---

[3] You should also see this from the process of repeatedly doing an integer division by 2. No matter what size list you start with, if you keep dividing by 2 (throwing away the fractional portion), you will eventually wind up with a list of one element.

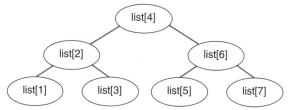

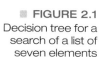

■ **FIGURE 2.1**
Decision tree for a
search of a list of
seven elements

Building a decision tree for the search process can also help with this analysis. The nodes of the decision tree would have the element that is checked at each pass. Those elements that would be checked if the target is less than the current element would go into the left subtree and those checked when the target is greater would go into the right subtree. If our list had just seven elements, the tree that would result is shown in Fig. 2.1. In general, we know that this tree is relatively balanced because we always choose the middle of the various parts of the list. So, we can use formulas related to binary trees from Section 1.3.2 to get the number of comparisons.

Because we chose $N = 2^k - 1$, the resulting decision tree will be complete. There will be k levels in the resulting tree, where $k = \lg(N + 1)$. Because we do one comparison on each level, the most we do is $\lg(N + 1)$ comparisons.

■ 2.2.2 Average-Case Analysis

As with sequential search, we will consider two situations when doing an average-case analysis. In the first, the target will always be in the list, and in the second, the target may not be in the list.

The first situation will have N possible locations for the target. We will consider each of these to be equivalent and so will give each a probability of $1/N$. If we consider the binary tree that represents this search process, we will see that one comparison is done to find the element that is in the root of the tree on level 1. Two comparisons are done to find the elements that are in the nodes on level 2, and three comparisons are done to find the elements that are in the nodes on level 3. In general, i comparisons are done to find the elements that are in the nodes on level i. Section 1.3.2 showed that for a binary tree there are 2^{i-1} nodes on level i, and when $N = 2^k - 1$, there are k levels in the tree. This means that we can determine the total number of comparisons done for every possible case by adding, for every level, the product of the number of nodes on each level and the number of comparisons for that level. This gives an average case of analysis of

$$A(N) = \frac{1}{N}\sum_{i=1}^{k} i2^{i-1} \qquad \text{for } N = 2^k - 1$$

$$A(N) = \frac{1}{N} * \frac{1}{2}\sum_{i=1}^{k} i2^{i}$$

We can use Equation 1.19 to simplify this equation to

$$A(N) = \frac{1}{N} * \frac{1}{2} * [(k-1)2^{k+1} + 2]$$

$$A(N) = \frac{1}{N}[(k-1)2^{k} + 1]$$

$$A(N) = \frac{1}{N}[k\ 2^{k} - 2^{k} + 1]$$

$$A(N) = \frac{[k\ 2^{k} - (2^{k} - 1)]}{N}$$

$$A(N) = \frac{[k\ 2^{k} - N]}{N}$$

$$A(N) = \frac{k\ 2^{k}}{N} - 1$$

Because $N = 2^k - 1$, $2^k = N + 1$.

$$A(N) = \frac{k(N+1)}{N} - 1$$

$$A(N) = \frac{k * N + k}{N} - 1$$

As N gets larger, k/N becomes zero, giving

$$A(N) \approx k - 1 \qquad\qquad \text{for } N = 2^k - 1$$
$$A(N) \approx \lg(N+1) - 1 \qquad \text{for } N = 2^k - 1$$

Now, let's consider the second situation where we include the possibility that the target is not in the list of elements. We still have N possibilities for the target being in the list, but now we have to add in the $N + 1$ possibilities that the target is not in the list. There are $N + 1$ of these possibilities because the target can be smaller than the element in location 1, larger than the element in location 1 but smaller than the one in location 2, larger than the element in location 2 but smaller than the one in location 3, and so on, through the possibility that the target is larger than the element in location N. In each of these cases, it takes k comparisons to learn that the target is not in the list. There are now $2 * N + 1$ possibilities to include in our calculation. Putting all of this together, we get

$$A(N) = \frac{1}{2N+1}\left[\left(\sum_{i=1}^{k} i\, 2^{i-1}\right) + (N+1)k\right] \quad \text{for } N = 2^k - 1$$

By a simiar series of substitutions as above, we get

$$A(N) = \frac{[(k-1)2^k + 1] + (N+1)k}{2N+1}$$

$$A(N) = \frac{[(k-1)2^k + 1] + (2^k - 1 + 1)k}{2(2^k - 1) + 1}$$

$$A(N) = \frac{(k\,2^k - 2^k + 1) + 2^k k}{2^{k+1} - 1}$$

$$A(N) = \frac{k\,2^{k+1} - 2^k + 1}{2^{k+1} - 1}$$

$$A(N) \approx \frac{k\,2^{k+1} - 2^k + 1}{2^{k+1}}$$

$$A(N) \approx k - \frac{1}{2} = \lg(N+1) - \frac{1}{2} \quad \text{for } N = 2^k - 1$$

This is just a little larger than the average case for when the key is known to be in the list. So, if the list has 1,048,575 ($2^{20} - 1$) elements, the first average case is about 19 and the second is 19.5.

■ 2.2.3 EXERCISES

1. Draw the decision tree for the binary search algorithm for a list of 12 elements. For the internal nodes of your decision tree, the node should be labeled with the element checked, the left child should represent what happens if the target is less than the element checked, and the right child should represent what happens if the target is greater than the element checked.

2. The analysis of binary search in this chapter assumed that the size was always $2^k - 1$ for some value of k. For this question, we will explore other possibilities for the size:

   a. What is the worst case when $N \neq 2^k - 1$?
   b. What is the average case when $N \neq 2^k - 1$, assuming that the key is in the list? *Hint:* Think about what this change in size means for the bottom of the search tree.
   c. What is the average case when $N \neq 2^k - 1$, if the key might not be in the list? *Hint:* Think about what this change in size means for the bottom of the search tree.

3. When the collection of data is large, there can still be a large number of comparisons needed to do a binary search. For example, a telephone directory of a large city could easily take about 25 comparisons per search. To improve this, multiway searching uses a general tree, which is a tree data structure that can have more than two children. In multiway searching, we store a few keys in each tree node, and the children represent the subtrees containing (a) the entries smaller than all the keys, (b) the entries larger than the first key but smaller than the rest, (c) the entries larger than the first two keys but smaller than the rest, and so on. The following figure shows an example of a general tree that can be used for multiway searching. In the root of this tree we have the keys of 6 and 10, so if we are looking for a key less than 6, we would take the left branch. If we are looking for a key between 6 and 10, we would take the middle branch, and for a key larger than 10, we would take the right branch.

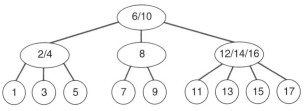

Write an algorithm to do a multiway search. For your answer, you can assume that each node has two arrays called `Keys[3]` and `Links[4]` and that you have a function called `Compare(keyList, searchKey)` that returns a positive integer indicating the key that matches or a negative integer indicating the link to take. (For example, `Compare([2, 6, 10], 6)` would return a value of 2 because the second key matches, and `Compare([2, 6, 10], 7)` would return a value of −3 because 7 would be found on the third link associated with the gap between the second and third key value.) When you have finished your algorithm, do a worst- and average-case analysis assuming that the tree is complete and each internal node has four children. (You might want to draw a sample tree.) What would be the impact on your two analyses if the tree was not complete or if some internal nodes had less than four children?

2.3 SELECTION

There are situations where we are interested in finding an element in a list that has a particular property, instead of a particular value. In other words, instead of finding a record with a particular key value, we may be interested in the record with the largest, smallest, or median value. More generally, we want to find the Kth largest value in the list.

One way to accomplish this would be to sort the list in decreasing order, and then the Kth largest value will be in position K. This is a lot more work than we need to do, because we don't really care about the values that are smaller than the one we want. A related technique to this would be to find the largest value and then move it to the last location in the list. If we again look for the largest value in the list, ignoring the value we already found, we get the second largest value, which can be moved to the second last location in the list. If we continue this process, we will find the Kth largest value on the Kth pass. This gives the algorithm

```
FindKthLargest( list, N, K )
list   the values to look through
N      the size of the list
K      the element to select

for i = 1 to K do
   largest = list[1]
   largestLocation = 1
```

```
      for j = 2 to N-(i-1) do
         if list[j] > largest then
            largest = list[j]
            largestLocation = j
         end if
      end for
      Swap( list[N-(i-1)], list[largestLocation] )
   end for
return largest
```

What is the complexity of this process? On each pass, we initialize `largest` to the first element of the list, and then we compare `largest` to every other element. On the first pass, we do $N - 1$ comparisons. On the second pass, we do $N - 2$ comparisons. On the Kth pass, we do $N - K$ comparisons. So, to find the Kth largest element, we will do

$$\sum_{i=1}^{K} N - i = N * K - \frac{K * (K - 1)}{2}$$

comparisons, which is $O(K * N)$. You should also see that if K is greater than $N/2$, it would be faster to look for the $N - K$th smallest value. This process will be reasonably efficient for values of K that are close to either end of the list, but there is a more efficient way to accomplish this process for values of K in the middle of the list.

Because we only want the Kth largest value, we don't really need to know the exact position for the values that are the largest through the $K - 1$st largest; we only need to know that they are larger. If we choose an element of the list, we can partition the list into two parts—those values that are greater than the one chosen and those values that are less than it. If we rearrange the list so that all of the larger values are after the chosen value and all of the smaller ones are before it, the chosen value will wind up in some position P in our list, meaning it is the Pth largest value. To do this partitioning, we will need to compare this value with all of the others, doing $N - 1$ comparisons. If we are lucky and $P = K$, we are done. If K is less than P, we want a larger value and will repeat this process on the second partition. If K is greater than P, we want a smaller value and will use the first partition, but we need to reduce K by the number of values we have eliminated in the larger partition. This gives the following recursive algorithm:

```
KthLargestRecursive( list, start, end, K )
list   the list of values
```

```
start   the index of the first value to consider
end     the value of the last value to consider
K       the element of this list that we want.

if start < end then
   Partition( list, start, end, middle )
   if middle = K then
      return list[middle]
   else
      if K < middle then
         return KthLargestRecursive( list, middle+1, end, K )
      else
         return KthLargestRecursive( list, start, middle-1, K-middle )
      end if
   end if
end if
```

If we assume that on average the partition process will divide the list into two roughly equal halves, we will do about $N + N/2 + N/4 + N/8 + \cdots + 1$ comparisons, which is about $2N$ comparisons. So, this process is linear and independent of K. We will see the partitioning process in more detail when we discuss quicksort in Chapter 3 and will do a more detailed analysis of it at that time.

■ 2.3.1 EXERCISES

1. Given five distinct values, the median would be the value in the third position if they were sorted. We will see in Chapter 3 that sorting a list of five elements would take seven comparisons. Prove that the median can be found more efficiently, namely, with no more than six comparisons.

2. The algorithms in this section can also be used to find the median of a list by looking for the $N/2$ largest element. Show that the worst case for this choice will take $O(N^2)$ time.

2.4 PROGRAMMING EXERCISE

1. Create a function based on sequential search and a program that will test it. Use method 3 of Appendix C to generate a list of random numbers in the range of 1 to N that you can use for your search, where N could be any number between 100 and 1000. Your program should have a global counter, which should be initialized to zero at the beginning of the program and

should be incremented just before the key comparison in your sequential search routine. Your main program should then call sequential search for each number between 1 and N. After doing this, the total count of comparisons divided by N will be the average number of comparisons done by sequential search.

2. Repeat Step 1 for binary search, using an ordered list.

3. Write a report that compares your output from parts 1 and 2 with the results you would predict based on the analysis in this chapter.

CHAPTER 3

Sorting Algorithms

PREREQUISITES

Before beginning this chapter, you should be able to

- Read and create iterative and recursive algorithms
- Use summations and probabilities presented in Chapter 1
- Solve recurrence relations
- Describe growth rates and order

GOALS

At the end of this chapter, you should be able to

- Explain insertion sort and its analysis
- Explain bubble sort and its analysis
- Explain shellsort and its analysis
- Explain radix sort and its analysis
- Trace the heapsort and `FixHeap` algorithms
- Explain the analysis of heapsort
- Explain merge sort and its analysis
- Explain quicksort and its analysis
- Explain external polyphase merge sort and its analysis

STUDY SUGGESTIONS

As you are working through the chapter, you should rework the examples to be sure you understand them. It will be especially helpful to trace insertion sort, bubble sort, shellsort, heapsort, merge sort, and quicksort using the lists [6, 2, 4, 7, 1, 3, 8, 5] and [15, 4, 10, 8, 6, 9, 16, 1, 7, 3, 11, 14, 2, 5, 12, 13]. You should trace radix sort using three buckets for 1, 2, and 3, and the list [1113, 2231, 3232, 1211, 3133, 2123, 2321, 1312, 3223, 2332, 1121, 3312]. Additionally, you should try to answer any questions before reading on. A hint or the answer is in the sentences following the question.

I n this chapter, we will consider another class of fundamental algorithms from computing: sorting algorithms. Because of the significant time savings of binary search over sequential search, software designers will frequently choose to keep information sorted so that searches can be done by binary or other nonsequential methods.

As in Chapter 2, we will work with a list of records, which have a special field called the key. All of our sort algorithms will sort the list into increasing order based on this key value. We will use standard comparisons with these keys with the full knowledge that when they are used, we might be comparing integers, strings, or more complex key types. For the sake of simplicity, we will assume that each of the values in the list is distinct, because the presence of duplicates will not significantly change any of the analyses that we do in this chapter. The reader should recognize that changing the comparison of keys would result in a different ordering. For example, if the less than and greater than comparisons are swapped, the list will be sorted in decreasing order.

The eight sorting algorithms discussed in this chapter are only a sampling of the possible sorts, but they exhibit a wide range of behaviors. The first, insertion sort, accomplishes sorting by inserting new elements into the correct place in a list that is already sorted. Bubble sort compares pairs of elements, swapping those that are out of order, until the list is sorted. Shellsort is a multipass sort that breaks the list into sublists that are sorted, and on each successive pass the number of sublists is decreased as their size is increased. Radix sort is a multipass sort that separates the list into buckets, each pass using a different part of the key. Heapsort builds a binary tree with list elements so that each node has a value larger than its children. This places the largest element at the root so that when it is removed and the heap is fixed, the next largest element moves to the root. This is repeated until all of the elements are back in the now-sorted list. Merge sort starts with two sorted lists and creates one sorted list by merging these two. Quicksort is a recursive sort that picks a pivot element from the list and then subdivides the list into two parts that contain the elements that are smaller and larger than the pivot.

The last sort considered is different in that it works with lists that are so large that they cannot be reasonably held in a computer's memory all at once. This external sort works with groups of records in sequential files and is designed to limit the file accesses, which would be an operation much slower than a comparison. The reader should note that even with expanded memory in today's computers, holding all of a database's records in memory at once may be possible but may incur delays due to virtual memory swapping. In this case, even though writing to disk files is not part of the algorithm, the reliance on virtual memory incurs the same cost because swaps are written to temporary disk files by the operating system.

3.1 INSERTION SORT

The basic idea of insertion sort is that if you have a list that is sorted and need to add a new element, the most efficient process is to put that new element into the correct position instead of adding it anywhere and then resorting the entire list. Insertion sort accomplishes its task by considering that the first element of any list is always a sorted list of size 1. We can create a two-element sorted list by correctly inserting the second element of the list into the one-element list containing the first element. We can now insert the third element of the list into the two-element sorted list. This process is repeated until all of the elements have been put into the expanding sorted portion of the list.

The following algorithm carries out this process:

```
InsertionSort( list, N )
list   the elements to be put into order
N      the number of elements in the list

for i = 2 to N do
   newElement = list[ i ]
   location = i - 1
   while (location ≥ 1) and (list[ location ] > newElement) do
      // move any larger elements out of the way
      list[ location + 1] = list[ location ]
      location = location - 1
```

```
       end while
    list[ location + 1 ] = newElement
end for
```

This algorithm copies the next value to be inserted into `newElement`. It then makes space for this new element by moving all elements that are larger one position over in the array. This is done by the `while` loop. The last copy of the loop moved the element in position `location + 1` to position `location + 2`. This means that position `location + 1` is available for the "new" element.

■ 3.1.1 Worst-Case Analysis

When we look at the inner `while` loop, we see that the most work this loop will do is if the new element to be added is smaller than all of the elements already in the sorted part of the list. In this situation, the loop will stop when location becomes 0. So, the most work the entire algorithm will do is in the case where every new element is added to the front of the list. For this to happen, the list must be in decreasing order when we start. This is a worst-case input, but there are others.

Let's look at how this input set will be handled. The first element to be inserted is the one in the second location of the list. This is compared to one other element at most. The second element inserted (that's at location 3) will be compared to the two previous elements, and the third element inserted will be compared to the three previous elements. In general, the ith element inserted will be compared to i previous elements. This process is repeated for $N - 1$ elements. This means that the worst-case complexity for insertion sort is given by

$$W(N) = \sum_{i=1}^{N-1} i = \frac{(N-1)N}{2} = \frac{N^2 - N}{2}$$

$$W(N) = O(N^2)$$

■ 3.1.2 Average-Case Analysis

Average-case analysis will be a two-step process. We first need to figure out the average number of comparisons needed to move one element into place. We can then determine the overall average number of operations by using the first step result for all of the other elements.

We begin by determining on average how many comparisons it takes to move the ith element into position. We said that adding the ith element to the sorted part of the list does at most i comparisons. It should be obvious that we do at least one comparison even if the element stays in its current position.

How many positions is it possible to move the ith element into? Let's look at small cases and see if we can generalize from there. There are two possible positions for the first element to be added—either in location 1 or location 2. There are three possible positions for the second element to be added—either in locations 1, 2, or 3. It appears that there are $i + 1$ possible positions for the ith element. We consider each of these equally likely.

How many comparisons does it take to get to each of these $i + 1$ possible positions? Again we look at small cases and generalize from there. If we are adding the fourth element, and it goes into location 5, the first comparison will fail. If it goes into location 4, the first comparison will succeed, but the second will fail. If it goes into location 3, the first and second comparisons will succeed, but the third will fail. If it goes into location 2, the first, second, and third comparisons will succeed, but the fourth will fail. If it goes into location 1, the first, second, third, and fourth comparisons will succeed, and there will be no further comparisons because location will have become zero. This seems to imply that for the ith element, it will do $1, 2, 3, \ldots, i$ comparisons for locations $i + 1, i, i - 1, \ldots, 2$, and it will do i comparisons for location 1. The average number of comparisons to insert the ith element is given by the formula

$$A_i = \frac{1}{i + 1}\left[\left(\sum_{p=1}^{i} p\right) + i\right]$$

$$A_i = \frac{1}{i + 1}\left[\frac{i(i + 1)}{2} + i\right]$$

$$A_i = \frac{i}{2} + \frac{i}{i + 1}$$

$$A_i = \frac{i}{2} + 1 - \frac{1}{i + 1}$$

This is just the average amount of work to insert the ith element. This now needs to be summed up for each of the 1 through $N - 1$ elements that gets "added" to the list. The final average case result is given by the formula

$$A(N) = \sum_{i=1}^{N-1} A_i = \sum_{i=1}^{N-1}\left(\frac{i}{2} + 1 - \frac{1}{i + 1}\right)$$

By two applications of Equation 1.11, we get

$$A(N) = \sum_{i=1}^{N-1} \frac{i}{2} + \sum_{i=1}^{N-1} 1 - \sum_{i=1}^{N-1} \frac{1}{i+1}$$

Notice that by using Equations 1.9 and 1.10, we have

$$\sum_{i=1}^{N-1} \frac{1}{i+1} = \sum_{i=2}^{N} \frac{1}{i} = \left(\sum_{i=1}^{N} \frac{1}{i} \right) - 1$$

By applications of Equations 1.15, 1.14, 1.20, and the last formula, we get

$$A(N) \approx \frac{1}{2} \left(\frac{(N-1)N}{2} \right) + (N-1) - (\ln N - 1)$$

$$A(N) \approx \frac{N^2 - N}{4} + (N-1) - (\ln N - 1)$$

$$A(N) \approx \frac{N^2 + 3N - 4}{4} - (\ln N - 1)$$

$$A(N) \approx \frac{N^2}{4}$$

$$A(N) = O(N^2)$$

■ 3.1.3 EXERCISES

1. Show the results of each pass of InsertionSort applied to the list [7, 3, 9, 4, 2, 5, 6, 1, 8].

2. Show the results of each pass of InsertionSort applied to the list [3, 5, 2, 9, 8, 1, 6, 4, 7].

3. Section 3.1.1 showed that a list in decreasing order leads to the worst case. This means that the list [10, 9, 8, 7, 6, 5, 4, 3, 2, 1] would give the worst case of 45 comparisons. Find one other list of these 10 elements that will give the worst-case behavior. What more can you say generally about the class of input that generates the worst case for this algorithm.

4. When you look closely at the InsertionSort algorithm, you will notice that the insertion of a new element basically does a sequential search for the new location. We saw in Chapter 2 that binary searches are much faster. Consider a variation on insertion sort that does a binary search to find the

correct position to insert this new element. You should notice that for unique keys the standard binary search would always return a failure. So for this problem, assume a revised binary search that returns the location at which this key belongs.

a. What is the worst-case analysis of this new insertion sort?
b. What is the average-case analysis of this new insertion sort?

3.2 BUBBLE SORT

The second sort we will consider is bubble sort. The general idea is to allow smaller values to move toward the top of the list while larger values move to the bottom. There are a number of varieties of bubble sort. This section will deal with one of these, and the others will be left as exercises.

The bubble sort algorithm makes a number of passes through the list of elements. On each pass it compares adjacent element values. If they are out of order, they are swapped. We start each of the passes at the beginning of the list and compare the elements in locations 1 and 2, then the elements in locations 2 and 3, then 3 and 4, and so on, swapping those that are out of order. On the first pass, once the algorithm reaches the largest element, it will be swapped with all of the remaining elements, moving it to the end of the list after the first pass. The second pass, therefore, no longer needs to look at the last element in the list. The second pass will move the second largest element down the list until it is in the second to last location. The process continues with each additional pass moving one more of the larger values down in the list. During all of this, the smaller values are also moving toward the front of the list. If on any pass there are no swaps, all of the elements are now in order and the algorithm can stop. It should be noted that each pass has the potential of moving a number of the elements closer to their final position, even though only the largest element on that pass is guaranteed to wind up in its final location.

The following algorithm carries out this bubble sort version:

```
BubbleSort( list, N )
list   the elements to be put into order
N      the number of elements in the list

numberOfPairs = N
swappedElements = true
```

```
while swappedElements do
   numberOfPairs = numberOfPairs - 1
   swappedElements = false
   for i = 1 to numberOfPairs do
      if list[ i ] > list[ i + 1 ] then
         Swap( list[i], list[i + 1] )
         swappedElements = true
      end if
   end for
end while
```

■ 3.2.1 Best-Case Analysis

We look quickly at the best case because the swappedElements flag might give the wrong impression of how this algorithm functions. Consider what will cause this algorithm to do the least amount of work. On the first pass, the for loop must fully execute, and so this algorithm does at least $N - 1$ comparisons. There are two possibilities that should be considered: There is at least one swap or there are no swaps. In the first case, the swap will cause swappedElements to be set to true, which will cause the while loop to execute a second time, which will do another $N - 2$ comparisons. In the second case, because there are no swaps, swappedElements will still be false and the algorithm will end.

So the best case is $N - 1$ comparisons, and this occurs when there are no swaps on the first pass. This means that the input data associated with the best case would be when the data values are already in order.

■ 3.2.2 Worst-Case Analysis

If the best case is when the input data starts in order, we might want to see if having the input data in reverse order will lead us to the worst case. If the largest value is first, it will be swapped with every other element down the list until it is in the last position. At the start of the first pass, the second largest element was in the second position, but you should see that the first comparison on the first pass swapped it into the first position of the list. At the start of the second pass, the second largest element is now in the first position, and it will be swapped with every other element in the list until it is in the second to last position. This gets repeated for every other element, and so the algorithm has to execute the `for` loop $N - 1$ times. This indicates that an input data set that is in the reverse order does lead to the worst case.[1]

How many comparisons are done in this worst case? We have said that the first pass will do $N - 1$ comparisons of adjacent values, and the second pass will do $N - 2$ comparisons. Further examination will show that each successive pass reduces the number of comparisons by 1. This means that the worst case is given by the formula

$$W(N) = \sum_{i=N-1}^{1} i = \sum_{i=1}^{N-1} i = \frac{(N-1)N}{2} = \frac{N^2 - N}{2}$$

$$W(N) \approx \frac{1}{2}N^2 = O(N^2)$$

■ 3.2.3 Average-Case Analysis

We have already said that in the worst case, there would be $N - 1$ repetitions of the inner `for` loop. For the average case, we will assume that it is equally likely that on any of these passes there will be no swaps done. We need to know how many comparisons are done in each of these possibilities. If we stop after one pass, we have done $N - 1$ comparisons. If we stop after two passes, we have done $N - 1 + N - 2$ comparisons. For now, let's say that $C(i)$ will calculate how many comparisons are done on the first i passes. Because the algorithm stops when there are no swaps done, the average case is found by looking at all of the places bubble sort can stop. This gives the equation

$$A(N) = \frac{1}{N-1}\sum_{i=1}^{N-1} C(i)$$

---

[1] This case does the largest number of comparisons and swaps, but because we are only interested in counting the number of comparisons, there are other data sets that will lead us to this worst case. The reader should be able to show that any list of elements with the smallest element in the last position, for example, will also produce this worst-case result. Can you find any others?

where, again, $C(i)$ is the number of comparisons done in the first i passes of the for loop before we stop. So, how many comparisons is this? $C(i)$ is given by the equation

$$C(i) = \sum_{j=N-1}^{i} j = \sum_{j=i}^{N-1} j = \sum_{j=1}^{N-1} j - \sum_{j=1}^{i-1} j \quad \text{the last step by Equation 1.10}$$

$$C(i) = \frac{(N-1)N}{2} - \frac{(i-1)i}{2} = \frac{N^2 - N - i^2 + i}{2}$$

Substituting this back into the first equation gives the following

$$A(N) = \frac{1}{N-1} \sum_{i=1}^{N-1} \left(\frac{N^2 - N - i^2 + i}{2} \right)$$

Because N is a constant relative to i, by using Equations 1.11 and 1.14 we can get

$$A(N) = \frac{1}{N-1} \left[(N-1) * \frac{N^2 - N}{2} + \sum_{i=1}^{N-1} \left(\frac{-i^2 + i}{2} \right) \right]$$

Again using Equation 1.11 and some basic algebra, we get

$$A(N) = \frac{N^2 - N}{2} + \frac{1}{2(N-1)} \left[\sum_{i=1}^{N-1} -i^2 + \sum_{i=1}^{N-1} i \right]$$

Now, we apply Equations 1.15 and 1.16 to get

$$A(N) = \frac{N^2 - N}{2} + \frac{1}{2(N-1)} \left[-\frac{(N-1)N(2N-1)}{6} + \frac{(N-1)N}{2} \right]$$

$$A(N) = \frac{N^2 - N}{2} - \frac{N(2N-1)}{12} + \frac{N}{4}$$

$$A(N) = \frac{6N^2 - 6N - 2N^2 + N + 3N}{12}$$

$$A(N) = \frac{4N^2 - 2N}{12}$$

$$A(N) \approx \frac{1}{3} N^2 = O(N^2)$$

■ 3.2.4 EXERCISES

1. Show the results of each pass of BubbleSort applied to the list [7, 3, 9, 4, 2, 5, 6, 1, 8].

2. Show the results of each pass of BubbleSort applied to the list [3, 5, 2, 9, 8, 1, 6, 4, 7].

3. A different version of bubble sort keeps track of where the last exchange occurred, and on the next pass, it will not go past this point. If the last change was made in the swap of locations i and $i + 1$, the next pass will not look at any elements past location i.

   a. Write this new version of bubble sort.
   b. Write a short paragraph that explains exactly why this new version of bubble sort will work.
   c. Does this new version of bubble sort change the worst-case analysis? Give an analysis or justification for your answer.
   d. This new version of bubble sort does change the average-case analysis. Give a detailed explanation of what is involved in calculating this new average-case analysis.

4. Another version of bubble sort alternates passes so that the odd passes are like the original, but the even passes move from the bottom of the array to the top. On the odd passes the larger elements move toward the bottom, and on the even passes the smaller elements move toward the top.

   a. Write this new version of bubble sort.
   b. Write a short paragraph that explains exactly why this new version of bubble sort will work.
   c. Does this new version of bubble sort change the worst-case analysis? Give an analysis or justification for your answer.
   d. This new version of bubble sort does change the average-case analysis. Give a detailed explanation of what is involved in calculating this new average-case analysis.

5. A third version of bubble sort combines the ideas of Questions 1 and 2. This bubble sort moves back and forth through the array but adjusts its upper and lower range of the sort based on where the last changes were made.

   a. Write this third version of bubble sort.

    b. Write a short paragraph that explains exactly why this third version of bubble sort will work.

    c. Does this third version of bubble sort change the worst-case analysis? Give an analysis or justification for your answer.

    d. This third version of bubble sort does change the average-case analysis. Give a detailed explanation of what is involved in calculating this new average-case analysis.

6. Develop a formal argument that proves that the largest element must be in the correct place after the first pass of the `BubbleSort` loop.

7. Develop a formal argument that proves that if there are no swaps done on any pass of `BubbleSort`, the list must now be in the correct order.

3.3 SHELLSORT

Shellsort was developed by Donald L. Shell. It is unusual in that it begins by considering the full list of values as a set of interleaved sublists. On the first pass, it may deal with sublists that are just pairs of elements. On the second pass, it could deal with groups of four elements each. The process repeats, increasing the number of elements per sublist and, therefore, decreasing the number of sublists. Figure 3.1 shows the sublists that can be used in the process of sorting a list of 16 elements.

In Fig. 3.1(a), we see that there are eight sublists of two values each, which match up the first and ninth elements, the second and tenth elements, and so on. In Fig. 3.1(b), we see that there are now four sublists of four values each. The first sublist now has the elements in the first, fifth, ninth, and thirteenth locations. The second sublist has the elements in the second, sixth, tenth, and fourteenth locations. In Fig. 3.1(c), we see that there are two sublists, which have the odd and even location elements in them. In the last pass, shown in Fig. 3.1(d), we are back to one list.

The sorting of the sublists is done with just an insertion sort based on the one in Section 3.1. This makes the algorithm

```
Shellsort( list, N )
list   the elements to be put into order
N      the number of elements in the list
```

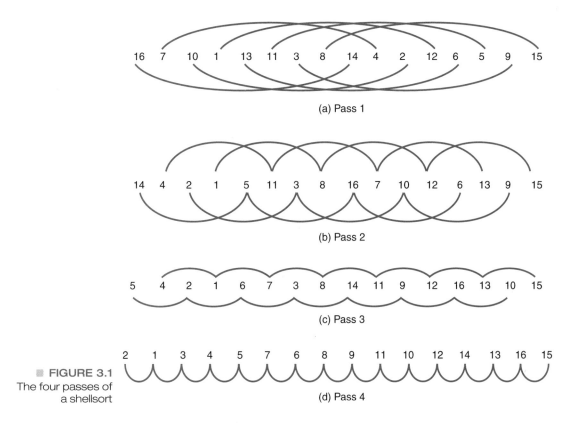

(a) Pass 1

(b) Pass 2

(c) Pass 3

(d) Pass 4

■ FIGURE 3.1
The four passes of
a shellsort

```
passes = ⌊lg N⌋
while (passes ≥ 1) do
    increment = 2^passes - 1
    for start = 1 to increment do
        InsertionSort( list, N, start, increment )
    end for
    passes = passes - 1
end while
```

The variable increment gives the spacing between the elements of the sublist. (In Fig. 3.1, the increments used are 8, 4, 2, and 1.) In the algorithm, we start with an increment that is 1 less than the largest power of 2 that is smaller than the size of the list. So, if our list has 1000 elements, our first increment will be 511. The increment also indicates the number of sublists that we have. If our first sublist has the elements in locations 1 and 1 + increment, the last sublist has to start in location increment. The last time the while loop is executed, passes will have a value of 1, which will make increment 1 for the last InsertionSort.

The analysis of this algorithm depends on the analysis that we did of InsertionSort. Before we begin the analysis of Shellsort, recall that in Section 3.1, we saw that for a list with N elements the worst case for insertion sort was $(N^2 - N)/2$ and the average case for insertion sort was $N^2/4$.

■ 3.3.1 Algorithm Analysis

In this analysis, we will first determine the number of times we call the InsertionSort function and the number of elements in the lists for those calls. Let's look at the specific case when the list size is 15. On the first pass, increment is 7 and so we make seven calls with lists of size 2. On the second pass, increment is 3, and so we make three calls with lists of size 5. On the third pass and last pass, increment is 1, and so we make one call with a list of size 15. From the above formulas, we see that for a list of size 2, Insertion-Sort will do one comparison in the worst case. For a list of size 5, it will do 10 comparisons in the worst case. For a list of size 15, it will do 105 comparisons in the worst case. If we add all of this up together, we find that we get a total of 142 comparisons (7 * 1 + 3 * 10 + 1 * 105). But is this a good estimate?

If you look back at the analysis of Section 3.1.1, you will see that we said the worst case for insertion sort occurs when each element to be added has to be put at the front of the list. On the last pass of our Shellsort algorithm, we know that this worst case cannot possibly occur because of the sorting that occurred in the earlier passes. Maybe a different approach will help us figure out how much work is left.

When analyzing sorting algorithms, we will sometimes consider the number of inversions in a list. An inversion is a pair of elements in the list that are out of order. For example, the list [3, 2, 4, 1] has four inversions, namely, (3, 2), (3, 1), (2, 1), and (4, 1). You should see that a list in reverse order has the worst number of inversions possible: $(N^2 - N)/2$.

One way to look at the work a sorting algorithm does is to count the number inversions between the current permutation of the elements and a sorted list. Each swap of elements will remove one or more of these inversions. For example, when bubble sort does a comparison and finds two adjacent elements out of order, it switches them, removing just one inversion. The same is true for insertion sort because the movement of each larger element up one location in the list is the removal of one inversion between it and the element we are inserting. So, in bubble and insertion sort ($O(N^2)$ sorts) each comparison can result in the removal of exactly one inversion.

Because shellsort relies on insertion sort, it would seem that its analysis must be the same, but when you consider that shellsort looks at sublists that are interleaved with each other, one comparison can cause a swap that removes more than just one inversion. On the first pass of Fig. 3.1, we compared 16 and 14, and because they were out of order they were swapped. By moving 16 from the first location to the ninth we removed 7 inversions of 16 with the values in locations 2 through 8 of the list. The analysis of shellsort gets complicated because that same swap moved 14 from the ninth location to the first and created seven new inversions, so that comparison didn't help at all. If you look at the swap of 7 and 4, you see the same thing. But overall, there are improvements. On the first pass, we did eight comparisons and removed 36 inversions. On the second pass, we did 16 comparisons and removed 20 inversions. On the third pass, we did 19 comparisons and removed 24 inversions. And on the last pass, we did 19 comparisons and removed the last 10 inversions. This is a total of 62 comparisons. If we just considered the average cases for the insertion sort calls that we did, you would still calculate 152 comparisons.

A complete analysis of the shellsort algorithm is very complex and beyond the scope of this book. With the sequence of increment values that we chose, it has been shown that shellsort in the worst case is $O(N^{3/2})$. A detailed analysis of shellsort and the impact of the increment sequence discussed in the next section are presented in the third volume of Donald Knuth's *The Art of Computer Programming* (Addison-Wesley, 1998).

▓ 3.3.2 The Effect of the Increment

The choice of the increment sequence can have a major effect on the order of shellsort, and attempts at finding an optimal increment sequence have not be successful. A number of different options have been considered, and their results are presented here.

If there are just two passes, it has been shown that using an increment of about $1.72 * \sqrt[3]{N}$ for the first pass and 1 for the second pass produces a sort of $O(N^{5/3})$.

Another set of increments would be $h_j = (3^j - 1) / 2$ for all h values less than N. These values also satisfy the relationship $h_{j+1} = 3h_j + 1$ and $h_1 = 1$, so once the largest value of h is identified, succeeding increments can be calculated by $h_j = (h_{j+1} - 1) / 3$. Using this sequence of increments results in a sort of $O(N^{3/2})$.

Another version will calculate all of the possible values of $2^i 3^j$ (for any integers $i \geq 0$ and $j \geq 0$) that are less than the size of the list and use those values in decreasing order. For example, if N is 40, we would have the following sequence of increments: 36 ($2^2 3^2$), 32 ($2^5 3^0$), 27 ($2^0 3^3$), 24 ($2^3 3^1$), 18 ($2^1 3^2$), 16 ($2^4 3^0$), 12 ($2^2 3^1$), 9 ($2^0 3^2$), 8 ($2^3 3^0$), 6 ($2^1 3^1$), 4 ($2^2 3^0$), 3 ($2^0 3^1$), 2 ($2^1 3^0$), and 1 ($2^0 3^0$). By using a sequence of values that follows this pattern, shellsort's order can be reduced to $O(N(\lg N)^2)$. It should be noted that the large number of passes introduces significant overhead, so this doesn't become a practical sequence unless the size of the list is very large.

Shellsort is unique in that its general algorithm stays the same, but the choices of its parameters can have a dramatic effect on its order.

■ 3.3.3 EXERCISES

1. Show the results of each of the passes of Shellsort using the increments of 7, 5, 3, and 1 with the initial list of values [16, 15, 14, 13, 12, 11, 10, 9, 8, 7, 6, 5, 4, 3, 2, 1]. How many comparisons are done?

2. Show the results of each of the passes of Shellsort using the increments of 8, 4, 2, and 1 with the initial list of values [16, 15, 14, 13, 12, 11, 10, 9, 8, 7, 6, 5, 4, 3, 2, 1]. How many comparisons are done?

3. Show the results of each pass of Shellsort using increments of 5, 2, and 1 applied to the list [7, 3, 9, 4, 2, 5, 6, 1, 8]. How many comparisons are done?

4. Show the results of each pass of Shellsort using increments of 5, 2, and 1 applied to the list [3, 5, 2, 9, 8, 1, 6, 4, 7]. How many comparisons are done?

5. Write the new version of InsertionSort used in this section.

6. This section looked at sorting as the removal of inversions in a list. For a list of N elements, what is the formula for the largest number of inversions that

can be removed by the exchange of two nonadjacent elements? Give an example for a list with 10 elements.

3.4 RADIX SORT

Radix sort uses key values to do the sort without actually comparing them to each other. In this sort, we will create a set of "buckets" and will distribute the entries into the buckets based on their key values. After collecting the values and repeating this process for successive parts of the key, we can create a sorted list. The distribution and collection has to be done very carefully for this to work.

A process similar to this was used to sort cards manually. In some libraries, before the days of computerized checkouts, when a book was taken out, a picture of it and a due date card was taken. The due date cards were numbered and had a series of holes punched along one side. Some of these holes were cut out to the side, creating notches along the edge that represented the number of the card. As books were returned, the due date cards were removed and just placed on a stack. A long needle was then placed through the first hole of the stack of cards and it was lifted. The cards with a notch would stay on the table and those without would remain on the needle. The two piles created were recombined by placing the cards on the needle behind those with the notches. The needle would then be moved to the next hole and the process repeated. As long as the process was done to the holes in order and the arrangement of the cards was never changed except for when the needle was raised, after processing the final hole, the cards would be in numerical order.

This manual process would separate the cards by their least significant digit at the beginning and by their most significant digit at the end. A computerized version of this process to sort a set of numeric keys would use 10 buckets and have the following algorithm:

```
RadixSort( list, N )
list  the elements to be put into order
N     the number of elements in the list

shift = 1
for loop = 1 to keySize do
   for entry = 1 to N do
```

```
            bucketNumber = (list[entry].key / shift) mod 10
            Append( bucket[bucketNumber], list[entry] )
        end for entry
        list = CombineBuckets()
        shift = shift * 10
end for loop
```

We'll begin by reviewing this algorithm. The calculation of `bucketNumber` will pull a single digit out of a key. The division by `shift` will cause the key value to be moved to the right some number of digits, and then the mod will eliminate all but the units digit of the resulting number. On the first pass with a shift value of 1, the division will do nothing, and the mod result will return just the units digit of the key. On the second pass, `shift` will now be 10, so the integer division and then the mod will return just the tens digit. On each succeeding pass, the next digit of the key will be used.

The `CombineBuckets` function will append the buckets back into one list starting with `bucket[0]` through `bucket[9]`. This recombined list is the starting point for the next pass. Because the buckets are recombined in order and because the numbers are added to the end of each bucket list, the keys will eventually be sorted. Figure 3.2 shows the three passes that would be done for keys with three digits. To make this example simpler, all of the keys just use the digits 0 through 3, so only four buckets are needed.

In looking at Fig. 3.2(c), you should see that if the buckets are again combined in order, the list will now be sorted.

■ 3.4.1 Analysis

An analysis of radix sort requires that we consider issues beyond just number of operations, because in this case they are significant. How this particular algorithm is implemented has an impact on its overall efficiency. We consider both the time and space efficiency of this algorithm.

Each key is looked at once for each digit (or letter if the keys are alphabetic) of the longest key. So, if the longest key has M digits and there are N keys, radix sort has order $O(M * N)$. But if we look at these two values, the size of the keys will be relatively small when compared to the number of keys. For example, if we have six-digit keys, we could have a million different records. Recalling the discussion of Section 1.4 on rates of growth, we see that the size of the keys is not significant, and this algorithm is of linear complexity, $O(N)$.

Original list

310 213 023 130 013 301 222 032 201 111 323 002 330 102 231 120

Bucket Number	Contents
0	310 130 330 120
1	301 201 111 231
2	222 032 002 102
3	213 023 013 323

(a) Pass 1, Units Digit

Pass 1 list

310 130 330 120 301 201 111 231 222 032 002 102 213 023 013 323

Bucket Number	Contents
0	301 201 002 102
1	310 111 213 013
2	120 222 023 323
3	130 330 231 032

(b) Pass 2, Tens Digit

Pass 2 list

301 201 002 102 310 111 213 013 120 222 023 323 130 330 231 032

Bucket Number	Contents
0	002 013 023 032
1	102 111 120 130
2	201 213 222 231
3	301 310 323 330

FIGURE 3.2
The three passes
of a radix sort   **(c)** Pass 3, Hundreds Digit

This is very efficient, and so you might wonder why any of the other sorting algorithms are even used.

The issue in this case becomes space efficiency. In sorts we've seen, we need extra space for at most one additional record as we are swapping. In this case, the space needs are more significant. If we use arrays for the buckets, these will need to be extremely large arrays. In fact, they will need to be the size of the original list, because we can't assume that the keys will be uniformly distributed among the buckets as in Fig. 3.2. The chance that the keys will be distributed equally among the buckets is the same as the chance that they will all be in the same bucket. Both can happen. Using arrays means that we will need $10N$ additional space if the keys are numeric, $26N$ additional space if the keys are alphabetic, and even more if the keys are alphanumeric or if case matters in alphabetic characters. If we use arrays, we also have the time to copy the records to the buckets in the distribution step and from the buckets back into the original list in the coalescing step. This means each record will be "moved" $2M$ times. If the records are large, this can take a substantial amount of time.

An alternative is to use a linked list structure for the records. Now, putting a record into a bucket just requires changing a link, and coalescing the buckets again just requires changing links. There is still significant space overhead, because most implementations of linked lists will require 2 to 4 bytes per link, making the total additional space needs $2N$ to $4N$ bytes.

■ 3.4.2 EXERCISES

1. Use the `RadixSort` algorithm to sort the list [1405, 975, 23, 9803, 4835, 2082, 7368, 573, 804, 746, 4703, 1421, 4273, 1208, 521, 2050]. Show the buckets for each pass and the list after each bucket coalescing step.

2. Use the `RadixSort` algorithm to sort the list [117, 383, 4929, 144, 462, 1365, 9726, 241, 1498, 82, 1234, 8427, 237, 2349, 127, 462]. Show the buckets for each pass and the list after each bucket coalescing step.

3. Another way of looking at radix sort is to consider the key as just a bit pattern. So, if the keys are 4-byte integers, they are just considered as 32 bits, and if the keys are strings of 15 alphanumeric characters (15 bytes), they are just considered as 120 bits. These bit streams are then subdivided into pieces, which determine the number of passes and the number of buckets. So, if we have 120-bit keys, we might do 12 passes with 10-bit pieces, 10 passes with 12-bit pieces, or 5 passes with 24-bit pieces.

a. If the key is a number in the range of 0 to 2^{64}, choose two options (one smaller and one larger) for the number of bits that will be used on each pass and indicate how many buckets and passes will be needed.

b. If the key is a string of 40 characters, choose two options (one smaller and one larger) for the number of bits that will be used on each pass and indicate how many buckets and passes will be needed.

c. Based on your answers to parts (a) and (b), can you give any general recommendations for how to make the choice of passes and key subdivisions?

3.5 HEAPSORT

Heapsort is based on a special type of binary tree called a heap where for every subtree the value at the root is larger than all the values in the two children. There is no ordering relationship between the two children, so sometimes the left child may be larger, and other times the right will be larger. A heap is constructed to be a complete tree where each level of the tree is filled before a new level is started, and all node positions on a level are filled in order from left to right.

The general idea of heapsort is to first construct a heap. The largest element will then be at the root of the tree, because all smaller elements must be in the children for this to be a heap. The root is then copied into the last location of the list, and the heap is reconstructed without this largest element. The second largest element will then be at the root, so we can remove it and reconstruct the heap. This process is repeated until all of the elements have been moved back to the list.

The general algorithm for this is

```
construct the heap
for i = 1 to N do
   copy the root to the list
   fix the heap
end for
```

There are a number of details that remain for this algorithm to be complete. We must first determine what is involved in the process of constructing and fixing the heap, because it will play a role in the efficiency of this algorithm.

We need to be concerned about how this algorithm will be implemented. The overhead of actually creating a binary tree would be a problem as the size

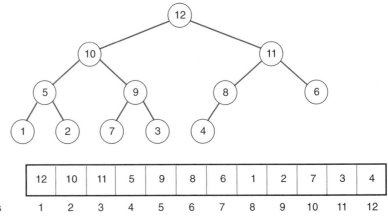

■ FIGURE 3.3
A heap and its list
implementation

Locations

of the list grows. We can, however, use the space for the list itself and do this sort without extra space. We can "build" the list into a heap if we notice that in a heap each internal node has two children, except for perhaps one node toward the bottom. If we consider the following mapping, we can use the list to hold these values. For the node at location i, we will store its two children at locations $2 * i$ and $2 * i + 1$. Notice that this process produces distinct locations for each node's children. We know that node i is a leaf if $2 * i$ is greater than N, and we know that node i has only one child if $2 * i$ is equal to N. Figure 3.3 shows a heap and its list version.

FixHeap

When we take the largest element out of the root and move it to the list, this leaves the root vacant. We know that the larger of its two children needs to be moved up, but then that child's node becomes vacant, and so we look at its two children, and so on. In this process, we need to maintain the heap as close to a complete tree as possible. When we fix the heap, we will also pass in the rightmost node from the bottom level, to be inserted back into the heap. This will remove nodes evenly from the bottom. If we don't do this and all of the large values are on one side of the heap, the heap will be unbalanced and the algorithm's efficiency will go down. This gives us the following algorithm:

```
FixHeap( list, root, key, bound )
list   the list/heap being sorted
root   the index of the root of the heap
```

```
key    the key value that needs to be reinserted in the heap
bound the upper limit (index) on the heap

vacant = root
while 2*vacant ≤ bound do
    largerChild = 2*vacant

    // find the larger of the two children
    if (largerChild < bound) and (list[largerChild+1] > list[largerChild]) then
        largerChild = largerChild + 1
    end if

    // does the key belong above this child?
    if key > list[ largerChild ] then
        // yes, stop looping
        break
    else
        // no, move the larger child up
        list[ vacant ] = list[ largerChild ]
        vacant = largerChild
    end if
end while
list[ vacant ] = key
```

When you look at this algorithm's parameters, you might wonder why we have chosen to pass in the root location. Because this routine is not recursive, the root of the heap should always be location 1. You will see, however, that this additional parameter will make it possible for us to use this function to construct the heap from the bottom up. We pass in the size of the heap, because as the elements get moved from the heap to the list, the heap shrinks.

Constructing the Heap

The way that we have chosen to implement the FixHeap function means that we can use this in the initial construction of the heap. Any two values can be treated as leaves of a vacant node. We do not need to do any work on the second half of the list because they are all leaves. We just need to construct small heaps from the leaves and then combine these until eventually all values are in the heap. This is accomplished by the following loop:

```
for i = N/2 down to 1 do
    FixHeap( list, i, list[ i ], N )
end for
```

Final Algorithm

Putting these pieces together, and adding the final details needed to move the elements from the heap to the list, gives the algorithm

```
for i = N/2 down to 1 do
   FixHeap( list, i, list[ i ], N )
end for
for i = N down to 2 do
   max = list[ 1 ]
   FixHeap( list, 1, list[ i ], i-1 )
   list[ i ] = max
end for
```

■ 3.5.1 Worst-Case Analysis

We begin by analyzing `FixHeap` because the rest of the algorithm depends on it. This algorithm will do, for each level of the heap, a comparison between the two children and then the larger child and the key. This means that for a heap of depth D, there will be no more than $2D$ comparisons. [2]

In the heap construction stage, we first call FixHeap for each node on the second level from the bottom, which means heaps of depth 1. Then it is called for each node on the third level from the bottom, which means heaps of depth 2. On the last pass at the root level, the heap will have depth $\lfloor \lg N \rfloor$. The only thing we need to consider is how many nodes is `FixHeap` called for at each pass. At the root level there is one node, and it has two children at the second level. The next level down has at most four nodes, and the level after that has eight. Putting all of this together gives the following formula:

$$W_{\text{Construction}}(N) = \sum_{i=0}^{D-1} 2(D-i)2^i$$

$$W_{\text{Construction}}(N) = 2D\sum_{i=0}^{D-1} 2^i - 2\sum_{i=0}^{D-1} i2^i$$

---

[2] The depth is 1 less than the level number. A heap with four levels will have a maximum depth of 3. The root is at depth 0, its children are at depth 1, their children are at depth 2, and so on.

Using Equations 1.17 and 1.19, we get

$$W_{\text{Construction}}(N) = 2D(2^D - 1) - 2[(D-2)2^D + 2]$$

$$W_{\text{Construction}}(N) = 2^{D+1}D - 2D - 2^{D+1}D + 2^{D+2} - 4$$

$$W_{\text{Construction}}(N) = 2^{D+2} - 2D - 4$$

We now substitute $D = \lg N$, giving

$$W_{\text{Construction}}(N) = 4 * 2^{\lg N} - 2\lg N - 4$$

$$W_{\text{Construction}}(N) = 4N - 2\lg N - 4 = O(N)$$

So the heap construction phase is linear with respect to the number of elements in the list.

Now we consider the main loop of the algorithm. In this loop, we remove one element from the heap and then call FixHeap. This gets repeated until there is only one element left in the heap. On each pass the number of elements decreases by 1, but how does this change the depth of the heap? We have already said that the entire heap has a depth of $\lfloor \lg N \rfloor$, and so it is easy to see that if there are K nodes left in the heap, it will have depth of $\lfloor \lg K \rfloor$, and the number of comparisons is twice this number. This means that the worst case for the loop is

$$W_{\text{loop}}(N) = \sum_{k=1}^{N-1} 2\lfloor \lg k \rfloor = 2\sum_{k=1}^{N-1} \lfloor \lg k \rfloor$$

The problem we now have is that there is no standard form for this summation. Let's think about how this breaks down. When k is 1, $\lfloor \lg k \rfloor$ will be 0. When k is 2 and 3, $\lfloor \lg k \rfloor$ will be 1. When k is 4 through 7, $\lfloor \lg k \rfloor$ will be 2. When k is 8 through 15, $\lfloor \lg k \rfloor$ will be 3. We notice that in each of these cases, when the result is j, there are 2^j values that give that result. This will be true for all but the last level of the heap if it is not complete. On that level, we see that there are $N - 2^{\lfloor \lg N \rfloor}$ elements.[3] This means that our equation can be represented as:

$$W_{\text{loop}}(N) = 2\left[\left(\sum_{k=1}^{d-1} k2^k\right) + d(N - 2^d)\right] \quad \text{where } d = \lfloor \lg N \rfloor$$

***

[3] Because there is a floor involved with the exponent of 2, $2^{\lfloor \lg N \rfloor} < N$, except when N is an exact power of 2, and then these are equal.

Using Equation 1.19, we get

$$W_{\text{loop}}(N) = 2[(d-2)2^d + 2 + d(N-2^d)]$$
$$W_{\text{loop}}(N) = d2^{d+1} - 2^{d+2} + 4 + 2d * N - d2^{d+1}$$
$$W_{\text{loop}}(N) = 2d * N - 2^{d+2} + 4$$

Now, substituting $\lfloor \lg N \rfloor$ for d, we get

$$W_{\text{loop}}(N) = 2\lfloor \lg N \rfloor N - 2^{\lfloor \lg N \rfloor + 2} + 4$$
$$W_{\text{loop}}(N) = 2\lfloor \lg N \rfloor N - 4\lfloor \lg N \rfloor + 4 = O(N \lg N)$$

Now, we have to add together the construction and loop stages to get our final result. This gives the equation

$$W(N) = W_{\text{construction}}(N) + W_{\text{loop}}(N)$$
$$W(N) = 4N - 2\lg N - 4 + 2\lfloor \lg N \rfloor N - 4\lfloor \lg N \rfloor + 4$$
$$W(N) \approx 4N + 2\lfloor \lg N \rfloor(N-3)$$
$$W(N) = O(N \lg N)$$

▥ 3.5.2 Average-Case Analysis

To get the average-case analysis for heapsort, we will take a different approach. Let's consider the best case, where the values are initially in the array in the reverse order. You should be able to see that this is automatically a correct heap. This means that each call to `FixHeap` in the construction phase will do only two comparisons to show the values are properly ordered. So, because `Fix-Heap` is called for about one-half of the elements and each call does two comparisons, the construction stage does about N comparisons, which is the same order as in the worst case.

Notice that no matter what order the elements are in at the start, after the construction stage we always have a heap. So, in every case, the `for` loop will have to execute the same number of times as in the worst case, because to get the sorted values we have to take each element out of the heap and then fix the heap. So, in the best case, heapsort does about $N + N \lg N$ comparisons. This means that the best case is $O(N \lg N)$.

For heapsort, the best and worst cases are both $O(N \lg N)$. This can only mean that the average case must also be $O(N \lg N)$.

1. Given the list of elements, [23, 17, 21, 3, 42, 9, 13, 1, 2, 7, 35, 4], what would be their order after the loop for the heap construction phase executes?

2. Given the list of elements, [3, 9, 14, 12, 2, 17, 15, 8, 6, 18, 20, 1], what would be their order after the loop for the heap construction phase executes?

3. We could shorten the second `for` loop in our heapsort by changing the ending condition to $i \geq 3$. What, if anything, would need to be added after this `for` loop to assure that the final list is sorted? Would this change reduce the number of comparisons (give a detailed reason for your answer)?

4. Prove that a list in reverse order is a heap.

3.6 MERGE SORT

Merge sort is the first of our recursive sort algorithms. It is based on the idea that merging two sorted lists can be done quickly. Because a list with just one element is sorted, merge sort will break a list down into one-element pieces and then sort as it merges those pieces back together. All of the work for this algorithm, therefore, occurs in the merging of the two lists.

Merge sort can be written as a recursive algorithm that does its work on the way up in the recursive process. In looking at the algorithm that follows, you will notice that it breaks the list in half as long as first is less than last. When we get to a point where first and last are equal, we have a list of one element, which is inherently sorted. When we return from the two calls to MergeSort that have lists of size 1, we then call MergeLists to put those together to create a sorted list of size 2. At the next level up, we will have two lists of size 2 that get merged into one sorted list of size 4. This process continues until we get to the top call, which merges the two sorted halves of the list back into one sorted list. We see that MergeSort breaks a list in halves on the way down in the recursive process and then puts the sorted halves together on the way back up. The algorithm to accomplish this is

```
MergeSort( list, first, last )
list    the elements to be put into order
first   the index of the first element in the part of list to sort
```

```
last    the index of the last element in the part of list to sort

if first < last then
   middle = ( first + last ) / 2
   MergeSort( list, first, middle )
   MergeSort( list, middle + 1, last )
   MergeLists( list, first, middle, middle + 1, last )
end if
```

It should be obvious that the work is all being done in the function Merge-Lists. We now will develop MergeLists.

Consider lists A and B, both sorted in increasing order. This ordering means that the smallest element of each list is in the first location, and the largest element of each list is in the last location. To merge these together into one list, we know that the smallest element overall must be either the first element of A or the first element of B, and the largest element overall must be either the last element of A or the last element of B. If we want to create a new list C that is the sorted combination of A and B, we will begin by moving the smaller of A[1] and B[1] into C[1]. But what gets moved into C[2]? If A[1] was smaller than B[1], A[1] was moved into C[1], and the next element might be B[1] unless A[2] is also smaller than B[1]. This is possible because all we really know is that A[2] is larger than A[1] and smaller than A[3], but we don't know how the elements of A relate in size to the elements of B. It seems that the best way to accomplish the merge would be to have two indices for A and B and increment the index for the list that has the smaller element. The general process keeps comparing the smallest elements of what is left of lists A and B and moves the smaller of these two into C. At some point, however, we will "run out" of elements in either list A or B. The elements "left over" will be those in one list that are greater than the last element of the other list. We need to make sure that these elements are moved to the end of the result list.

Putting these ideas together into an algorithm gives us

```
MergeLists( list, start1, end1, start2, end2 )
list     the elements to be put into order
start1   beginning of "list" A
end1     end of "list" A
start2   beginning of "list" B
end2     end of "list" B
// assumes that the elements of A and B are contiguous in list
finalStart = start1
```

```
finalEnd = end2
indexC = 1
while (start1 ≤ end1) and (start2 ≤ end2) do
   if list[start1] < list[start2] then
      result[indexC] = list[start1]
      start1 = start1 + 1
   else
      result[indexC] = list[start2]
      start2 = start2 + 1
   end if
   indexC = indexC + 1
end while

// move the part of the list that is left over
if (start1 ≤ end1) then
   for i = start1 to end1 do
      result[indexC] = list[i]
      indexC = indexC + 1
   end for
else
   for i = start2 to end2 do
      result[indexC] = list[i]
      indexC = indexC + 1
   end for
end if

// now put the result back into the list
indexC = 1
for i = finalStart to finalEnd do
   list[i] = result[indexC]
   indexC = indexC + 1
end for
```

■ 3.6.1 MergeLists Analysis

Because all of the element comparisons occur in MergeLists, we begin ana-lyzing there. Let's look at the case where all of the elements of list A are smaller than the first element of list B. What will happen in MergeLists? We will begin by comparing A[1] and B[1] and because A[1] is smaller we will move it to C. We then compare A[2] with B[1] and move A[2] because it is smaller. This process will continue comparing each element of A with B[1], because they are all smaller. This means that the algorithm does N_A comparisons, where

N_A is the number of elements in list A. Notice that if all of the elements of list B are smaller than the first element of A, the resulting number of comparisons would be N_B, where N_B is the number of elements in list B.

What if the first element of A is greater than the first element of B but all of the elements of A are smaller than the second element of B? We would compare A[1] and B[1] and move B[1] to C. We now find ourselves in the same position we were in the last case, where we will compare every element of A with B[2] as they are moved to the result. This time, however, we not only have done N_A comparisons of the elements of A with B[2], but we also did a comparison of A[1] and B[1], so the total number of comparisons in this case is $N_A + 1$. If we consider other arrangements, we start to see that the case presented in the first paragraph of this subsection might be the best case, and it is.

We saw that if all the elements of list A were between B[1] and B[2], we did more comparisons than if all of the elements of A were smaller than all of the elements of B. Let's see if taking this to the extreme gives the worst case. Consider what happens if the elements of A and B are "interleaved" based on their value. In other words, what happens if the value of A[1] is between B[1] and B[2], the value of A[2] is between B[2] and B[3], the value of A[3] is between B[3] and B[4], and so on. Notice that each comparison moves one element from either A or B into list C. Based on the example ordering above, we move an element of B, then one of A, then one of B, then one of A, until we have moved all but the last element of A. Because the comparisons resulted in moving all but the last element of A, we will have done $N_A + N_B - 1$ comparisons in this worst case.

■ 3.6.2 MergeSort Analysis

Now that we know the range of complexity of `MergeLists`, we can now look at `MergeSort`. Based on the techniques of Section 1.5, we look at the parts of the `MergeSort` algorithm. First, we notice that the function is called recursively as long as `first` is less than `last`. This means that if they are equal or if `first` is greater than `last`, there is no recursive call. If `first` is equal to `last`, this represents a list of size 1. If `first` is greater than `last`, this represents a list of size 0. In both of these cases, the algorithm does nothing, so the direct solution has zero comparisons.

The division of the list into two parts is done by the calculation of `middle`. We see this calculation is done without any comparisons, so the division step is zero. Because `middle` is calculated to be exactly between `first` and `last`, we see that we are breaking the list into two sublists, and each one is half the size of the original. If the list has N elements, we create two sublists with $N / 2$ elements. Based on the analysis of `MergeLists`, this means that the combine step will take $N / 2$ comparisons in the best case, and $N / 2 + N / 2 - 1$, or $N - 1$, comparisons in the worst case. Putting all of this together gives the two recurrence relations for the worst (W) and best (B) cases.

$$W(N) = 2W(N/2) + N - 1$$
$$W(0) = W(1) = 0$$
$$B(N) = 2B(N/2) + N/2$$
$$B(0) = B(1) = 0$$

We now apply the techniques of Section 1.6 to solve these recurrence relations. First, we solve the worst case:

$$W(N/2) = 2W(N/4) + N/2 - 1$$
$$W(N/4) = 2W(N/8) + N/4 - 1$$
$$W(N/8) = 2W(N/16) + N/8 - 1$$
$$W(N/16) = 2W(N/32) + N/16 - 1$$

Now we substitute:

$$W(N) = 2W(N/2) + N - 1$$
$$W(N) = 2(2W(N/4) + N/2 - 1) + N - 1$$
$$W(N) = 4W(N/4) + N - 2 + N - 1$$
$$W(N) = 4(2W(N/8) + N/4 - 1) + N - 2 + N - 1$$
$$W(N) = 8W(N/8) + N - 4 + N - 2 + N - 1$$
$$W(N) = 8(2W(N/16) + N/8 - 1) + N - 4 + N - 2 + N - 1$$
$$W(N) = 16W(N/16) + N - 8 + N - 4 + N - 2 + N - 1$$
$$W(N) = 16(2W(N/32) + N/16 - 1) + N - 8 + N - 4 + N - 2 + N - 1$$
$$W(N) = 32W(N/32) + N - 16 + N - 8 + N - 4 + N - 2 + N - 1$$

We see that the coefficient of W increases at the same rate as the denominator increases. Eventually, this term will become $W(1)$, which has a value of zero, and so this first term will eventually disappear. Notice that each substitution produced another addition of N and the subtraction of the next higher power of 2. How many of these will be included? We see in the last equation that we have five N terms, the sum of the powers of 2 from 0 ($1 = 2^0$) through 4 ($16 = 2^4$) and $W(N / 32) = W(N / 2^5)$. This means that when we get to the point of having $W(N / 2^{\lg N}) = W(N / N)$, the closed form of this equation becomes

$$W(N) = N * W(1) + N \lg N - \sum_{i=0}^{\lg N - 1} 2^i$$

$$W(N) = N \lg N - (2^{\lg N} - 1)$$
$$W(N) = N \lg N - N + 1$$

This means that $W(N) = O(N \lg N)$. When we look at $W(N)$ and $B(N)$, we see the difference between the two is that N becomes $N / 2$. When we look at the role that N played during our substitutions, the reader should see that $B(N) \approx (N \lg N) / 2$, so it is also the case that $B(N) = O(N \lg N)$.

This means that `MergeSort` is a very efficient sort, even in the worst case, but the problem is that the `MergeList` function needs extra space to accomplish the merge.

■ 3.6.3 EXERCISES

1. Show the results of each pass of `MergeSort` applied to the list [7, 3, 9, 4, 2, 5, 6, 1, 8].

2. Show the results of each pass of `MergeSort` applied to the list [3, 5, 2, 9, 8, 1, 6, 4, 7].

3. In the discussion of `MergeLists`, it was mentioned that the best case is when all of the values of list A are smaller than the values of list B. This, however, doesn't say anything about the operation of the entire algorithm for any initial input of values. Exactly how many key comparisons will be done by `MergeSort` on the list [1, 2, 3, 4, 5, 6, 7, 8]? In general, how many comparisons are done for a list of N elements that is already in increasing order? Show details of all work.

4. Exactly how many key comparisons will be done by `MergeSort` on the list [8, 7, 6, 5, 4, 3, 2, 1]? In general, how many comparisons are done for a list of N elements that is in decreasing order? Show details of all work.

5. Create an ordering of the numbers 1 through 8 that will cause `MergeSort` to do the worst-case number of comparisons of 17. (*Hint:* Work backward through the sorting process.)

3.7 QUICKSORT

Quicksort is another recursive sorting algorithm. It picks an element from the list and uses it to divide the list into two parts. The first part has all of the elements that are smaller than the one chosen, and the second part has all of the elements that are larger. We saw this process when we looked at the selection problem in Section 2.3. The Quicksort algorithm is different because it is then applied recursively to both parts. This is an efficient sort on average, but its worst case is the same as insertion and bubble sort.

Quicksort chooses an element of the list, called the pivot element, and then rearranges the list so that all of the elements smaller than the pivot are moved before it and all of the elements larger than the pivot are moved after it. The elements in each of the two parts of the list are not put in order. If the pivot element winds up in location i, all we know is that the elements in locations 1 through $i - 1$ are smaller than the pivot element and those in locations $i + 1$ through N are larger than the pivot. Quicksort is then called recursively for these two parts. If Quicksort is called with a list containing one element, it does nothing because a one-element list is sorted.

Because the determination of the pivot point and the movement of the elements into the proper section do all of the work, the main Quicksort algorithm just needs to keep track of the bounds of these two sections. Further, because splitting the list into two parts is where the keys are moved around, all of the sorting work is done on the way down in the recursive process. Recall that this is the opposite of merge sort, which does its work on the way back up in the recursive process.

The algorithm for quicksort is

```
Quicksort( list, first, last )
list   the elements to be put into order
first the index of the first element in the part of list to sort
last   the index of the last element in the part of list to sort

if first < last then
   pivot = PivotList( list, first, last )
   Quicksort( list, first, pivot-1 )
   Quicksort( list, pivot+1, last )
end if
```

Splitting the List

There are at least two versions of the `PivotList` function. The first is easy to program and understand and is presented in this section. The other is more complicated to write but is faster than this version. The second version will be considered in the exercises.

The function `PivotList` will pick the first element of the list as its pivot element and will set the pivot point as the first location of the list. It then moves through the list comparing this pivot element to the rest of the elements. Whenever it finds an element that is smaller than the pivot element, it will increment the pivot point and then swap this element into the new pivot point location. After some of the elements are compared to the pivot inside the loop, we will have four parts to the list. The first part is the pivot element in the first location. The second part is from location first + 1 through the pivot point and will be all of the elements we have looked at that are smaller than the pivot element. The third part is from the location after the pivot point through the loop index and will be all of the elements we have looked at that are larger than the pivot element. The rest of the list will be values we have not yet examined. This is shown in Fig. 3.4.

The algorithm for `PivotList` is as follows:

```
PivotList( list, first, last )
list   the elements to work with
first  the index of the first element
last   the index of the last element

PivotValue = list[ first ]
PivotPoint = first
for index = first + 1 to last do
    if list[ index ] < PivotValue then
```

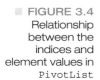

FIGURE 3.4 Relationship between the indices and element values in `PivotList`

```
      PivotPoint = PivotPoint + 1
      Swap( list[ PivotPoint ], list[ index ] )
   end if
end for
// move pivot value into correct place
Swap( list[ first ], list[ PivotPoint ] )
return PivotPoint
```

■ 3.7.1 Worst-Case Analysis

When `PivotList` is called with a list of N elements, it does $N - 1$ comparisons as it compares the PivotValue with every other element in the list. Because we have already said that quicksort is a divide and conquer algorithm, you might assume that a best case would be when `PivotList` creates two parts that are the same size and you would be correct. The worst case would then be when the lists are of drastically different sizes. The largest difference in the size of these two lists occurs if the `PivotValue` is smaller (or larger) than all of the other values in the list. In that case, we wind up with one part that has no elements and the other that has $N - 1$ elements. If the same thing happens each time we apply this process, we would only remove one element (the `Pivot-Value`) from the list at each recursive call. This means we would do the number of comparisons given by the following formula:

$$W(N) = \sum_{i=2}^{N}(i - 1) = \frac{N(N-1)}{2}$$

What original ordering of elements would cause this behavior? If each pass chooses the first element, that element must be the smallest (or largest). A list that is already sorted is one arrangement that would cause this worst case behavior! In all of the other sort algorithms we have considered, the worst and average cases have been about the same, but as we are about to see, this is not true for quicksort.

■ 3.7.2 Average-Case Analysis

You will recall that when we looked at shellsort, we considered the number of inversions that each comparison removed in our analysis. At that time, we pointed out that bubble sort and insertion sort didn't do well on average because they both removed only one inversion for each comparison.

So, how does quicksort do in removing inversions? Consider a list of N elements that the `PivotList` algorithm is working on. Let's say that the `PivotValue` is greater than all of the values in the list. This means that at the end of the routine `PivotPoint` will be N, and so the `PivotValue` will be switched from the first location to the last location. It is also possible that the element in the last location is the smallest value in the list. So swapping these two values will move the largest element from the first location to the last and will move the smallest element from the last location to the first. If the largest element is first, there are $N - 1$ inversions of it with the rest of the elements in the list, and if the smallest element is last, there are $N - 1$ inversions of it with the rest of the elements in the list. This one swap can remove $2N - 2$ inversions from the list. It is because of this possibility that quicksort has an average case that is significantly different from its worst case.

Notice that `PivotList` is doing all of the work, and so we first look at this algorithm to see what it does in the average case. We first notice that it is possible for each of the N locations in the list to be the location of the `PivotValue` when `PivotList` is done. To get the average case, we have to look at what happens for each of these possibilities and average the results. When looking at the worst case, we noticed that for a list of N elements there are $N - 1$ comparisons done by `PivotList` in dividing the list. There is no work done to put the lists back together. Lastly, notice that when `PivotList` returns a value of P, we call `Quicksort` recursively with lists of $P - 1$ and $N - P$ elements. Our average case analysis needs to look at all N possible values for P. Putting this together gives the recurrence relation

$$A(N) = (N-1) + \frac{1}{N}\left(\sum_{i=1}^{N}[A(i-1) + A(N-i)]\right) \quad \text{for } N \geq 2$$

$$A(1) = A(0) = 0$$

If you look closely at the summation, you will notice that the first term is used with values from 0 through $N - 1$, and the second term is used with values from $N - 1$ down to 0. This means that the summation adds up every value of A from 0 to $N - 1$ twice. This gives us the following simplification:

$$A(N) = (N-1) + \frac{1}{N}\left(2\sum_{i=0}^{N-1}A(i)\right) \quad \text{for } N \geq 2$$

$$A(1) = A(0) = 0$$

This is a very complicated form of recurrence relation because it depends on not just one smaller value of A, but rather on every smaller value for A. There are two ways to go about solving this. The first is to come up with an educated guess for the answer and to then prove that this answer does satisfy the recurrence relation. The second way is to look at the equations for both $A(N)$ and $A(N-1)$. Those two equations differ by only a few terms. We now compute $A(N) * N$ and $A(N-1) * (N-1)$ to get rid of the two fractions. This gives

$$A(N) * N = (N-1)N + 2\sum_{i=0}^{N-1} A(i)$$

$$A(N) * N = (N-1)N + 2A(N-1) + 2\sum_{i=0}^{N-2} A(i)$$

$$A(N-1) * (N-1) = (N-2)(N-1) + 2\sum_{i=0}^{N-2} A(i)$$

Now, we subtract the third equation above from the second and simplify to get

$$A(N) * N - A(N-1) * (N-1) = 2A(N-1) + (N-1)N - (N-2)(N-1)$$

$$A(N) * N - A(N-1) * (N-1) = 2A(N-1) + N^2 - N - (N^2 - 3N + 2)$$

$$A(N) * N - A(N-1) * (N-1) = 2A(N-1) + 2N - 2$$

Adding $A(N-1) * (N-1)$ to both sides, we get

$$A(N) * N = 2A(N-1) + A(N-1) * (N-1) + 2N - 2$$

$$A(N) * N = A(N-1) * (2 + N - 1) + 2N - 2$$

This gives our final recurrence relation:

$$A(N) = \frac{(N+1) * A(N-1) + 2N - 2}{N}$$

$$A(1) = A(0) = 0$$

Solving this is not difficult but does require care because of all of the terms on the right-hand side of the equation. If you work through all of the details, you will see the final result is $A(N) \approx 1.4 \, (N+1) \lg N$. Quicksort is, therefore, $O(N \lg N)$ on average.

■ 3.7.3 EXERCISES

1. Trace the operation of `Quicksort` on the list [23, 17, 21, 3, 42, 9, 13, 1, 2, 7, 35, 4]. Show the list order and the stack of (first, last, pivot) values at the start of every call. Count the number of comparisons and swaps that are done.

2. Trace the operation of `Quicksort` on the list [3, 9, 14, 12, 2, 17, 15, 8, 6, 18, 20, 1]. Show the list order and the stack of (first, last, pivot) values at the start of every call. Count the number of comparisons and swaps that are done.

3. We showed that the `Quicksort` algorithm performs poorly when the list is sorted because the pivot element is always smaller than all of the elements left in the list. Just picking a different location of the list would have the same problem because you could get "unlucky" and always pick the smallest remaining value. A better alternative would be to consider three values list[first], list[last], and list[(first + last) / 2] and pick the median or middle value of these three. The comparisons to pick the middle element must be included in the complexity analysis of the algorithm.

   a. Do Question 1 using this alternative method for picking the pivot element.

   b. Do Question 2 using this alternative method for picking the pivot element.

   c. In general, how many comparisons are done in the worst case to sort a list of N keys? (*Note:* You are now guaranteed to not have the smallest value for the `PivotValue`, but the result can still be pretty bad.)

4. An alternative for the `PivotList` algorithm would be to have two indices into the list. The first moves up from the bottom and the other moves down from the top. The main loop of the algorithm will advance the lower index until a value greater than the `PivotValue` is found, and the upper index is moved until a value less than the `PivotValue` is found. Then these two are swapped. This process repeats until the two indices cross. These inner loops are very fast because the overhead of checking for the end of the list is eliminated, but the problem is that they will do an extra swap when the indices pass each other. So, the algorithm does one extra swap to correct this. The full algorithm is

```
PivotList( list, first, last )
list   the elements to work with
first the index of the first element
last   the index of the last element
```

```
PivotValue = list[ first ]
lower = first
upper = last+1
do
    do upper = upper - 1 until list[upper] ≤ PivotValue
    do lower = lower + 1 until list[lower] ≥ PivotValue
    Swap( list[ upper ], list[ lower ] )
until lower ≥ upper
// undo the extra exchange
Swap( list[ upper ], list[ lower ] )
// move pivot point into correct place
Swap( list[ first ], list[ upper ] )
return upper
```

(*Note:* This algorithm requires one extra list location at the end to hold a special sentinel value that is larger than all of the valid key values.)

a. Do Question 1 using this alternative method for PivotList.

b. Do Question 2 using this alternative method for PivotList.

c. What operation is done significantly less frequently for this version of PivotList?

d. How many key comparisons does the new PivotList do in the worst case for a list of N elements? (*Note:* It is not $N - 1$.) How does this affect the overall worst case for quicksort?

5. How many comparisons will Quicksort do on a list of N elements that all have the same value?

6. What is the maximum number of times that Quicksort will move the largest or smallest value?

3.8   EXTERNAL POLYPHASE MERGE SORT

In some cases, a list that needs to be sorted may be so large that it cannot be held in memory at one time. You should note that even though our sorting algorithms have only been concerned with placing keys in the correct order, it is assumed that those keys are connected to entire records of information. You should see that in many instances, the size of the full record will be significantly larger than the size of the key. In some instances, the record size is so significant that the process of swapping two records becomes so time consuming that the efficiency of a sorting algorithm is both the number of comparisons and the number of swaps.

It is also possible to be able to declare an array large enough to hold all of the data but that the logical memory needs of the program are much greater than the physical memory available in the computer. This places a reliance on the computer to effectively implement virtual memory, but in even the best of circumstances there may be a large amount of data that needs to be swapped between physical memory and a disk drive. Even with an effective sorting algorithm like Quicksort, the relationship between the bounds of a partition and the blocks of logical memory that can be and are loaded may be such that a large number of blocks will have to be swapped in and out of physical memory. This problem may not be seen until a program is implemented and runs so slowly that computer-based analysis tools are needed to identify the problem. Even in that case, the problem may not be found unless system profiling tools are available that track virtual memory use.

Our analysis looked at comparison operations to determine what was an efficient sort algorithm. But the amount of time that can be spent writing information to and from the disk in the process of a virtual memory block swap will be much more significant than any logical or arithmetic operation. Because this is handled by the operating system, we have no real control over when swaps may occur.

An alternative thought might be to use a direct access file on disk and convert each array access into a seek operation to move to the correct location of the file, followed by a read. This reduces the amount of logical memory needed and so reduces the reliance on virtual memory. This still translates to a significant amount of disk input and output, which is what is costly, whether done by the program or the operating system.

All of this makes the sorting algorithms in the last seven sections impractical when the data set gets extremely large. We will now look at an alternative that will use four external sequential files and a merging process to accomplish a sort.

We first identify how many records can reasonably be held in memory when we account for the size of the executable code and the available memory. We will declare an array of this size, call it S, that will be used for the two steps of our sort process. In the first step, we will read in S records and use an appropriate internal sort to put these records in order. This set of now sorted records will be written to file A. We read in a second set of S records, sort them, and write them to file B. We continue this process, alternating where we write the sorted list between file A and file B. An algorithm to accomplish this first step would be

```
CreateRuns( S )
S  is the size of the runs to be created

CurrentFile = A
while not at the end of the input file do
   read S records from the input file
   sort the S records
   write the records to file CurrentFile
   if CurrentFile = A then
      CurrentFile = B
   else
      CurrentFile = A
   end if
end while
```

Once we have processed the entire original file into sorted runs, we are now ready to start the second step, which is to merge these runs. If you think about the process, you will realize that both files A and B have some number of runs of S records that are in order. But, as in merge sort, we can't really say anything about the relationship between the records that are in two separate runs.

Our merging process will be similar to the MergeLists function of Section 3.6, however, in this case, instead of moving the records to a new array, we will move them to a new file. So we begin by reading in half of the first runs from files A and B. We can only read in half of each run because we have already identified that we can only hold S records at a time, and we need records from both files A and B. We now begin to merge them into a new file C. If we run through the first half of records from either file, we will then read in the second set of records for this run. When we have completed one of the two runs, the rest of the other run is written to the file. Once the first runs of files A and B have been merged, we then merge the second two runs, but this time the output is written to file D. This process continues to merge runs and write them alternately to files C and D. On the completion of this pass, you should see that we now have runs of $2S$ records in files C and D. We repeat the process again, but this time we read runs from C and D and write them to files A and B, which will then have runs with $4S$ records. You should see that eventually we will have merged the runs into one list that is now sorted. An algorithm to accomplish this second step would be

```
PolyphaseMerge( S )
S  is the size of the initial runs
Size = S
Input1 = A
Input2 = B
CurrentOutput = C
while not done do
   while more runs this pass do
      Merge one run of length Size from file Input1
         with one run of length Size from file Input2
         sending output to CurrentOutput
      if (CurrentOutput = A) then
         CurrentOutput = B
      elseif (CurrentOutput = B) then
         CurrentOutput = A
      elseif (CurrentOutput = C) then
         CurrentOutput = D
      elseif (CurrentOutput = D) then
         CurrentOutput = C
      end if
   end while
   Size = Size * 2
   if (Input1 = A) then
      Input1 = C
      Input2 = D
      CurrrentOutput = A
   else
      Input1 = A
      Input2 = B
      CurrentOutput = C
   end if
end while
```

Before we begin our analysis, we first look at what we have in terms of runs and the number of passes this translates to. If we have N records in our original file, and we can store S records at one time, this means that after CreateRuns we must have $R = \lceil N / S \rceil$ runs split between the two files. Each of the PolyphaseMerge passes joins pairs of runs, so it must cut the number of runs in half. After one pass there will be $\lceil R / 2 \rceil$ runs, after two passes there will be $\lceil R / 4 \rceil$ runs, and, in general, after j passes there will be $\lceil R / 2^j \rceil$ runs. Because we stop when we get down to one run, this will be when $\lceil R / 2^D \rceil$ is equal to 1, which will be when D is $\lceil \lg R \rceil$. This means we will do $\lceil \lg R \rceil$ passes of the merge process.

▨ 3.8.1 Number of Comparisons in Run Construction

Because the algorithm used for the run construction phase is not specified, we will assume that an $O(N \lg N)$ sort is used. Because there are S elements in each run, each one will take $O(S \lg S)$ to construct. There are R runs, giving $O(R * S * \lg S) = O(N \lg S)$ comparisons in total for the construction of all of the runs. The run construction phase is $O(N \lg S)$.

▨ 3.8.2 Number of Comparisons in Run Merge

In Section 3.6.1, we saw that `MergeLists` does $A + B - 1$ comparisons in the worst case with two lists of A and B elements. In our case, we have R runs of size S on the first pass that get merged, so there are $R / 2$ merges, each of which will take at most $2S - 1$ comparisons, or $R / 2 * (2S - 1) = R * S - R / 2$ comparisons. On the second pass, we have $R / 2$ runs of size $2S$, so there are $R / 4$ merges, each of which will take at most $2(2S) - 1$ comparisons, or $R / 4 * (4S - 1) = R * S - R / 4$ comparisons. On the third pass, we have $R / 4$ runs of size $4S$, so there are $R / 8$ merges, each of which will take at most $2(4S) - 1$ comparisons, or $R / 8 * (8S - 1) = R * S - R / 8$ comparisons.

If we recall that there will be $\lg R$ merge passes, the total number of comparisons in the merge phase will be

$$\sum_{i=1}^{\lg R} (R * S - R/2^i) = \sum_{i=1}^{\lg R} (R * S) - \sum_{i=1}^{\lg R} (R/2^i)$$

$$= (R * S) * \lg R - R * \sum_{i=1}^{\lg R} 1/2^i$$

$$\approx (R * S) * \lg R - R$$

$$= N \lg R - R$$

In the second equation, you should note that if you add $1/2 + 1/4 + 1/8 +, \ldots$, you will get a number that is less than 1, but it will get closer to 1 the more terms that you have. To visualize this, imagine that you stand 1 foot away from a wall, and you repeatedly keep moving closer to the wall by one-half your current distance from the wall. Because you only move one-half the distance each step, you will never reach the wall, but you will keep getting closer to it. In the same way, if you do the above addition, you are adding one-half the distance between your current total and the number 1 each time. This means that the sum will keep getting closer to 1, but never larger. This can also be shown by the application of Equation 1.18 using $A = 0.5$ and an adjustment because the above summation begins at 1, where the summation in Equation 1.18 begins at 0.

The run merge phase is $O(N \lg R)$. This makes the entire algorithm

$$
\begin{aligned}
O(N \lg S + N \lg R) &= O[N * (\lg S + \lg R)] \\
&= O[N * \lg (S * R)] \quad \text{by Equation 1.5} \\
&= O[N * \lg (S * N / S)] \\
&= O(N \lg N)
\end{aligned}
$$

■ 3.8.3 Number of Block Reads

Reading large blocks of data is significantly faster than reading each of the items in the block one after another. For this reason, a polyphase merge sort will be most efficient if all data is read as larger blocks. We are still, however, interested in how many blocks of data will be read in this sort.

In the run construction step, we will read one block of data for each run, resulting in R block reads. Because we can only fit S records in memory, and we need records from two runs for the merge step, we will read blocks of size $S / 2$ in the merge phase. Each pass of the merge step will have to read all of the data as part of some run, meaning that there will be $N / (S / 2) = 2R$ block reads. Because there are $\lg R$ passes, there are $2R \lg R$ block reads in the merge step.

In the entire algorithm, there are $R + 2R \lg R = O(R \lg R)$ block reads.

■ 3.8.4 EXERCISES

1. What would be involved in rewriting the external polyphase merge sort algorithm so that it only used three files instead of four? What impact would this change have on the number of comparisons and block reads? (*Hint:* This new version can't alternate back and forth in the merge step.)

2. What would be involved in rewriting the external polyphase merge sort algorithm so that it used six files instead of four and the merging of three lists was done simultaneously? What impact would this change have on the number of comparisons and block reads? Would there be any additional change if we used eight files and merged four lists simultaneously?

3.9   ADDITIONAL EXERCISES

1. Selection sort will scan the list of values looking for the largest (or smallest) key value. This value is swapped into the last (or first) location of the list.

The process is repeated for a list one element smaller that doesn't include the element just put into the correct position. This is continued until the entire list is sorted.

a. Write a formal algorithm that will accomplish this selection sort by looking for the largest element on each pass.
b. Do a worst-case analysis of your algorithm from part (a).
c. Do an average-case analysis of your algorithm from part (a).

2. A counting sort can be used on a list that has no duplicate keys. In a counting sort, you would compare the first key in the list with every other element (including itself), counting the number of values that are less than or equal to this key. If we find that there are X keys that are less than or equal to this key, it belongs in location X. We can repeat this for all of the other keys, storing the values we get into a separate array that has the same number of elements as our list. When we have completed the counting, the extra array has all of the locations where the elements need to be for the list to be sorted, and it can be used to create the new sorted list.

a. Write a formal algorithm that will accomplish this counting sort.
b. Do a worst-case analysis of your algorithm from part (a).
c. Do an average-case analysis of your algorithm from part (a).

3. When a sorting algorithm is applied to a list of values, we are sometimes interested in knowing what happens when there are duplicate entries in the list. This is important in an application that sorts large records on a number of different fields and doesn't want the efforts of a previous sort lost. For example, let's say that records store a person's first and last names in two separate fields. We could first sort the records based on the first name field and then sort them again on the last name field. If the sort algorithm keeps records with the same last name in the same order they were in after the first sort, the entire list would be properly sorted by full name.

If for every case where list[i] = list[j] ($i < j$), the sorting algorithm moves list[i] into location i', moves list[j] into location j', and $i' < j'$, the sorting algorithm is called stable. In other words, if there are two records with the same key, a sorting algorithm is stable when those keys stay in the same relative order in the list even though they may move.

Prove which of the following sorting algorithms are stable:

a. Insertion sort
b. Bubble sort

c. Shellsort

d. Radix sort

e. Heapsort

f. Merge sort

g. Quicksort

3.10 PROGRAMMING EXERCISES

You can test the complexity of a sorting algorithm in the following way:

- Write a function or functions that will do the sorting algorithm.

- Put in two global counters called compareCount and swapCount. The first should be incremented before every comparison of list values in every routine. The second should be incremented whenever list elements are exchanged or moved.

- Write a main program with a loop that generates a random list and then sorts it. In each pass of this loop, you should keep track of the maximum, minimum, and total values for both compareCount and swapCount. At the end, you can report the overall maximum, minimum, and averages for these two counters. The more times you perform this loop, the more accurate your results will be.

- If you are trying to compare sort routines, you should run them on the same list or lists. The easiest way to do this is to have a set of counters for each sort, and then when you generate a random list, make a copy of the list to pass into each sort. You would then run all of the sorts on the first list before generating the next list.

1. Use the technique above with insertion sort and bubble sort. Even though both are $O(N^2)$ sorts, does your test show any differences? How do your results relate to the analysis done in this chapter? Try to explain any differences.

2. Use the technique above with heapsort, merge sort, and quicksort. Even though all are $O(N \lg N)$ sorts on average, does your test show any differences? How do your results relate to the analysis done in this chapter? Try to explain any differences.

3. Use the technique above with the version of bubble sort given in the chapter and one or more of the versions described in the exercises in Section

3.2.4. Does your test show any differences? How do your results relate to the analysis done in this chapter and as part of the exercises? Try to explain any differences.

4. Use the technique above with quicksort using the versions of `PivotList` given in the chapter and in the exercises in Section 3.7.3. Does your test show any differences? How do your results relate to the analysis done in this chapter and as part of the exercises? Try to explain any differences.

5. Using the previous general technique, investigate the impact of the increment on shellsort. You should create a version of the `ShellSort` function that has an additional parameter, which is just an array with the increment values to use in decreasing order. You will need to alter this function so it uses the values passed in instead of the increments that are calculated based on the powers of 2. You should work with random lists of 250 elements and make sure that each of the sets of increments discussed in Section 3.3 is used with each list generated. How do your results relate to the analysis done in Section 3.3? Try to explain any differences.

6. Some people find it easier to understand an algorithm if they can visualize it in action. The numeric values in a list can be visualized by drawing a vertical bar for each list element with the first element to the left and the last to the right. The height of each bar is based on the value stored at that element. For example, if we have a list with the values from 1 to 500, the location where the 1 is stored would have a bar 1 unit high and the location where the 500 is stored would have a bar 500 units high. A random list would have the bars all mixed up, but a list sorted in increasing order would appear as a triangle with the shortest bar to the left and the largest to the right.

The operation of a sorting algorithm can be seen if the list is displayed as described above after each pass of the sorting algorithm. This allows the viewer to watch as the elements are moved into their proper position by the sort algorithm. Write a program (or programs) using randomly arranged lists for the cases below. You should use lists of between 250 and 500 elements, depending on capabilities of the computer(s) you are using. On fast computers, you may need to put in a short delay so that the visualization does not happen too quickly.

a. Insertion sort—displaying the list at the end of each pass of the outer loop

b. Bubble sort—displaying the list at the end of each pass of the outer loop

c. Shellsort—displaying the list after each call to the modified insertion sort

d. Heapsort—displaying the list after each call to `FixHeap`

e. Merge sort—displaying the list after each call to `MergeLists`

f. Quicksort—displaying the list after each call to `PivotList`

CHAPTER 4

Numeric Algorithms

PREREQUISITES

Before beginning this chapter, you should be able to

- Do simple algebra
- Evaluate polynomials
- Describe growth rates and order

GOALS

At the end of this chapter, you should be able to

- Evaluate a polynomial by Horner's method
- Evaluate a polynomial by preprocessing its coefficients
- Explain the analysis of preprocessed coefficients
- Explain matrix multiplication
- Trace Winograd's matrix multiplication
- Explain the analysis of Winograd's matrix multiplication
- Use Strassen's matrix multiplication

STUDY SUGGESTIONS

As you are working through the chapter, you should rework the examples to make sure you understand them. In addition, you should trace Horner's method and calculate the preprocessed coefficients for the polynomials $x^3 + 4x^2 - 3x + 2$ and $x^7 - 8x^6 + 3x^5 + 2x^4 - 4x^3 + 5x - 7$. You should trace the standard matrix multiplication algorithm, Winograd's matrix multiplication algorithm, and Strassen's matrix multiplication with

$$\begin{bmatrix} 1 & 4 \\ 5 & 8 \end{bmatrix} \quad \text{and} \quad \begin{bmatrix} 6 & 7 \\ 3 & 2 \end{bmatrix}$$

You should trace the Gauss–Jordan method with the equations $3x_1 + 9x_2 + 6x_3 = 21$, $5x_1 + 3x_2 + 22x_3 = 23$, and $2x_1 + 8x_2 + 7x_3 = 26$. You should also try to answer any questions before reading on. A hint or the answer is in the sentences following the question.

M athematical calculation forms the basis for a wide range of programs. Computer graphics and vision both require a large number of calculations involving polynomials and matrices. Because these are typically done for each location in an image, small improvements can have a great impact. A typical image can be created with 1024 pixels per row and 1024 pixels per column. Improving the calculation for each of these locations by even one multiplication would reduce the creation of this image by 1,048,576 multiplications overall. So, even though the techniques in this chapter don't seem to show a dramatic improvement, the real savings come from the number of times that these are used.

Some software will repeatedly evaluate complex polynomial equations. This can be part of a monitoring task where input from an external device is the value "plugged into" the equation, and the result tells if there is some condition that needs attention. Another application is trigonometric functions. What most programmers do not realize is that standard trigonometric functions like sine and cosine have power series expansions that take the form of polynomial equations, and it is these equations that a computer will use when calculating trigonometric function results. These calculations need to be fast, and so, we begin by looking at methods for more rapidly calculating polynomials.

Matrix multiplication plays a role in a number of applications. Models of physical objects for computer graphics and computer-aided design and manufacturing can be moved and manipulated through matrix operations. Image analysis will use matrices in convolution operations to improve the quality of an image and to identify the bounds of objects in a picture. Fourier analysis will describe complex wave patterns in terms of simpler sine waves through matrix manipulation.

The common issue in all of these cases is that the matrix operations are done frequently, and so faster matrix multiplication results in faster programs. Object transformations use 4×4 matrices, convolutions can use square matrices from 3×3 up to 11×11 or bigger, but they are used a very large number of times. Convolutions, for example, will take a matrix and multiply it by blocks of pixels in an image for every possible location. This means that for a 5×5 template used with a small image of 512×512 pixels (about one-quarter of a typical computer screen), a convolution will multiply this matrix by 258,064 different locations (508×508). If the standard matrix multiplication algorithm is used, this will result in 32,258,000 multiplications. A more efficient matrix multiplication algorithm can save significant time in this application.

In this chapter we will investigate ways to make polynomial evaluation and matrix multiplication more efficient. Because we are interested in how many calculations are done, we will be counting additions and multiplications. When we considered searching and sorting, we found equations that were based on the size of the list. In analyzing numeric algorithms, we will base our equations on the power of the highest order term in a polynomial equation, or the dimensions of the matrices we are multiplying.

4.1   CALCULATING POLYNOMIALS

For our discussion of polynomial evaluation, we will use a generic polynomial of the form

$$p(x) = a_n x^n + a_{n-1} x^{n-1} + a_{n-2} x^{n-2} + \cdots + a_2 x^2 + a_1 x + a_0 \qquad (4.1)$$

We will assume that the coefficient values of a_n through a_0 are all known, constant, and will be stored in an array. This means that our evaluation of a polynomial has only the value of x as its input and will return the resulting polynomial value as its output.

The standard evaluation algorithm is very straightforward:

```
Evaluate( x )
x  the value to use for evaluation of the polynomial

result = a[0] + a[1]*x
xPower = x
for i = 2 to n do
   xPower = xPower * x
   result = result + a[i]*xPower
end for
return result
```

This algorithm is very clear and its analysis is obvious. The `for` loop has two multiplications and is done $N - 1$ times. There is one multiplication done before the loop, giving a total of $2N - 1$ multiplications. There is one addition done inside the loop and one done before it, giving N additions.

4.1.1 Horner's Method

Horner's method gives a better way to do this evaluation without making the process very complex. This method is based on recognizing that the polynomial equation can be factored into the following form:

$$p(x) = (\{\dots[(a_n x + a_{n-1}) * x + a_{n-2}] * x + \dots + a_2\} * x + a_1) * x + a_0 \quad \textbf{(4.2)}$$

The reader should be able to easily see that this calculates the same value as Equation 4.1. This can be expressed in algorithmic form as

```
HornersMethod( x )
x  the value to use for evaluation of the polynomial

result = a[n]
for i = n - 1 down to 0 do
   result = result * x
   result = result + a[i]
end for
return result
```

We see that the loop is done N times and that there is one addition and one multiplication done in the loop. This means that there are N multiplications and N additions done by Horner's method. This method saves almost half of the multiplications done by the standard algorithm.

4.1.2 Preprocessed Coefficients

It is possible to do even better than this by preprocessing the coefficients. The basic idea here is that it is possible to express a polynomial as a factorization into two polynomials of lesser degree. For example, if you want to calculate x^{256}, you could use a loop like the one in the function `Evaluate` at the start of this section and do 255 multiplications. An alternative would be to set `result = x * x` and then do the statement `result = result * result` three times. We get the same answer with just four multiplications. After the first, `result` will hold x^4. After the second, it will hold x^{16}, and after the third, it will hold x^{256}.

For preprocessed coefficients to work, we need our polynomial to be monic ($a_n = 1$) and to have its largest degree equal to 1 less than a power of 2 ($n = 2^k - 1$ for some $k = 1$).[1] If this is the case, we can factor the polynomial so that

$$p(x) = (x^j + b) * q(x) + r(x) \qquad \text{where } j = 2^{k-1} \qquad \textbf{(4.3)}$$

There will be half as many terms in $q(x)$ and $r(x)$ as in $p(x)$. To get the results we want, we would evaluate $q(x)$ and r(x) and then do one additional multiplication and two additions. The interesting thing about this process is that if we choose the value of b carefully, both $q(x)$ and $r(x)$ will be monic polynomials with the proper degree for this process to be applied again. After all of this is done, we will see that this process does save calculations.

Instead of looking at just generic polynomials, consider the following:

$$p(x) = x^7 + 4x^6 + 8x^4 + 6x^3 + 9x^2 + 2x + 3$$

We first need to determine the value of $(x^j + b)$ for Equation 4.3. Looking at $p(x)$ we see that its largest degree is 7, which is $2^3 - 1$, so that means k is 3. This makes $j = 2^2 = 4$. We choose a value of b so that both of the equations, $q(x)$ and $r(x)$, are monic. To achieve that, we need to look at the coefficient of the $j - 1$ term in the equation and make $b = a_{j-1} - 1$. For our above equation, this means that b will have the value of $a_3 - 1$, or 5. We now need to find the values of $q(x)$ and $r(x)$ that satisfy the equation

$$x^7 + 4x^6 - 8x^4 + 6x^3 + 9x^2 + 2x - 3 = (x^4 + 5) * q(x) + r(x)$$

---

[1] The savings of this method can be large enough that it is sometimes faster to add the terms necessary to be able to use this method and then subtract those values from the result returned. In other words, if we had an equation with degree 30, we would add x^{31}, determine the factorization, and then subtract x^{31} from every answer. This would still save time over using another method for the calculation.

If we divide $p(x)$ by $x^4 + 5$, we will get a quotient and remainder polynomials, and those are the values of $q(x)$ and $r(x)$, respectively. So, we need to divide as follows:

$$
\begin{array}{r}
x^3 + 4x^2 + 0x + 8 \\
\hline
x^4 + 5\overline{)\ x^7 + 4x^6 + 0x^5 + 8x^4 + 6x^3 + 9x^2 + 2x + 3} \\
-x^7 - 4x^6 - 0x^5 - 8x^4 - 5x^3 - 20x^2 - 0x - 40 \\
\hline
x^3 - 11x^2 + 2x - 37
\end{array}
$$

This gives the equation

$$
p(x) = (x^4 + 5) * (x^3 + 4x^2 + 0x + 8) + (x^3 - 11x^2 + 2x - 37)
$$

But we can apply this process to each of the polynomials for $q(x)$ and $r(x)$:

$$
\begin{array}{r}
x + 4 \\
\hline
x^2 - 1\overline{)\ x^3 + 4x^2 + 0x + 8} \\
-x^3 - 4x^2 + x + 4 \\
\hline
x + 12
\end{array}
\qquad
\begin{array}{r}
x - 11 \\
\hline
x^2 + 1\overline{)\ x^3 - 11x^2 + 2x - 37} \\
-x^3 + 11x^2 - x + 11 \\
\hline
x - 26
\end{array}
$$

The results of all of this would be

$$
p(x) = (x^4 + 5) * [(x^2 - 1)(x + 4) + (x + 12)] + [(x^2 + 1)(x - 11) + (x - 26)]
$$

If we look at this polynomial, we will see that there is one multiplication to calculate x^2 and another to calculate x^4 (done as $x^2 * x^2$). There are also three additional multiplications done in the equation, for a total of five multiplications. There are 10 additions done in this equation as well. Comparing this to the other methods, we get the table in Fig. 4.1. This doesn't look like a great saving, but this is just for a limited case. We can get a general equation for the amount of work done by looking carefully at the process. We first notice that we do only one multiplication and two additions in Equation 4.3. This gives the following set of recurrence relations for the number of multiplications, $M(k)$, and the number of additions, $A(k)$, where $N = 2^k - 1$:

$$M(1) = 0 \qquad\qquad\qquad A(1) = 0$$

$$M(k) = 2M(k-1) + 1 \quad \text{for } k > 1 \qquad A(k) = 2A(k-1) + 2 \quad \text{for } k > 1$$

Method	Multiplications	Additions
Standard	13	7
Horner's	7	7
Preprocessed coefficients	5	10

FIGURE 4.1
Work done for a polynomial of degree 7

Method	Multiplications	Additions
Standard	$2N - 1$	N
Horner's	N	N
Preprocessed coefficients	$\dfrac{N}{2} + \lg N$	$\dfrac{3N - 1}{2}$

FIGURE 4.2
Work done for a polynomial of degree N

Solving these equations we find that we will do approximately $N / 2$ multiplications and $(3N - 1) / 2$ additions. This doesn't, however, include the multiplications to get the sequence of values x^2, x^4, x^8, ..., $x^{2^{k-1}}$, which takes an additional $k - 1$ multiplications. Thus, there are about $N / 2 + \lg N$ total multiplications.

Figure 4.2 gives a comparison of the standard algorithm, Horner's method, and preprocessed coefficients. In comparing the last two, we see that we have saved $N / 2 - \lg N$ multiplications but at a cost of $(N - 1) / 2$ additions. By most standards, trading a multiplication for an addition will result in a time savings, so using preprocessed coefficients is more efficient.

■ 4.1.3 EXERCISES

1. Give the factorization of the equation $x^7 + 2x^6 + 6x^5 + 3x^4 + 7x^3 + 5x + 4$ that results from

   a. Horner's method

   b. Preprocessed coefficients

2. Give the factorization of the equation $x^7 + 6x^6 + 4x^4 - 2x^3 + 3x^2 - 7x + 5$ that results from

   a. Horner's method

   b. Preprocessed coefficients

4.2   MATRIX MULTIPLICATION

A matrix is a mathematical structure of numbers arranged in rows and columns that is equivalent to a two-dimensional array. Two matrices can be added or subtracted element by element if they are the same size. Two matrices can be multiplied if the number of columns in the first is equal to the number of rows in the second. The resulting matrix will have the same number of rows as the first matrix and the same number of columns as the second. If we multiply a 3 × 4 matrix by a 4 × 7 matrix, we will get a 3 × 7 matrix as our answer. Matrix multiplication is not commutative, so if two matrices, called A and B, are square, we could calculate the products AB or BA, but those two resulting matrices may not be equal. (Notice that because multiplication of numbers is commutative, if A and B are numbers, AB will always equal BA.)

Two matrices are multiplied by taking each row of the first and multiplying it, element by element, with each column of the second. The sum of each of these products is taken and that becomes the value in the corresponding location of the result. Figure 4.3 shows the result of multiplying two matrices.

If you look at Fig. 4.3, you will count 24 multiplications and 16 additions. In general, the standard matrix multiplication algorithm will do $a * b * c$ multiplications and $a * (b - 1) * c$ additions for two matrices of sizes $a \times b$ and $b \times c$. This general algorithm for multiplying matrix G (size $a \times b$) and matrix H (size $b \times c$) to get resulting matrix R (size $a \times c$) is given by

```
for i = 1 to a do
    for j = 1 to c do
        R_{i,j} = 0
        for k = 1 to b
            R_{i,j} = R_{i,j} + G_{i,k} * H_{k,j}
        end for k
    end for j
end for i
```

It would seem that this is the minimum work that is required to successfully multiply two matrices. But researchers could not prove that this amount of

FIGURE 4.3
Multiplication of a
2 × 3 matrix and a
3 × 4 matrix

$$\begin{bmatrix} a & b & c \\ d & e & f \end{bmatrix} \begin{bmatrix} A & B & C & D \\ E & F & G & H \\ I & J & K & L \end{bmatrix} = \begin{bmatrix} aA+bE+cI & aB+bF+cJ & aC+bG+cK & aD+bH+cL \\ dA+eE+fI & dB+eF+fJ & dC+eG+fK & dD+eH+fL \end{bmatrix}$$

work was absolutely necessary, and they eventually found algorithms that multiply matrices faster.

■ 4.2.1 Winograd's Matrix Multiplication

If you look at each element of the result of a matrix multiplication, you will see that it is nothing more than the dot product of the corresponding row and column of the original matrices. We can also notice something more in that this multiplication can be factored in a way that allows us to preprocess some of the work.

Consider two of these vectors: $\mathbf{V} = (v_1, v_2, v_3, v_4)$ and $\mathbf{W} = (w_1, w_2, w_3, w_4)$. Their dot product is given by

$$\mathbf{V} \bullet \mathbf{W} = v_1 * w_1 + v_2 * w_2 + v_3 * w_3 + v_4 * w_4$$

But this can be factored into the following:

$$\mathbf{V} \bullet \mathbf{W} = (v_1 + w_2) * (v_2 + w_1) + (v_3 + w_4) * (v_4 + w_3)$$
$$- v_1 * v_2 - v_3 * v_4 - w_1 * w_2 - w_3 * w_4$$

The reader should be able to show that these two are the same. It would appear that the second of these equations actually does more work because we can count six multiplications verses four and ten additions verses three. What might not be obvious is that the last few terms can be preprocessed and stored for each row of the first matrix and for each column of the second. This means that in practice we will only have to do the first two multiplications and five additions along with an additional two additions to include the preprocessed values.

The full Winograd's matrix multiplication algorithm for multiplying G (size $a \times b$) and H (size $b \times c$) to get result R (size $a \times c$) is

```
d = b/2
// calculate rowFactors for G
for i = 1 to a do
   rowFactor[i] = G_{i,1} * G_{i,2}
   for j = 2 to d do
      rowFactor[i] = rowFactor[i] + G_{i,2j-1} * G_{i,2j}
   end for j
end for i

// calculate columnFactors for H
for i = 1 to c do
   columnFactor[i] = H_{1,i} * H_{2,i}
```

```
        for j = 2 to d do
            columnFactor[i] = columnFactor[i] + H₂ⱼ₋₁,ᵢ * H₂ⱼ,ᵢ
        end for j
    end for i

    // calculate R
    for i = 1 to a do
        for j = 1 to c do
            R_{i,j} = -rowFactor[i] - columnFactor[j]
            for k = 1 to d do
                R_{i,j} = R_{i,j} + (G_{i,2k-1} + H_{2k,j})*(G_{i,2k} + H_{2k-1,j})
            end for k
        end for j
    end for i

    // add in terms for odd shared dimension
    if (2 * (b / 2) ≠ b) then
        for i = 1 to a do
            for j = 1 to c do
                R_{i,j} = R_{i,j} + G_{i,b} * H_{b,j}
            end for j
        end for i
    end if
```

Analysis of Winograd's Algorithm

Let's look at the case where the shared dimension (b) is even. We can count the multiplications and additions as follows:[2]

	Multiplications	**Additions**
Preprocessing of G	$a * d$	$a * (d - 1)$
Preprocessing of H	$c * d$	$c * (d - 1)$
Computing elements of R	$a * c * d$	$a * c * (2d + d + 1)$
Total	$\dfrac{a * b * c + a * b + b * c}{2}$	$\dfrac{a(b-2) + c(b-2) + a * c * (3b+2)}{2}$

---

[2] Under Additions and Computing elements of R, the $2d$ is from the two additions in the terms of the product, d is from the sum of the products, and the 1 is from the initialization of the result.

■ 4.2.2 Strassen's Matrix Multiplication

For Strassen's algorithm, we will work with matrices that are square. In actuality, Strassen's algorithm is fast enough that expanding matrices to be square can sometimes still result in enough improvement to offset the extra elements.

Strassen's algorithm uses a set of seven formulas to multiply two 2×2 matrices. These formulas are quite unusual, and it is unfortunate that Strassen's original paper presenting this method gave no indication of how he arrived at these formulas. What is notable is that these formulas and their use don't rely on the base elements being commutative under multiplication. This means that each of the elements could be matrices and, therefore, this method can be applied recursively. Strassen's formulas are

$$x_1 = (G_{1,1} + G_{2,2}) * (H_{1,1} + H_{2,2}) \qquad x_5 = (G_{1,1} + G_{1,2}) * H_{2,2}$$

$$x_2 = (G_{2,1} + G_{2,2}) * H_{1,1} \qquad x_6 = (G_{2,1} - G_{1,1}) * (H_{1,1} + H_{1,2})$$

$$x_3 = G_{1,1} * (H_{1,2} - H_{2,2}) \qquad x_7 = (G_{1,2} - G_{2,2}) * (H_{2,1} + H_{2,2})$$

$$x_4 = G_{2,2} * (H_{2,1} - H_{1,1})$$

The entries of R would then be calculated by

$$R_{1,1} = x_1 + x_4 - x_5 + x_7 \qquad R_{1,2} = x_3 + x_5$$

$$R_{2,1} = x_2 + x_4 \qquad R_{2,2} = x_1 + x_3 - x_2 + x_6$$

For two 2×2 matrices, we see that this algorithm does 7 multiplications and 18 additions. This doesn't appear to be a saving because we trade 1 multiplication for 14 additions relative to the standard algorithms. A full analysis of this would show that the number of multiplications done for two $N \times N$ matrices would be approximately $N^{2.81}$ and the number of additions would be about $6N^{2.81} - 6N^2$. For two 16×16 matrices, Strassen's algorithm would save about 1677 multiplications at a cost of 9138 additions.

Putting together our three results gives the following chart (for ease of comparison, the results are all shown for two $N \times N$ matrices):

	Multiplications	Additions
Standard algorithm	N^3	$N^3 - N^2$
Winograd's algorithm	$\dfrac{N^3 + 2N^2}{2}$	$\dfrac{3N^3 + 4N^2 - 4N}{2}$
Strassen's algorithm	$N^{2.81}$	$6N^{2.81} - 6N^2$

Strassen's algorithm is rarely used in actual practice because of the book-keeping necessary to use it recursively. Its importance is that it was the first algorithm for multiplying matrices that was faster than the $O(N^3)$ algorithms. Improving the efficiency of matrix multiplication and perhaps identifying a lower bound continues to be an active area of research.

■ 4.2.3 EXERCISES

1. How many multiplications and additions are done by Winograd's algorithm for an odd value of the shared dimension?
2. Show that Strassen's algorithm works by using it to multiply the two matrices

$$\begin{bmatrix} 1 & 9 \\ 7 & 3 \end{bmatrix} \quad \text{and} \quad \begin{bmatrix} 5 & 2 \\ 4 & 11 \end{bmatrix}$$

Compare the result with that of the standard algorithm. Show all work.

4.3 LINEAR EQUATIONS

A system of linear equations is a set of N equations with N unknown quantities. Typically these equations are written as

$$a_{11}x_1 + a_{12}x_2 + a_{13}x_3 + \cdots + a_{1N}x_N = b_1$$
$$a_{21}x_1 + a_{22}x_2 + a_{23}x_3 + \cdots + a_{2N}x_N = b_2$$
$$\vdots$$
$$a_{N1}x_1 + a_{N2}x_2 + a_{N3}x_3 + \cdots + a_{NN}x_N = b_N$$

These equations can come from a number of sources, but typically the constants (represented by the a coefficients) are some settings on equipment that give the indicated results (represented by the b values in the equations). We are interested in knowing what values of the unknowns (represented by the x values) will produce these results. Consider the following example:

$$2x_1 + 7x_2 + 1x_3 + 5x_4 = 70$$
$$1x_1 + 5x_2 + 3x_3 + 2x_4 = 45$$
$$3x_1 + 2x_2 + 4x_3 + 1x_4 = 33$$
$$8x_1 + 1x_2 + 5x_3 + 3x_4 = 56$$

One way to try to find the value for each x would be to do substitutions of the equations. In other words, we could take the second equation and rewrite it as $x_1 = 45 - 5x_2 - 3x_3 - 2x_4$ and then substitute this into the other three equations in place of x_1. This would give three equations with three unknowns. We could then take one of the remaining three equations and do the same for x_2, which would give us two equations with two unknowns. Doing this one more time with x_3 would give one equation with one unknown (x_4). We would now know the value for x_4 and could substitute this back into one of the two equations in the previous step, which would allow us to solve for the value of x_3. Substituting x_3 and x_4 into one of the three equations we got after the first substitution would allow us to determine the value of x_2, and then using these three values in one of our original equations would give us the value of x_1.

This process works extremely well, but a lot of algebra is needed, and it would be easy for a mistake to occur. As the number of equations and unknowns increases, this algebra work can take quite a while to complete. This process is not easily programmed as described, but it is the basis for the Gauss-Jordan method, which will be described next.

■ 4.3.1 Gauss-Jordan Method

We could consider the system of linear equations as a matrix with N rows and $N + 1$ columns. For the previous example, this would give the matrix

$$\begin{bmatrix} 2 & 7 & 1 & 5 & 70 \\ 1 & 5 & 3 & 2 & 45 \\ 3 & 2 & 4 & 1 & 33 \\ 8 & 1 & 5 & 3 & 56 \end{bmatrix}$$

We can now do a series of operations based on the rows to reach the result. When the first n rows and columns represent the identity matrix, the final column will have the x values that we want. This would look like the following:

$$\begin{bmatrix} 1 & 0 & 0 & 0 & x_1 \\ 0 & 1 & 0 & 0 & x_2 \\ 0 & 0 & 1 & 0 & x_3 \\ 0 & 0 & 0 & 1 & x_4 \end{bmatrix}$$

The basic plan is to divide the first row by the value in the first column and then subtract multiples of this new first row from each of the other rows. In our example, the second row would have the new first row subtracted from it, the third row would have 3 times the new first row subtracted from it, and the fourth row would have 8 times the new first row subtracted from it. You should recognize that this would create the proper first column. This new matrix is

$$\begin{bmatrix} 1 & 3.5 & 0.5 & 2.5 & 35 \\ 0 & 1.5 & 2.5 & -0.5 & 10 \\ 0 & -8.5 & 2.5 & -6.5 & -72 \\ 0 & -27 & 1 & -17 & -224 \end{bmatrix}$$

We now repeat this process for the second row. After we divide each of the values in this row by the number in the second column (1.5), we use the values in the second column of the other rows to determine how much this row is multiplied by for each subtraction. The new matrix is now (values shown are rounded)

$$\begin{bmatrix} 1 & 0 & -5.33 & 3.66 & 11.7 \\ 0 & 1 & 1.67 & -0.33 & 6.67 \\ 0 & 0 & 16.7 & -9.3 & -15.3 \\ 0 & 0 & 46 & -26 & -44 \end{bmatrix}$$

We now repeat this process, using the third row to clear out the third column and the fourth row to clear out the fourth column. This gives the next two matrices:

$$\begin{bmatrix} 1 & 0 & 0 & 0.68 & 6.76 \\ 0 & 1 & 0 & 0.6 & 8.2 \\ 0 & 0 & 1 & -0.56 & -0.92 \\ 0 & 0 & 0 & -0.24 & -1.68 \end{bmatrix}$$

$$\begin{bmatrix} 1 & 0 & 0 & 0 & 2 \\ 0 & 1 & 0 & 0 & 4 \\ 0 & 0 & 1 & 0 & 3 \\ 0 & 0 & 0 & 1 & 7 \end{bmatrix}$$

The final matrix gives us the x values of $x_1 = 2$, $x_2 = 4$, $x_3 = 3$, and $x_4 = 7$. The problem with this process is that on a computer, we will get round-off errors that may give inaccurate results. Round-off errors can multiply within a computer program so that a minor round-off difference in one calculation will cause the next to be more inaccurate than the last. In a large system of linear equations, round-off errors can be rather significant. There are other algorithms to solve or at least control these round-off errors, but the description of those algorithms is more appropriate for a text on numerical analysis and will not be discussed further.

A second concern with this process is what happens if two rows are just multiples of each other. In that case, we will wind up with one row that is entirely zero, and that will lead to a divide by zero error in our algorithm. This problem is called singularity, and modifying this algorithm to handle singularity is beyond the scope of this book.

■ 4.3.2 EXERCISES

1. Show the steps in the Gauss–Jordan algorithm for the following system of linear equations:

$$3x_1 + 6x_2 + 12x_3 + 9x_4 = 78$$
$$2x_1 + 3x_2 + 5x_3 + 7x_4 = 48$$
$$1x_1 + 7x_2 + 2x_3 + 3x_4 = 27$$
$$4x_1 + 9x_2 + 1x_3 + 2x_4 = 45$$

2. Show the steps in the Gauss–Jordan algorithm for the following system of linear equations:

$$2x_1 + 4x_2 + 5x_3 = 23$$
$$1x_1 + 5x_2 + 3x_3 = 16$$
$$3x_1 + 1x_2 + 6x_3 = 25$$

3. From the description of Section 4.2.1, do an analysis of the Gauss–Jordan method for solving a system of N linear equations with N unknowns. Your analysis should determine the number of multiplications and the number of additions that are done.

CHAPTER 5

Matching Algorithms

PREREQUISITES

Before beginning this chapter, you should be able to

- Create finite automata
- Use character strings
- Use one- and two-dimensional arrays
- Describe growth rates and order

GOALS

At the end of this chapter, you should be able to

- Explain the substring matching problem
- Explain the straightforward algorithm and its analysis
- Explain the use of finite automata for string matching
- Construct and use a Knuth-Morris-Pratt automaton
- Construct and use slide and jump arrays for the Boyer-Moore algorithm
- Explain the method of approximate string matching

STUDY SUGGESTIONS

As you are working through the chapter, you should rework the examples to make sure you understand them. Using the string "abccbaabcabcbccabc" as the text, you should trace the straightforward algorithm and the Knuth-Morris-Pratt algorithm using the pattern "abcabc" and trace the Boyer-Moore algorithm using the pattern "abcbccabc." You should also try to answer any questions before reading on. A hint or the answer is in the sentences following the question.

L ooking for a substring in a longer piece of text is an important utility in text editors and word processors. This chapter begins with an examination of four ways this can be done. Presentation of matching techniques will be done from the perspective of character strings. These techniques could, however, be used to search for any string of bits or bytes in a binary file. Virus checking is an example of a binary-based use that searches for the known pattern of bytes that appear in a computer virus.

Word processing programs typically have spelling checkers that will not only identify words that appear to be misspelled but also suggest possible correct spellings for the word. One process for spell checkers is to produce a sorted list of words in the document. This list is then compared to the words stored in both the system dictionary and the user's dictionary, and words that do not appear are flagged as potentially incorrect. The process of identifying suggested alternative spellings can involve approximate string matching.

The discussion of approximate string matches will be based on looking for a substring in a given piece of text. This technique can, however, also be applied to looking for approximate matches with a dictionary.

5.1 STRING MATCHING

Our problem is to find the first occurrence of a substring within a larger piece of text. Finding later occurrences can use the same techniques by just changing the starting point in the text. This problem is complex because the entire substring has to match in order. In the standard algorithm, we begin by comparing the first character of the text with the first character of the substring. If they match, we move to the next character of each. This process continues until the entire substring matches the text or the next characters do not match.

Text:	there they are
Pass 1:	they
Text:	there they are
Pass 2:	they
Text:	there they are
Pass 3:	they
Text:	there they are
Pass 4:	they
Text:	there they are
Pass 5:	they
Text:	there they are
Pass 6:	they
Text:	there they are
Pass 7:	they

■ **FIGURE 5.1**
Match of substring "they" in text "there they are." The first pass matches three characters of the substring, but only the seventh pass matches completely. (There are 13 character comparisons done to find the match.)

In the first case we are done, but in the second, we move the starting point in the text by one character and begin matching with the substring again. This process can be seen in Fig. 5.1.

The following algorithm accomplishes this standard string match:

```
subLoc = 1          // current match point in substring
textLoc = 1         // current match point in text
textStart = 1       // location where this match attempt starts

while textLoc ≤ length(text) and subLoc ≤ length(substring) do
   if text[ textLoc ] = substring[ subLoc ] then
      textLoc = textLoc + 1
      subLoc = subLoc + 1
   else
      // begin again but move the start by 1
      textStart = textStart + 1
      textLoc = textStart
      subLoc = 1
   end if
end while
```

```
if (subLoc > length(substring))
   return textStart // found a match
else
   return 0          // indicates no match found
end if
```

It should be obvious that the important task is to compare characters, and that is what we will count. In the worst case, each time we compare the substring we match all of the characters but fail on the last one. How many times could this happen? It could happen once for each character in the text. If S is the length of the substring and T is the length of the text, the worst case would seem to take $S * (T - S + 1)$ comparisons.[1] We have to consider whether this arrangement of characters is at all possible. Consider a substring of "XX...XXY" and text of "XX...XXXXX," where the substring is a set of $S - 1$ Xs followed by one Y and the text is a set of T Xs. This set of characters will cause this worst-case behavior. It should be noted that natural language is not usually like this, and so it can be expected that if this algorithm is used with actual words, it will perform much better. In fact, studies have shown that this algorithm averages a little over T comparisons on a natural language text.[2]

The problem with the standard algorithm is that it can waste a lot of effort. If we have matched the beginning part of the substring, we can use that information to tell us how far to move in the text to start the next match. For example, if we look at pass 1 in Fig. 5.1, we see that the mismatch occurred with the fourth character of the substring. That means the first three matched. When we examine the substring, we see that the third symbol doesn't appear anywhere else, so we could have skipped past the first three symbols and had our second pass start with the fourth symbol of the text instead of the second. The following techniques take advantage of this fact.

■ 5.1.1 Finite Automata

The area of theory of computation shows that finite automata are used to decide whether a word is in a given language. A finite automaton (the singular

---

[1] The $T - S + 1$ is because we can stop if there are fewer characters left in the text than there are in the substring.

[2] Because of the limited number of characters and the uneven distribution of their occurrence (i.e.; in English, e occurs much more frequently than z or q), performance on natural language will always be better than our general measures.

form of the word "automata") is a simple machine that has a current state and a transition function. The transition function examines the state and the next character of input and then decides on a new state for the automaton. Some states are labeled as accepting states, and if the automaton is in one of these when it has finished the input, the input word is said to be accepted.

We can use finite automata to do string matching by having an automata set up to match just one word, and when we get to the final state, we know we have found the substring in the text. This technique is very efficient because a finite automata functions by looking at each input symbol once. This means that we can do the matching with a finite automaton in no more than T comparisons. The problem becomes developing an algorithm to construct a deterministic finite automaton for any possible substring. This is not an easy task, and although algorithms are available that can do this, they take a lot of time. Because of this, finite automata are not a good general-purpose solution to string matching.

■ 5.1.2 Knuth-Morris-Pratt Algorithm

When constructing a finite automaton to look for a substring in a piece of text, it is easy to build the links that move us from the start state to the final accepting state, because they are just labeled with the characters of the substring (see Fig. 5.2). The problem occurs when we begin to add additional links for the other characters that don't get us to the final state.

The Knuth-Morris-Pratt algorithm is based on finite automata but uses a simpler method of handling the situation of when the characters don't match. In Knuth-Morris-Pratt, we label the states with the symbol that should match at that point. We then only need two links from each state—one for a successful match and the other for a failure. The success link will take us to the next node in the chain, and the failure link will take us back to a previous node based on the word pattern. A sample Knuth-Morris-Pratt automaton for the substring "ababcb" is given in Fig. 5.3.

■ **FIGURE 5.2**
The beginning of a finite automaton to look for the substring "hello"

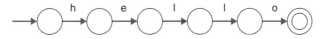

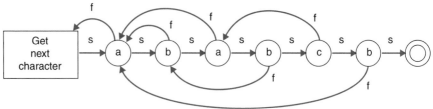

■ FIGURE 5.3
A completed Knuth-
Morris-Pratt
automaton
for the substring
"ababcb"

Each success link of a Knuth-Morris-Pratt automaton causes the "fetch" of a
new character from the text. Failure links do not get a new character but reuse
the last character fetched. If we reach the final state, we know that we found the
substring. To assure that you understand how this process works, you should try
it with the text string "ababababcbab" and the automaton in Fig. 5.3 to see how it
successfully finds the substring. The full algorithm for this process is

```
subLoc = 1     // current match point in substring
textLoc = 1    // current match point in text

while textLoc ≤ length(text) and subLoc ≤ length(substring) do
   if subLoc = 0 or text[ textLoc ] = substring[ subLoc ] then
      textLoc = textLoc + 1
      subLoc = subLoc + 1
   else    // no match so follow fail link
      subLoc = fail[ subLoc ]
   end if
end while

if (subLoc > length(substring)) then
   return textLoc - length(substring) + 1  // found a match
else
   return 0                                 // no match
end if
```

Before we can analyze this process, we need to consider how these fail links
are determined. Notice that we do not need to do anything special for the success links because they just move us to the next successive location. The failure
links, however, are calculated by looking at how the substring relates to itself.
For example, if we look at the substring "ababcb," we see that if we fail when
matching the c, we shouldn't back up all the way. If we got to character 5 of

the substring, we know that the first four characters matched, and so the "ab" that matched substring characters 3 and 4 should perhaps match substring characters 1 and 2 for a successful search. The following algorithm determines these relationships in the substring:

```
fail[ 1 ] = 0
for i = 2 to length(substring) do
   temp = fail[ i - 1 ]
   while (temp > 0) and (substring[ temp ] ≠ substring[ i - 1 ]) do
      temp = fail[ temp ]
   end while
   fail[ i ] = temp + 1
end for
```

Analysis of Knuth-Morris-Pratt

We first consider the failure link construction phase of the algorithm. If we look at the while loop, we see that it will run until we find two substring characters that match. On a cursory look at the process, you see that temp follows the fail links, and those are in decreasing order. This might lead you to believe that, for the kth pass of the for loop, the while loop does as many as $k - 1$ comparisons and this entire process takes about $S^2 / 2$ comparisons. If we look closer, we will find a better approximation of the number of comparisons. We notice the following facts:

1. There are at most $S - 1$ times that the ≠ character comparisons will be false.
2. The fail links are all smaller than their index (i.e., fail[x] < x for every x) because they indicate where to back up to on a failed text character match.
3. Every time the ≠ comparison is true, temp is decreased because of fact 2.
4. On the first pass of the for loop, the while is not done because temp = fail[1]=0.
5. The combination of the final statement of the for loop, the increment of i, and then the first statement of the next pass of the for loop means that temp is incremented by 1 each subsequent pass of the for loop.
6. Effectively by fact 5, because there are $S - 2$ "subsequent passes" of the for loop, temp is incremented $S - 2$ times.
7. Because fail[1]=0, temp never becomes negative.

We now know that temp starts at a value of 0 (fact 4), and is incremented no more than $S - 2$ times (fact 6). Because each time the characters don't match temp is decreased (fact 3) and temp never becomes negative (fact 7), there can be no more than $S - 2$ mismatched character comparisons. This means a total of $2S - 3$ matched (fact 1) and mismatched character comparisons. So, the construction of the links is linear relative to the length of the substring.

Now we consider the matching algorithm. We notice that the `while` loop has at most one character comparison per pass. On each pass, either `textLoc` and `subLoc` are incremented or `subLoc` is decremented. Because `textLoc` starts at 1 and never becomes greater than the length of the text, we know that there are at most T increments of `textLoc` and `subLoc`. The index `subLoc` also starts at 1, never becomes negative, and is never increased more than T times, so it can be decreased at most T times. Putting all of this together tells us that because there are at most T increments of `textLoc` and `subLoc` and T decreases of `subLoc`, there are at most $2T$ comparisons of characters.

So, we see that the Knuth-Morris-Pratt algorithm in total does $2T + 2S - 3$ character comparisons, which is of order $O(T + S)$. This is an improvement over the standard algorithm, which is of order $O(T * S)$. Studies of these two algorithms on natural language text have shown that they operate at roughly the same level of complexity, although Knuth-Morris-Pratt is slightly better because it doesn't back up in the text.

■ 5.1.3 Boyer-Moore Algorithm

The Boyer-Moore algorithm is different from the previous two algorithms in that it matches the pattern from the right instead of left end. By examining the pattern we are looking for, we should be able to make better jumps through the text when a mismatch has occurred.

For example, in Fig. 5.4 (the same match as Fig. 5.1), we first compare the y with the r and find a mismatch. Because r doesn't appear in the pattern at all, we know the pattern can be moved to the right a full four characters (the size of the pattern). We next compare the y with the h and find a mismatch. This

■ FIGURE 5.4 Match of substring "they" in text "there they are" (there are six character comparisons done to find the match)

```
Text:    there they are
Pass 1:  they
Text:    there they are
Pass 2:      they
Text:    there they are
Pass 3:       they
```

FIGURE 5.5
A problem with
sliding

```
Text:      the tinkle of a bell
Pattern:       think
Text:      the tinkle of a bell
Pattern:         think
```

time because the h does appear in the pattern, we move the pattern only two characters to the right so that the h characters line up. We then begin the match from the right side and find a complete match for the pattern. In the Boyer-Moore algorithm, we did 6 character comparisons verses 13 for the first simple algorithm.

There is a problem with this one improvement. If you look at Fig. 5.5, you see that we will match the k, n, and i, but the t of tinkle doesn't match the h of think. With just the above change, we would then slide the pattern to the right one character so that the t characters line up. The problem is that because we matched the "ink" part of the pattern, shifting just one character will cause a quick mismatch that we could predict will occur.

The Boyer-Moore algorithm will process the pattern in two ways. In the first, we will calculate a slide value that will tell us how much the pattern has to be shifted to line up the mismatched text character with where it next appears in the pattern. In the second, we will calculate a jump value that is based on character sequences at the end of the pattern that also appear earlier. We first look at the matching process that uses these values before we look at how to calculate them.

The Match Algorithm

We have described generally how the slide and jump arrays will be used. In the slide array, we have the amount that the pattern can be shifted in the text to line up the mismatched character if possible. In the jump array, we have the amount that the pattern can be shifted to line up previously matched characters with another matching place in the pattern. There are two possibilities when the pattern character and the text character don't match. The slide array could indicate a larger move than the jump array, or the jump array could indicate a larger move than the slide array. (The possibility that they are the same is easiest because they are both indicating the same shift.) What do these two possibilities tell us? If the slide array is larger, it means that the mismatched character appears "closer" to the front than the repetition of the end characters of the pattern. If the jump array is larger, it means that the end characters of the pattern that matched appear closer to the front of the pattern than the mismatched character. In either of these two cases, we should use the larger shift, because the smaller shift will definitely fail again because of what we know from the other value. For example, if the slide array has a value of 4 and the jump array has a value of 2, if we just move by two characters, we know this will fail because the mismatched character is still not lined up. But if we move by the four characters, the mismatched character will line up correctly in the pattern, and there is a possibility that the end matching characters might match in their new location as well.

Because we are just taking the larger of the two values, the algorithm is rather simple:

```
textLoc = length(pattern)
patternLoc = length(pattern)
while (textLoc ≤ length(text)) and (patternLoc > 0) do
    if text[ textLoc ] = pattern[ patternLoc ] then
        textLoc = textLoc - 1
        patternLoc = patternLoc - 1
    else
        textLoc = textLoc + MAXIMUM(slide[text[textLoc]], jump[patternLoc])
        patternLoc = length(pattern)
    end if
end while

if patternLoc = 0 then
    return textLoc + 1    // found a match
else
    return 0
end if
```

The Slide Array

We now look at the operation of the slide array. In Fig. 5.6(a), we begin the match with textLoc = 6 and patternLoc = 6. Because those two characters match, both textLoc and patternLoc are decremented. The next two characters also match, so textLoc and patternLoc are both decremented again and now have a value of 4. There is a mismatch in the next character. We want to slide the pattern so that the b character of the text lines up with the b

```
                         ↓ textLoc
            Text:      baabacacbacb
            Pattern: abacac
                           ↑ patternLoc
         (a)
```

```
                         ↓ textLoc
            Text:      baabacacbacb
            Pattern:    abacac
                               ↑ patternLoc
         (b)
```

■ FIGURE 5.6
Deciding on a
slide value

character of the pattern as shown in Fig. 5.6(b). Then we begin the matching process from the right end again. To do this, we need to reset `patternLoc` to be the size of the pattern, and `textLoc` has to be increased by 4, which is what really moves the pattern.

To accomplish this method of movement, we therefore need to determine how much to increase `textLoc` based on the character that didn't match. We will use an array called `slide` that is as large as the character set that can appear in the text. We initialize each element of the slide array to the size of the pattern, because any characters not in the pattern should move the pattern that amount. We then update the values for each character that does appear. If a character appears more than once, the slide value will move the pattern so the alignment is with the last occurrence. Alignment with characters earlier in the pattern would be done by the jump factor, which will be discussed next. The algorithm to calculate the slide values is

```
for every ch in the character set do
   slide[ ch ] = length(pattern)
end for

for i = 1 to length(pattern) do
   slide[ pattern[i] ] = length(pattern) - i
end for
```

If you trace this algorithm with the pattern "datadata," you will find that slide[d] = 3, slide[a] = 0, and slide[t] = 1, and the slide value is 8 for all other characters.

The Jump Array

We will create a second array called jump (the same size as our pattern) that will encode information about the pattern relative to itself. This new array will be able to let us know, for example, that when the h and t in Fig. 5.5 don't match, we need to move the pattern completely past where we currently are. This new array will also know if there are repetitions of the characters at the end of the pattern that might be good alternates for a match. For example, let's say our pattern is "abcdbc" and in the matching process we were able to match the last two characters of the pattern with the text. If we now fail on the third to last character, our jump array will tell us how much to shift the pattern so the next time the text characters that matched the "bc" in positions 5 and 6 of the pattern are now lined up with the "bc" in positions 2 and 3 of the pattern. So, the jump array tells us the smallest move necessary to line up characters we have already matched with the next place they appear in the pattern.

Let's say that we have a pattern where a mismatch of a character means that the pattern has to be shifted all the way past where we started. In Fig. 5.7, we show a piece of text and a pattern. The X symbols in the pattern could be any character and are used to help illustrate the process.

If we need to move the pattern completely past where we started, we would want the X symbols to line up with the text from f to j, meaning that the new starting value for textLoc would be 10. If the mismatch occurs at the e character when textLoc is 5, we would need to add 5 to textLoc to reposition the pattern. If this mismatch occurs at the d character (textLoc = 4), we would need to add 6. With a mismatch at characters c, b, or a, we would need

■ FIGURE 5.7   Text: abcdefghijklmn
Determining a   Pattern: XXXXX
jump value

to add 7, 8, or 9, respectively. Thinking about this in general shows the amount we add for a mismatch on the last character of the pattern is the pattern length, and a mismatch on the first character is twice the length minus 1. This is the basis for the `jump` array initialization.

Now, we need to look at a pattern where there is some repetition of character sequences that are at the end of the pattern. We need to look at how much to increase `textLoc` to move the pattern the correct amount (ignoring the possibilities handled by the `slide` array). To do that, imagine we are matching the pattern with the pattern. Consider the pattern "abcdbc" again. If the last character doesn't match, we can just increase `textLoc` by 1 and start again. If the last character matched but the second to last didn't, we can see that because both c characters are preceded by b characters, we need to move the pattern completely past where we started. If the last two characters match, but the third to last doesn't, we increase `textLoc` by 5, which will line up the "bc" that matches the last two pattern characters with the second and third pattern characters.

The calculation of the `jump` array is handled by the following algorithm. The first loop handles the initialization of the `jump` array. The second loop updates the array based on end characters that are repeated earlier. The third (and fourth) loop adjusts the maximum moves of the front (end) of the jump array based on where the pattern repetitions were found. The complete algorithm is

```
// initialize jump to the largest possible movement
for i = 1 to length(pattern) do
   jump[ i ] = 2 * length(pattern) - i
end for

// match the end of the pattern with characters earlier in the pattern
test = length(pattern)
target = length(pattern) + 1
while test > 0 do
   link[test] = target
   while target ≤ length(pattern) and pattern[test] ≠ pattern[target] do
      jump[target] = MINIMUM( jump[target], length(pattern)-test )
      target = link[target]
   end while
```

```
    test = test - 1
    target = target - 1
end while

for i = 1 to target do
    jump[ i ] = MINIMUM( jump[ i ], length(pattern) + target - i )
end for

temp = link[ target ]
while target ≤ length(pattern) do
    while target ≤ temp do
        jump[target] = MINIMUM(jump[target], temp-target+length(pattern))
        target = target + 1
    end while
    temp = link[temp]
end while
```

Figure 5.8 shows the values of the jump and link arrays after each of the loops for the pattern value "datadata."

First loop

jump

| 15 | 14 | 13 | 12 | 11 | 10 | 9 | 8 |

Second loop

link

| 5 | 6 | 7 | 8 | 7 | 8 | 8 | 9 |

jump

| 15 | 14 | 13 | 12 | 11 | 10 | 3 | 1 |

Third loop

jump

| 11 | 10 | 9 | 8 | 11 | 10 | 3 | 1 |

Fourth loop

jump

| 11 | 10 | 9 | 8 | 11 | 10 | 3 | 1 |

■ FIGURE 5.8
Calculation of the
jump array for
"datadata"

Analysis

In the following analysis, we will use *P* to represent the number of characters in the pattern, *T* to represent the number of characters in the text, and *A* to represent the number of characters in the alphabet.

The calculation of the slide array values does an assignment for each array location and another for each character of the pattern. This does $O(A + P)$ assignments.

The calculation of the jump array will at worst compare each character to all of the ones that appear later in the pattern. From past experience, you should quickly see that this does $O(P^2)$ comparisons. Because there could be an assignment to the jump array for each of these, there are also $O(P^2)$ assignments.

The details of an analysis of the number of comparisons done by the matching algorithm are beyond the scope of this book. Studies have shown that for natural language text with patterns of six or more characters, the match algorithm will compare a character of the pattern with about 40% of the characters or less. As the length of the pattern increases, the percentage decreases to a lower value of about 25% of the characters.

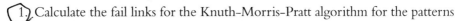

■ 5.1.4 EXERCISES

1. Calculate the fail links for the Knuth–Morris–Pratt algorithm for the patterns
   a. ABABBC
   b. ABCABC
   c. CBCBBACA
   d. BBABBCAC

2. In the text, we indicated that the worst case for the standard algorithm was a substring consisting of a string of Xs with one Y at the end and a text consisting of a string of Xs. If the substring has *S* characters ($S - 1$ Xs and 1 Y) and the text has *T* characters, we saw that the standard algorithm would take $S * T$ character comparisons. What would the fail links look like for the substring "XXXXY" and how many comparisons would be done to construct them? In general, what would the fail links look like for strings of this form, and how many comparisons would be done to construct them? How many character comparisons would the Knuth–Morris–Pratt algorithm do attempting to match the substring and text? (Show all work used to get your answer.)

3. Calculate the slide array values for the Boyer-Moore algorithm for the patterns below. For simplicity, you should assume an alphabet of {A, B, C, D, E}.

   a. ABBCBB

   b. ACBDCB

   c. CABCDB

   d. BACAACA

4. Calculate the jump array values for the Boyer-Moore algorithm for the patterns

   a. ABBCBB

   b. ACBDCB

   c. CABCDB

   d. BACAACA

5.2 APPROXIMATE STRING MATCHING

It is typical to identify a set of common problems that might have caused mismatches between the substring and the text with which it is being matched. Those differences are that the corresponding characters in the substring and text are different, the substring has a character the text doesn't have, or the text has a character the substring doesn't have. Typically, typing errors fall into one of these three types, with a common error of transposed characters being treated as two character differences of the first type.

We will typically look for a k-approximate match for the substring, where k represents the maximum number of differences of the kind mentioned in the previous paragraph. There are a number of possibilities that we will need to keep track of. For example, what does it mean if the first character of the substring and text do not match? It could mean that there is a mismatch of characters, there is a character missing from the substring, or a character is missing from the text. If the characters do match, getting a better overall match of the entire substring may still require that we consider the case of a character missing from the pattern or the text.

For example, consider the attempt to match the substring "ad" with the text "read." The first position has two possible 2-approximate matches. (The a is changed to an r and the d is changed to an e, or there could be an "re" added to the front of the string.) There is also a 3-approximate match at the first position. (Add an r and change the "ad" to an "ea".) The second position has a 2-approximate match (change the "ad" to an "ea") and a 1-approximate match (add an e to the front).

Notice that there can be a lot of possibilities and they build very quickly. If the first few characters matched, but then we hit a sequence that didn't, we might find a better match if we changed some characters or put some extra characters into the substring, into the text, or into both. How can we consider the possibilities and still do this with a reasonable algorithm and data structure? If the algorithm has to test all possibilities, it will be too complex. Therefore, we make the algorithm simple but have a larger data structure.

We will solve this problem by creating a matrix that we will call `diffs` to hold the information that we have gathered so far. Each row of this matrix will be associated with one of the characters in the substring, and each column will be associated with one of the characters in the text. The values in the matrix will give us an idea of how well the matching process is going at that point. So, if the value in row 5 column 27 is a 4, in matching the first five characters of the substring with the portion of the text ending at location 27, we have found four differences.

The number of differences for any location will be based on the three possible values that are immediately above, to the left, and to the left and diagonally up. If we use the value above, we are implying that the text is missing a character of the substring. If we use the value to the left, we are implying that the substring is missing a character of the text. Use of the diagonal value is related to the match or mismatch of the characters. More specifically, for any value of diffs$[i, j]$, we will look at the minimum of three values.[3]

1. diffs$[i - 1, j - 1]$ if substring$_i$ = text$_j$, otherwise diffs$[i - 1, j - 1] + 1$
2. diffs$[i - 1, j] + 1$ (substring$_i$ is missing from the text)
3. diffs$[i, j - 1] + 1$ (text$_j$ is missing from the substring)

To get this process started, if we refer to any location above the matrix (in other words, $i = 0$), that location will be considered to have a zero stored in it. If we refer to any location to the left of the matrix (in other words, $j = 0$), that location will be considered to have the corresponding value of i stored in it. A

_____

[3] Notice that diffs$[i - 1, j - 1]$ represents the value diagonally up and to the left, diffs$[i - 1, j]$ represents the value above, and diffs$[i, j - 1]$ represents the value to the left.

■ **FIGURE 5.9**

The diffs matrix for the substring "trim" and the text "try the trumpet"

		t	r	y		t	h	e		t	r	u	m	p	e	t
	0	0	0	0	0	0	0	0	0	0	0	0	0	0	0	0
t	1	0	1	1	1	0	1	1	1	0	1	1	1	1	1	0
r	2	1	0	1	2	1	1	2	2	1	0	1	2	2	2	1
i	3	2	1	1	2	2	2	2	3	2	1	1	2	3	3	2
m	4	3	2	2	2	3	3	3	3	3	2	2	1	2	3	3

sample of this for the substring "trim" and the text "try the trumpet" is given in Fig. 5.9.

If we look at the bottom row for the character y in the text, we see the value 2, which represents the fact that to match "trim" so that it ends at the y would require two differences of the kind discussed before. Those two differences would represent an m missing from the text after the y and the mismatch of the y with the i *or* an i missing from the text before the y and the mismatch of the y with the m. So, the bottom row gives us the best possible matches of the substring ending at that point in the text. We see that the closest match of "trim" in the text, with one difference, would end at the m in trumpet and represents the mismatch of the i and u.

If this process were used in practice, we would specify not only the substring and text but also the maximum number of differences for which we were looking. The algorithm would fill in the matrix column by column until the bottom value of a column was less than or equal to the number given. This means that the algorithm does not need to store $S * T$ integers for this matrix (where S is the number of characters in the substring and T is the number of characters in the text), but rather it just needs to store $2S$ integers for the column being calculated and for the previous column on which it depends.

This style of algorithm is classified as "dynamic programming," which will be discussed again in Chapter 9.

■ 5.2.1 Analysis

This process is easy to analyze because of the nature of the matrix. We see that for each location in the matrix, we do one character comparison. This means that in the worst case there will be $S * T$ comparisons. Notice that even with all of the possible differences that could occur, this process operates as efficiently as the straightforward exact string match algorithm.

■ 5.2.2 EXERCISES

1. Construct the approximate matches matrix for substring "their" and text "hello there friends."
2. Construct the approximate matches matrix for substring "where" and text "were they here."
3. When we looked for an exact match, we could determine the starting point easily, because we knew the start had to be S characters from the end. With approximate matching, finding the start of the match is not so easy because of the possibility of characters missing from the substring, the text, or both. Give a detailed description of what data structure and process you would add to the algorithm described in this lesson to have that information available when a k-approximate match is found. (*Hint:* One way to see if the parenthesis in an expression match is to keep a counter as you scan the expression, adding 1 to it on every open parenthesis, subtracting 1 from it on every close parenthesis, and not changing it for other characters. Can you do something similar to keep track of missing characters?)

5.3 PROGRAMMING EXERCISES

You can get a large block of text to use for these programming problems by saving a term paper you wrote using a word processor in text-only format. To be able to test special cases, put in a word that is not already there. Options for this word might be a plant or flower, the name of a place, or a color name. Be careful in your choice of words, because a short word may appear as part of other words. For example, red is part of bothered. Using this technique, you could put the word "banyan" someplace in the middle of the text and the word "potato" at the end, and then search for those words.

1. Program up the Knuth-Morris-Pratt algorithm and count the number of character comparisons done for a few different cases. Don't forget to count the comparisons done in the calculation of the failure links. Be sure to test both long and short patterns. Your program should output the location in the text (distance from the start) where the pattern was found and how many comparisons were done. How do your results compare to the analysis done in the text?

2. Program up the Boyer-Moore algorithm and count the number of character comparisons done for a few different cases. Don't forget to count the comparisons done in the calculation of the slide and jump arrays. Be sure to test both long and short patterns. Your program should output the location in the text (distance from the start) where the pattern was found and how many comparisons were done. How do your results compare to the analysis done in the text?

CHAPTER 6

Graph Algorithms

PREREQUISITES

Before beginning this chapter, you should be able to

- Describe a set and set membership
- Use two-dimensional arrays
- Use stack and queue data structures
- Use linked lists
- Describe growth rates and order

GOALS

At the end of this chapter, you should be able to

- Describe and define graph terms and concepts
- Create data structures for graphs
- Do breadth-first and depth-first traversals and searches
- Find the minimum spanning tree for a connected graph
- Find the shortest path between two nodes of a connected graph
- Find the biconnected components of a connected graph

STUDY SUGGESTIONS

As you are working through the chapter, you should rework the examples to make sure you understand them. You should do a breadth-first and depth-first traversal starting at node A for the following graph:

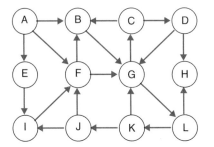

You should trace the Dijkstra-Prim minimum spanning tree algorithm starting at node A, Kruskal's minimum spanning tree algorithm, and Dijkstra's shortest-path algorithm starting at node A for the following graph:

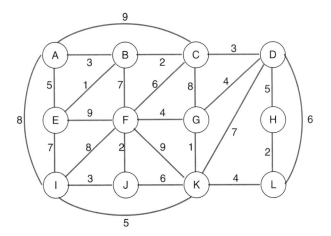

You should also try to answer any questions before reading on. A hint or the answer is in the sentences following the question.

G raphs are a formal description for a wide range of familiar situations. The most common example is a road map, which shows the location of intersections and the roads that run between them. In graph terminology, the intersections are the nodes of the graph, and the roads are the edges. Sometimes our graphs are directed (like one-way streets) or weighted with a travel cost associated with each edge (like toll roads). As we give more details on the terminology and concepts in graphs, the similarity to road maps will be even clearer.

After we have explored the mathematical concepts of graphs, we will look at methods of storing them so that they can be used and manipulated by our algorithms. We will see that there are alternatives for graph storage that vary in the amount of overhead, which depends on the graph itself.

There are times when information needs to be distributed to a large number of people or to the computers on a large network. We would like this information to get to everywhere, but we also don't want it going any place twice. Some groups of people will accomplish this by setting up a "phone tree" where each person has a small number of people to call to pass on news. If everyone appears once in the tree and if the tree is not very deep, information will travel to everyone very quickly. For graphs, this is a bit more complicated, because there are typically many more connections between nodes than in a tree. We will look at two graph traversal methods, depth-first and breadth-first, to accomplish this.

A spanning tree is a connected subset of a graph that has no cycles and contains all of the graph nodes and a subset of the edges. A minimum spanning tree is a spanning tree where the sum of the weights for the edges included has the smallest total possible. One use of a minimum spanning tree is in the construction of a company intranet with routers to be placed at strategic points throughout some geographic area. If we wish to minimize the cost of connecting the routers, we could build a graph with each router as a node and the weights on the edges set as the cost of connecting each pair of routers. The minimum spanning tree of this graph will tell us which pairs of routers to connect with wires so that our intranet is completely connected at the cheapest cost.

A similar application is to find the shortest path between two nodes of a graph. This has a practical application in planning a route for a car trip or sending a message through a computer network.

An important consideration in large computer networks is reliability. We would like the network to continue to function if one of the routers should fail. In simple terms, this requires multiple paths between any two routers in the network so that if something fails along one of the paths, there is still a way

to get information through. The last section of this chapter looks at a biconnected components algorithm. It will identify nodes in a graph that are on
every path from one part of the graph to another. These nodes are points in a
computer network, for example, where a failure could cause the network to
become disconnected.

6.1 GRAPH BACKGROUND AND TERMINOLOGY

Formally, a graph is an ordered pair, $G = (V, E)$, of two sets representing the
nodes or vertices of the graph and the edges of the graph. An edge specifies
which nodes have a connection between them. When working with graphs,
we are frequently interested in how these edges can be put together to move
through the graph. For this reason, we will often talk of traveling an edge,
which means that we have changed our node of interest by following one of
the edges connected to it. In other words, if our graph has nodes A and B that
are connected by an edge, we will talk of "moving from A to B," "traveling
from A to B," or "traversing the edge from A to B" to represent the fact that
our focus has changed from node A to node B. For the ease of discussion, we
will just write the two node labels as shorthand for the edge that connects
them. So, AB would represent the edge between node A and node B, and we
will say that B is adjacent to A.

A graph can either be undirected or directed. An undirected graph, typically
just called a graph, has edges that can be traversed in either direction. In this
case, an edge is a set, which contains the labels of the nodes that are at the two
ends of the edge.[1] A directed graph, also called a digraph, has edges that can
only be traversed in one direction. For a digraph, our set of edges will have
ordered pairs in which the first item is where the edge starts and the second is
where the edge ends.[2] In our discussion, we will use the shorthand above for
our edges, with the context indicating if this is a directed edge or if you can
travel in either direction between the two nodes.

---

[1] If a set representing an edge has just one element, that represents an edge that "loops,"
or in other words, starts and ends at the same node.

[2] In a digraph, an ordered pair that has the same label for both components represents
an edge that starts and ends on the same node.

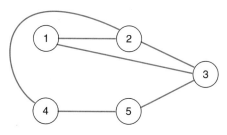

FIGURE 6.1A
The graph G = ({1, 2, 3, 4, 5}, {{1, 2}, {1, 3}, {2, 3}, {2, 4}, {3, 5}, {4, 5}})

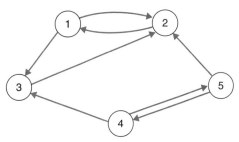

FIGURE 6.1B
The directed graph G = ({1, 2, 3, 4, 5}, {(1, 2), (1, 3), (2, 1), (3, 2), (4, 3), (4, 5), (5, 2), (5,4)})

After this section, we will specify graphs by drawing them instead of giving these sets. In our drawings, we will use circles to represent the nodes of the graph and lines connecting the circles to represent the edges. We will put the node labels inside the circles. If we want to represent a directed graph, we will use arrows to show the direction the edge can be traveled. Figure 6.1 shows the drawing of a graph (Fig. 6.1(a)) and directed graph (Fig. 6.1(b)) with their formal set definitions.

■ 6.1.1 Terminology

A complete graph is a graph with an edge between every pair of nodes. If there are N nodes, there will be $(N^2 - N) / 2$ edges in a complete graph without loop edges. A complete digraph is a digraph with an edge allowing traversal between every pair of nodes. Because the edges of a graph allow travel in two directions, whereas a digraph's edges allow travel in only one, a digraph with N nodes will have twice as many edges, specifically $N^2 - N$.

A subgraph (V_s, E_s) of a graph or digraph (V, E) is one that has a subset of the vertices $(V_s \subseteq V)$ and edges $(E_s \subseteq E)$ of the full graph.

A path between two nodes of a graph or digraph is a sequence of edges that can be traveled consecutively. In other words, a path between node A and node B would begin at node A and traverse a set of edges until node B was reached. Formally, we say that a path from node v_i to v_j is the sequence of edges $v_i v_{i+1}$, $v_{i+1} v_{i+2}, \ldots, v_{j-1} v_j$ that are in the graph. We require that all of the nodes along this path be unique. A path is said to have a length that represents the number of edges that make up the path. The path AB, BC, CD, DE has length 4.

A weighted graph or digraph is one where each edge has a value, called the weight, associated with it. In graph drawings, the weight will be written near the edge. In formal definitions, the weight will be an extra component in the set of an edge or the ordered "pair" (now a triplet). When working with weighted graphs, we consider the weight to be the cost for traversing the edge. A path through a weighted graph has a cost that is the sum of the weights of each edge in the path. In a weighted graph, the shortest path between two nodes is the path with the smallest cost, even if it doesn't have the fewest edges. For example, if path P_1 has five edges with a total cost of 24, and path P_2 has three edges with a total cost of 36, path P_1 will be considered the shorter path because its cost is less.

A graph or digraph is called connected if there is at least one path between every pair of nodes. A cycle is a path that begins and ends at the same node. An acyclic graph or digraph is one that has no cycles. A graph that is connected and acyclic is called an unrooted tree. An unrooted tree has the structure of a tree except that no node has been specified as the root (but every node could serve as the root).

■ 6.1.2 EXERCISES

1. Draw the following graph: G = ({1, 2, 3, 4, 5, 6}, {{1, 2}, {1, 4}, {2, 5}, {2, 6}, {3, 4}, {3, 5}, {3, 6}, {4, 5}, {4, 6}, {5, 6}}).

2. Draw the following digraph: G = ({1, 2, 3, 4, 5}, {(1, 2), (1, 4), (1, 5), (2, 3), (2, 4), (2, 5), (3, 2), (3, 4), (3, 5), (4, 1), (4, 2), (4, 5), (5, 2), (5, 3), (5, 4)}).

3. Give the set description for the following graph:

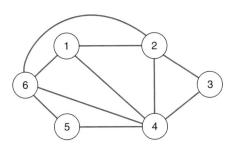

4. Give the set description for the following digraph:

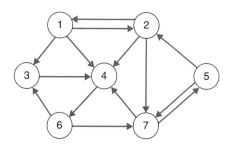

5. List all of the paths between node 1 and node 5 in the graph in question 3.
6. List all of the paths between node 1 and node 4 in the digraph in question 4.
7. List all of the cycles that start at node 3 in the graph in question 3.
8. List all of the cycles that start at node 7 in the digraph in question 4.

6.2   DATA STRUCTURE METHODS FOR GRAPHS

There are two ways that we can store the graph or digraph information: an adjacency matrix or an adjacency list. In this section, there is no difference between how these methods are used for graphs and digraphs. For this reason, the term *graph* should be interpreted as meaning digraphs as well. As you will see, these storage methods will also neutralize the differences between graphs and digraphs, and so the algorithms that use these structures will not need to differentiate between graphs and digraphs either.

An adjacency matrix gives us the ability to quickly access edge information, but if the graph is far from being a complete graph, there will be many more empty elements in the array than there are full elements. An adjacency list uses space that is proportional to the number of edges in the graph, but the time to access edge information may be greater.

There is no clear benefit to either of these methods. The choice between these two will be closely linked to knowledge of the graphs that will be input to the algorithm. In situations where the graph has many nodes, but they are each connected to only a few other nodes, an adjacency list would be best because it uses less space, and there will not be long edge lists to traverse. In situations were the graph has few nodes, an adjacency matrix would be best because it would not be very large, so even a sparse graph would not waste many entries. In situations where the graph has many edges and begins to approach a complete graph, an adjacency matrix would be best because there would be few empty entries.

The following sections give the details on adjacency matrix and list methods.

■ 6.2.1 The Adjacency Matrix

An adjacency matrix, AdjMat, for a graph $G = (V, E)$, with $|V| = N$, will be stored as a two dimensional array of size $N \times N$. Each location $[i, j]$ of this array will store a 0, except if there is an edge from node v_i to node v_j, the location will store a 1. More formally,

$$\text{AdjMat}[i, j] = \begin{cases} 1 & \text{if } v_i v_j \in E \\ 0 & \text{if } v_i v_j \notin E \end{cases} \qquad \text{for all } i \text{ and } j \text{ in the range 1 to } N$$

The adjacency matrices for the graph and digraph in Fig. 6.1 are given in Fig. 6.2.

For weighted graphs and digraphs, the adjacency matrix entries would be ∞ if there is no edge and the weight for the edge in all other cases. The diagonal elements would be 0, because there is no cost to travel from a node to itself.

	1	2	3	4	5
1	0	1	1	0	0
2	1	0	1	1	0
3	1	1	0	0	1
4	0	1	0	0	1
5	0	0	1	1	0

■ FIGURE 6.2A
The adjacency matrix for the graph in Fig. 6.1(a)

	1	2	3	4	5
1	0	1	1	0	0
2	1	0	0	0	0
3	0	1	0	0	0
4	0	0	1	0	1
5	0	1	0	1	0

■ FIGURE 6.2B
The adjacency matrix for the digraph in Fig. 6.1(b)

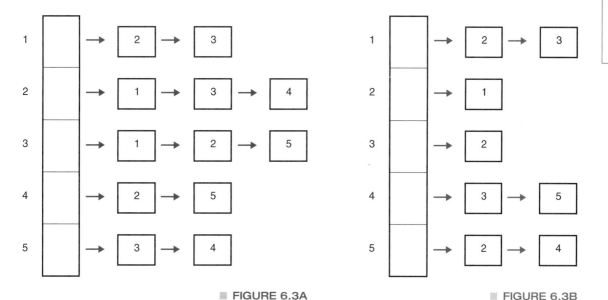

■ **FIGURE 6.3A**
The adjacency list for the graph in Fig. 6.1(a)

■ **FIGURE 6.3B**
The adjacency list for the graph in Fig. 6.1(b)

■ 6.2.2 The Adjacency List

An adjacency list, AdjList, for a graph G = (V, E), with |V| = N, will be stored as a one-dimensional array of size N, with each location being a pointer to a linked list. There will be one list for each node, and that list will have one entry for each adjacent node. Figure 6.3 shows the adjacency lists for the graph and digraph in Fig. 6.1.

For weighted graphs and digraphs, the adjacency list entries would have an additional field to hold the weight for that edge.

■ 6.2.3 EXERCISES

1. Give the adjacency matrix for the graph in question 1 of Section 6.1.2.
2. Give the adjacency matrix for the digraph in question 2 of Section 6.1.2.
3. Give the adjacency matrix for the graph in question 3 of Section 6.1.2.
4. Give the adjacency matrix for the digraph in question 4 of Section 6.1.2.
5. Give the adjacency list for the graph in question 1 of Section 6.1.2.
6. Give the adjacency list for the digraph in question 2 of Section 6.1.2.
7. Give the adjacency list for the graph in question 3 of Section 6.1.2.
8. Give the adjacency list for the digraph in question 4 of Section 6.1.2.

6.3   DEPTH-FIRST AND BREADTH-FIRST TRAVERSAL ALGORITHMS

When we work with graphs, there may be times that we wish to do something to each node in the graph exactly once. For example, there may be a piece of information that needs to be distributed to all of the computers on a network. We want this information to get to each computer, and we do not want to give it to any computer twice. The same thing would be true if we were looking for information instead of distributing it.

There are two techniques that we will examine that accomplish this traversal. In depth-first, our traversal will go as far as possible down a path before considering another, and in breadth-first, our traversal will go evenly in many directions. We now look at these two methods in more detail. For these two traversal methods, we choose one node in the graph as our starting point. In our discussion, we use the phrase "visit the node" to represent the action that needs to be done at each node. For example, if we are searching, visiting the node would mean that we check it for the information we want. These methods work with both directed and undirected graphs without any changes. We will illustrate them with undirected graphs.

Either of these traversal methods can also be used to determine if a graph is connected. If we create a list of the nodes we visit during our traversal, this list can be compared to the set of nodes in the graph. If they are the same, the graph is connected. If they are not, there are some nodes that cannot be reached from where we started, meaning that the graph is not connected.

■ 6.3.1 Depth-First Traversal

In depth-first traversal, we visit the starting node and then proceed to follow links through the graph until we reach a dead end. In an undirected graph, a node is a dead end if all of the nodes adjacent to it have already been visited. In a directed graph, if a node has no outgoing edges, we also have a dead end.

When we reach a dead end, we back up along our path until we find an unvisited adjacent node and then continue in that new direction. The process will have completed when we back up to the starting node and all the nodes adjacent to it have been visited. In illustrating this algorithm and all others in this chapter, if presented with a choice of two nodes, we will choose the node with the numerically or alphabetically smaller label. When this algorithm is implemented, that choice will depend on how the edges of the graph are stored.

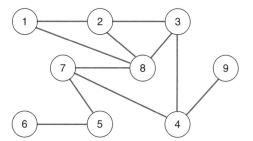

FIGURE 6.4
A graph

Consider the graph in Fig. 6.4. If we begin the depth-first traversal at node 1, we then visit, in order, the nodes 2, 3, 4, 7, 5, and 6 before we reach a dead end. We would then back up to node 7 to find that node 8 hasn't been visited, but that immediately leads to a dead end. We next back up to node 4 and find that node 9 hasn't been visited, but again we have an immediate dead end. We then continue to back up until we reach the starting node, and because all nodes adjacent to it have been visited, we are done.

The recursive algorithm for depth-first traversal is

```
DepthFirstTraversal(G, v)
G   is the graph
v   is the current node

Visit( v )
Mark( v )
for every edge vw in G do
   if w is not marked then
      DepthFirstTraversal(G, w)
   end if
end for
```

This recursive algorithm relies on the system stack of the computer to keep track of where it has been in the graph so that it can properly back up when it reaches dead ends. We could create a similar nonrecursive algorithm by using a stack data structure and pushing and popping graph vertices ourselves.

■ 6.3.2 Breadth-First Traversal

In a breadth-first traversal, we visit the starting node and then on the first pass visit all of the nodes directly connected to it. In the second pass, we visit nodes that are two edges "away" from the starting node. With each new pass, we visit nodes that are one more edge away. Because there might be cycles in the graph, it is possible for a node to be on two paths of different lengths from the starting node. Because we will visit that node for the first time along the shortest path from the starting node, we will not need to consider it again. We will, therefore, either need to keep a list of the nodes we have visited or we will need to use a variable in the node to mark it as visited to prevent multiple visits.

Consider again the graph in Fig. 6.4. If we begin our traversal at node 1, we will visit nodes 2 and 8 on the first pass. On the second pass, we will visit nodes 3 and 7. (Even though nodes 2 and 8 are also at the end of paths of length 2, we will not return to them because they were visited in the first pass.) On the third pass, we visit nodes 4 and 5, and on the last pass we visit nodes 6 and 9.

Where the depth-first traversal depended on a stack, our breadth-first traversal is based on a queue. The algorithm for breadth-first traversal is

```
BreadthFirstTraversal(G, v)
G   is the graph
v   is the current node

Visit( v )
Mark( v )
Enqueue( v )
while the queue is not empty do
   Dequeue( x )
   for every edge xw in G do
      if w is not marked then
         Visit( w )
         Mark( w )
         Enqueue( w )
      end if
   end for
end while
```

This algorithm will add the root of the breadth-first traversal tree to the queue but then immediately remove it. As it looks at the nodes that are adjacent to the root, they will be added to the end of the queue. Once all of the nodes adjacent to the root have been visited, we will return to the queue and get the first of those nodes. You should notice that because nodes are added to the end of the queue, no node that is two edges away from the root will be considered again until all of the nodes one edge away have been taken off of the queue and processed.

■ 6.3.3 Traversal Analysis

Our goal for these two traversal algorithms was to create a process that would visit each node of a connected graph exactly once. We begin our analysis to see if this has been accomplished. In breadth-first, we moved out from the starting node. We followed all available edges, unless they led to a node we had already visited. Does this cause any problem? Any nodes that could be reached from that node will still be visited but just from a more direct route. Looking back at Fig. 6.4, we see that we didn't revisit node 8 after nodes 2 or 3. But anything that we could reach from node 8 is already being visited because node 8 was reached in an earlier pass. Looking at it another way, is it possible for there to be a node in a connected graph that wasn't visited? Because on each pass we take one step from a node visited on the last pass, the only way for a node not to be visited is for it to not be adjacent to a visited node of the graph. But that would mean that the graph is not connected, which contradicts our statement that the graph is connected, so all of the nodes must be visited.

A similar thing is true for a depth-first search. In this case, we travel deeply into the graph until we reach a dead end. Do we then visit all of the remaining nodes in the process of backtracking? Is it possible that we may have missed a node in this process? Each time that we reach a dead end, we back up to the first node that has an unvisited adjacent node. We move to that node and again begin to travel deeply into the graph. A dead end again causes us to back up to the first node with an unvisited adjacent node that we find. For a node in the graph to not be visited at the end of this process means that it must not be adjacent to any of the nodes visited in the graph. But again, this would mean that the graph is not connected, which contradicts our statement that it is. All of the nodes must be visited in this traversal as well.

What about the efficiency of this algorithm? Our assumption is that the work done as we visit each node is the most complex part of this process. So, the work done to check to see if an adjacent node has been visited and the work to traverse the edges is not significant in this case. So the order of the algorithm is the number of times a node is visited. Because we have said that these algorithms visit each node exactly one time, for a graph with N nodes, the visit process will be done N times. These traversals are, therefore, of order $O(N)$.

■ 6.3.4 EXERCISES

1. For the following graphs, give the order that the nodes will be first visited when doing a breadth-first traversal starting at the node labeled with a 1.

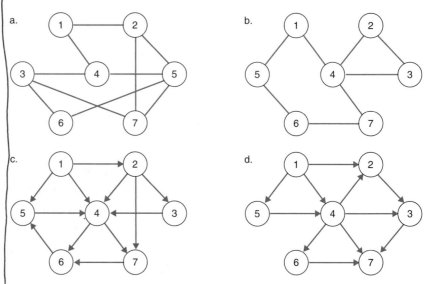

a.

b.

c.

d.

2. For the graphs in question 1, give the order that the nodes will be first visited when doing a depth-first traversal starting at the node labeled with a 1.

3. Write a detailed algorithm for depth-first traversal using an adjacency matrix that just prints the node label as the visit operation. You should trace it using the graphs in this section to make sure you get the same answer.

4. Write a detailed algorithm for breadth-first traversal using an adjacency matrix that just prints the node label as the visit operation. You should trace it using the graphs in this section to make sure you get the same answer.

5. Write a detailed algorithm for depth-first traversal using an adjacency list that just prints the node label as the visit operation. You should trace it using the graphs in this section to make sure you get the same answer.

6. Write a detailed algorithm for breadth-first traversal using an adjacency list that just prints the node label as the visit operation. You should trace it using the graphs in this section to make sure you get the same answer.

7. Prove that each edge in a connected graph will be part of the depth-first traversal tree or will be an edge pointing to a predecessor in the tree.

8. Prove that each edge in a connected graph will be part of the breadth-first traversal tree or will be an edge pointing to a node in the tree that is neither a predecessor or descendent.

6.4 MINIMUM SPANNING TREE ALGORITHM

The minimum spanning tree (MST) of a weighted connected graph is a sub-graph that contains all of the nodes of the original and a subset of the edges so that the subgraph is connected and the total of the edge weights is the smallest possible. If the original graph is not connected, the processes below can be used on each of the separate components to produce a spanning tree for each one.

There is a brute force way that the MST could be found for a connected graph. Because the edges in the MST are a subset of the edges in the entire graph, we could look at all of the possible subsets of the edge set until we find the MST. You should see that this is a very time-consuming process. First, if there are N edges, there would be 2^N subsets. For each of these subsets, we would need to first check that it spans all of the nodes and has no cycles. Then we could calculate its total weights. We could speed up the process once we find the first spanning tree. Any edge subset with a total weight that is greater than that of our current best spanning tree can't possibly be better, so there is no need to check to see if it spans all of the nodes and is acyclic. Even with this improvement, this brute force method would be of order $O(2^N)$.

6.4.1 The Dijkstra-Prim Algorithm

The following algorithm to find the MST was developed by Edsger Dijkstra and R. C. Prim in the late 1950s; they worked and published their results independently.

To find the MST, we will use what is called a "greedy" algorithm. Greedy algorithms work by looking at a subset of the larger problem and making the best decision based on that information. In this case, we will, at each step of the process, look at a collection of potential edges to add to the spanning tree and pick the one with the smallest weight. By doing this repeatedly, we will grow a spanning tree that has a minimum overall total.

To accomplish this process, we will consider the nodes of the graph to be in one of three categories: in the tree, on the fringe of the tree, and not yet con-sidered. We begin by picking one node of the graph and putting that into the spanning tree. Because our result is an unrooted tree, the choice of an initial node has no impact on our final result (unless there are multiple MSTs). We then place all of the nodes that are connected to this initial one into the fringe category. We loop through the process of picking the smallest weighted edge connecting a tree node with a fringe node, adding the new node to the tree, and then updating the nodes in the fringe category. When all the nodes have been added to the tree, we are done.

Our general algorithm for this process is as follows

```
select a starting node
build the initial fringe from nodes connected to the starting node
while there are nodes left do
    choose the edge to the fringe of the smallest weight
    add the associated node to the tree
    update the fringe by:
        adding nodes to the fringe connected to the new node
        updating the edges to the fringe so that they are the smallest
end while
```

Figure 6.5 gives an example of this algorithm in operation. We have arbitrarily chosen node A to begin the process. As we said, a different choice for the starting node will not change the result, unless there is more than one MST.

The original graph is shown in Fig. 6.5(a), and as was mentioned, we choose to start the construction of the MST at node A. All of the nodes directly connected to node A become the starting fringe set. We see that the

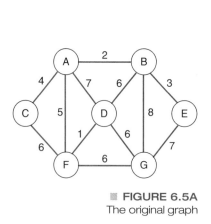

FIGURE 6.5A
The original graph

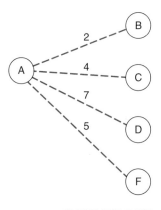

FIGURE 6.5B
First node added. (Dashed lines show edges to fringe nodes.)

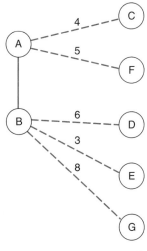

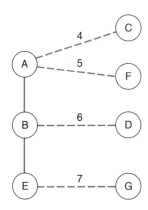

■ FIGURE 6.5C
Second node added.
Edges to nodes D, E, and
G updated. (Solid lines
show edges in the MST.)

■ FIGURE 6.5D
Third node added. Edge
to node G updated.

edge with the smallest weight connects nodes A and B, so B is added to the
MST along with the edge AB.

When node B is added to the tree (Fig. 6.5(c)), we need to determine if
there are any nodes that need to be added to the fringe set, and we find that
nodes E and G must be added. Because the only tree node they are connected
to is node B, we add those edges to the ones we will consider next. At this
time, we also need to check to see if the edges from node A to nodes C, D, and
F are still the shortest or if there are better edges from node B to these three
nodes. In the original graph, there are no direct connections from node B to
nodes C and F, so those will not change. But the edge from node B to node D
has a smaller weight than the one from node A, and so the edge BD now
replaces the edge AD.

Of the five edges to fringe nodes, we see that BE has the smallest weight,
and so it and node E are added to the tree (Fig. 6.5(d)). The edge EG has a
smaller weight than the edge BG, so it is now used. Of the four current edges
to the fringe, we see that AC has the smallest weight and so it is added next.

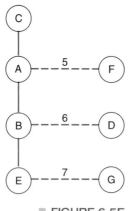

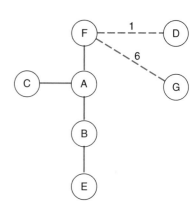

FIGURE 6.5E
Node C added to the tree

FIGURE 6.5F
Node F added to the tree and edges to nodes D and G are updated

The addition of node C and edge AC to the spanning tree (Fig. 6.5(e)) did not cause any edges to be updated. We next choose the edge AF, so it and the node F are added to the tree. We also update the links because the edge FD has a smaller weight than BD and edge FG has a smaller weight than EG. In the resulting fringe (Fig. 6.5(f)), we see that the edge FD is now the remaining edge with the smallest weight, so it is added next.

We now just have one node that has not been added to the tree (Fig. 6.5(g)). When it is added, the process is complete, and we have determined the MST rooted at node A (Fig. 6.5(h)).

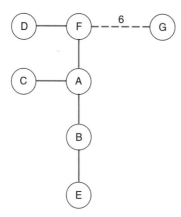

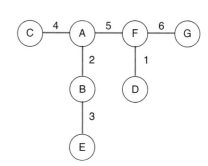

FIGURE 6.5G
Only one node is left in the fringe

FIGURE 6.5H
The complete minimum spanning tree rooted at node A

■ 6.4.2 The Kruskal Algorithm

Where the Dijkstra-Prim algorithm began at a particular node and built the minimum spanning tree outward, Kruskal's algorithm concentrates instead on the edges of the graph.

In this algorithm, we begin with an empty spanning tree and add edges in order of increasing weight until all nodes are connected to the graph. If we run out of edges before all of the nodes are connected, the original graph wasn't connected, and the result we have generated is the MSTs of each of the connected components of the original graph.

We begin in Fig. 6.6(a) with the same graph that we used for the Dijkstra-Prim algorithm. In this case, we first add the edge with the lowest weight, which is the one between nodes D and F, giving the partial results in Fig. 6.6(b).

The edge with weight 2 is added next (Fig. 6.6(c)) between the nodes A and B, and then the edge with weight three is added, giving us Fig. 6.6(d).

The edges with weights of 4 and 5 are next added to our result, as you can see in Figs. 6.6(e) and 6.6(f). Only node G is still unconnected. The next edges to consider are those with a weight of 6.

Of the four edges with a weight of 6, two are discarded because they would form a cycle with edges already part of the MST. The edge between nodes C and F would form a cycle that includes node A, and the edge between node B and D would form a cycle that includes nodes A and F. The other two nodes are both good alternatives, and depending on the one chosen, we get the MST in either Fig. 6.6(g) or Fig. 6.6(h).

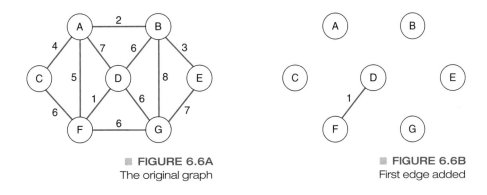

■ FIGURE 6.6A
The original graph

■ FIGURE 6.6B
First edge added

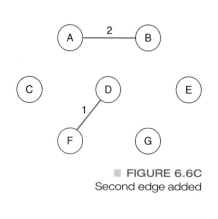

■ FIGURE 6.6C
Second edge added

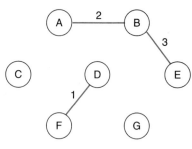

■ FIGURE 6.6D
Third edge added

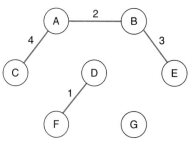

■ FIGURE 6.6E
Fourth edge added

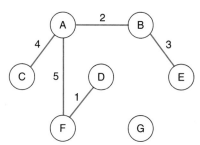

■ FIGURE 6.6F
Fifth edge added

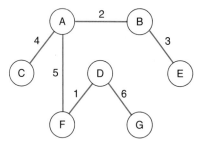

■ FIGURE 6.6G
A minimum spanning tree

■ FIGURE 6.6H
An alternative minimum spanning
tree

The general algorithm that will accomplish this is (where E represents the number of edges and N the number of vertices)

```
sort the edges in nondecreasing order by weight
initialize partition structure
edgeCount = 1
includedCount = 0
while edgeCount ≤ E and includedCount ≤ N-1 do
   parent1 = FindRoot( edge[edgeCount].start )
   parent2 = FindRoot( edge[edgeCount].end )
   if parent1 ≠ parent2 then
      add edge[edgeCount] to spanning tree
      includedCount = includedCount + 1
      Union( parent1, parent2 )
   end if
   edgeCount = edgeCount + 1
end while
```

Our main loop will continue until the `edgeCount` variable indicates that we have looked at all of the edges or the `includedCount` indicates that we have added enough edges to create the spanning tree. You should see that if we have N nodes in the graph, a spanning tree would have one less edge than nodes.

Inside the loop, we first find the parents of the two nodes that are connected by the next edge we are considering. If those nodes are in partitions with different roots, adding an edge between them will not create a cycle, so this current edge can be added to the MST and those two pieces can be joined so that they now have the same root. The details of the `FindRoot` and `Union` routines will be given in Section 6.7.

The complexity of this algorithm will be the complexity of the sort algorithm used because the `while` loop is linearly related to the number of edges. This makes the complexity of Kruskal's MST algorithm $O(E \lg E)$.

■ 6.4.3 EXERCISES

1. Find the minimum spanning tree using the Dijkstra–Prim algorithm for the following graphs starting at node A. Show all steps.

a.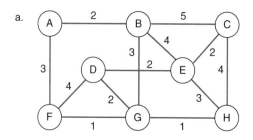

b.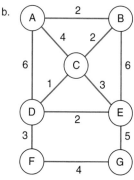

c.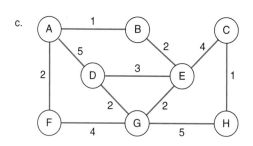

d.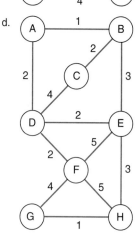

2. Find the minimum spanning tree using the Kruskal algorithm for the graphs in question 1. Show all steps.

3. Do an analysis of the Dijkstra–Prim minimum spanning tree algorithm, counting the number of times that an edge is considered for nodes added to the fringe, for updating edges to the fringe nodes, or to pick the node to move from the fringe to the minimum spanning tree.

4. Prove that if there is one edge with a weight smaller than all of the other edges, that edge will be part of every minimum spanning tree.

5. Prove that if a connected graph has edge weights that are all distinct (in other words, no two edges have the same weight), there is only one minimum spanning tree.

6. Prove whether it is always, never, or sometimes true that the order in which the nodes are added to the MST by the Dijkstra–Prim algorithm is the same as the order in which they are encountered in a breadth-first traversal.
7. Prove whether it is always, never, or sometimes true that the order in which the nodes are added to the MST by the Dijkstra–Prim algorithm is the same as the order in which they are encountered in a depth-first traversal.

6.5 SHORTEST-PATH ALGORITHM

The shortest-path algorithm will find for two nodes the series of edges between them that will result in the smallest total weight.

It might seem that we could use the minimum spanning tree algorithm to prune out some of the edges and then just look for the path between the nodes in the spanning tree. Unfortunately, that will not always produce the shortest path. Remember that the minimum spanning tree algorithm is trying to find an overall total that is smallest, so it is going to look for the smallest weights possible. For example, think of a graph that is "circular" in shape. In other words, the first node is connected to the second, which is connected to the third, and so on until the last node, which is connected to the first. This graph is just a ring where each node is just connected to the two nodes on either side of it. For example, Fig. 6.7(a) shows just such a graph with six nodes. Notice that weights on all of the edges are 1, except for the edge from node A to node B, which has a weight of 2. The minimum spanning tree algorithm will pick all of the edges with weight 1, and drop the one edge of weight 2. But that means that the path between node A and node B in the minimum spanning tree (Fig. 6.7(b)) must go through all of the other nodes for a path length of 5. This is

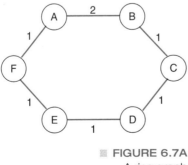

■ FIGURE 6.7A
A ring graph

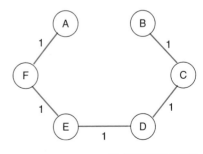

■ FIGURE 6.7B
Its minimum spanning tree

clearly not the shortest path, because you can see in Fig. 6.7(a) that there is a direct path between node A and node B that has length 2.

■ 6.5.1 Dijkstra's Algorithm

The minimum spanning tree algorithm will not work to find the shortest path because its greedy algorithm just considered the weight of one edge at each pass. If we modify the algorithm so that it chooses the edge to the fringe that is part of the shortest entire path from the starting node, we will get the result we want. More specifically, our algorithm becomes

```
select a starting node
build the initial fringe from nodes connected to the starting node
while we are not at the destination node do
    choose the fringe node with the shortest path to the starting node
    add that node and its edge to the tree
    update the fringe by:
        adding nodes to the fringe connected to the new node
        for each node in the fringe do
            update its edge to the one connected to the tree on the shortest
                path to the starting node
        end for
end while
```

Figure 6.8 shows an example execution of this algorithm. We begin with the same graph that we used for the minimum spanning tree algorithm (reproduced here as Fig. 6.8(a)) and will look for the shortest path starting at node A and ending at node G.

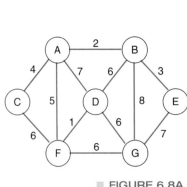

■ FIGURE 6.8A
The original graph

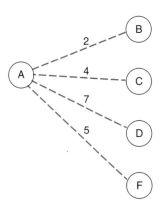

■ FIGURE 6.8B
The shortest path is to node B

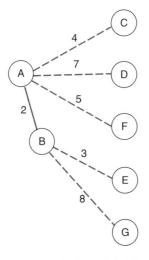

■ FIGURE 6.8C
Path of length 4 to node
C is the shortest of the
options

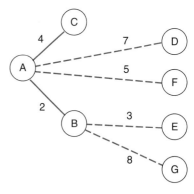

■ FIGURE 6.8D
The path of length 5 to either node
E or node F is shortest

Beginning our path at node A gives us four possible edges to consider. Of those four, the edge AB is the shortest.

Node B is added to our shortest path tree (Fig. 6.8(c)), and we now look at updating the paths. Nodes E and G can now be reached, so they are added. We also look at node D and compare its direct path from node A of length 7 with the path that goes through node B, which is of length 8. Because the direct path is shorter, there is no change to the edge for node D. In looking at the options, we see that the path from node A to node C is of length 4 and is the shortest. The edge BE is shorter, but we are now considering the entire path from node A and so the length of the path to node E is actually 5.

Node C is added to the shortest path tree (Fig. 6.8(d)). In examining the graph, we see that we can get to node F through node C, but that total path length is 10, which is longer than the current path to node F and so there are no changes.

Given the situation in Fig. 6.8(d), we could choose either the path from node A to node F or the path from node A to node E that goes through node B, because they are both of length 5. The one chosen during a program execution will depend on the way the data is stored. For our purposes, when presented with a choice, we will select the node that is alphabetically smaller to get Fig. 6.8(e). Because the addition of node E to the graph didn't change any

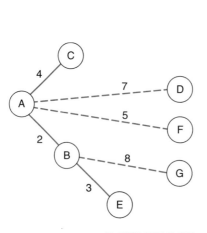

■ FIGURE 6.8E
The other path of length 5 to node F
is next

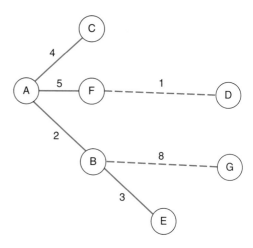

■ FIGURE 6.8F
The path of length 6 to node D is shorter
than the path to node G

of the other connections, we now choose node F to get Fig. 6.8(f). You should see that even though the selection of node F changed the edge for node D, if we had selected node F first, we would have chosen node E second.

In Fig. 6.8(f), it should be clear that the path to node D is shorter than the path to node G. Choosing node D results in Fig. 6.8(g), and then node G is the last to be added, giving the final shortest path tree in Fig. 6.8(h). The shortest path from node A to node G has length of 10. If you look back at Fig. 6.5(h), you will see another example of the minimum spanning tree not having the shortest path, because that figure has the path from node A to node G at length 11.

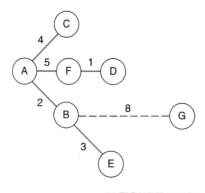

■ FIGURE 6.8G
The path to node G is the only
one left

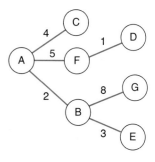

■ FIGURE 6.8H
The complete shortest
path tree starting at node A

In the example in Fig. 6.8, we have the full shortest-path tree for node A because our destination node was the last to be added. If we had reached node G earlier, the algorithm would have stopped at that point. There are applications where we might be interested in the shortest path from one node to every other node. For example, if we have a small computer network that has relatively stable transmission rates between the nodes, we could calculate the shortest path to every other node for each computer. Then when a message needs to be sent, we would not need to do anything but access our predetermined shortest-path table to find the quickest way to send the message.

■ 6.5.2 EXERCISES

1. Execute the shortest-path algorithm on the following graphs starting at node A to create the entire shortest-path tree for each one. Count how many edges you look at in the process (if you look at one edge more than once, count it each time).

a.
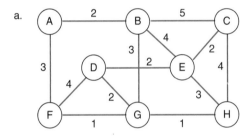

b.
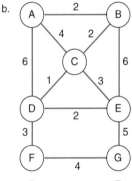

c.
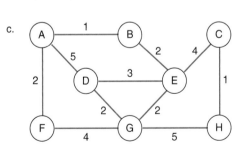

d.
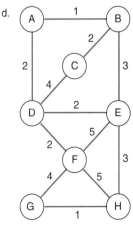

2. Alter the algorithm in this section so that it efficiently determines the shortest path from the start node to every node in the graph, instead of just to one destination.

3. Do an analysis of the shortest-path algorithm, counting the number of times that an edge is checked for nodes added to the fringe, for updating edges to the fringe nodes, or to pick the node to move from the fringe to the minimum spanning tree.

4. Prove that a breadth-first traversal produces a shortest-path tree for a graph without weights.

5. Prove whether it is always, never, or sometimes true that the order in which the nodes are added to the shortest-path tree is the same as the order in which they are encountered in a breadth-first traversal.

6. Prove whether it is always, never, or sometimes true that the order in which the nodes are added to the shortest-path tree is the same as the order in which they are encountered in a depth-first traversal.

6.6 BICONNECTED COMPONENT ALGORITHM

A biconnected component of a graph is the set of three or more nodes for which there are at least two paths between each node. A biconnected component can also have just two nodes and one edge connecting them. A biconnected component is a robust part of a graph because if one node and its edges are removed from the graph, all of the other nodes in the biconnected component can still reach any other. The graph in Fig. 6.9 shows a connected graph that has three biconnected components. The first biconnected component has the nodes labeled A, B, C, and D, the second has the nodes labeled D, E, F, G, and H, and the third has the nodes H and I.

■ FIGURE 6.9
A connected graph
with two
biconnected
components

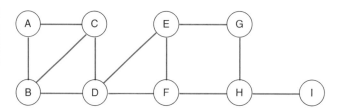

Determining the biconnected components of a network indicates how stable the network can be under degraded conditions. So, if all computers on a network are part of the biconnected component of the related graph, we know that the network will continue to function even if one of the computers is down. In airline scheduling, the biconnected component of the graph for the flight schedule indicates if passengers can be rerouted when an airport is closed because of weather problems.

An articulation point in a connected graph is a node that, when it is removed, causes the graph to no longer be connected. Articulation points of a graph are nodes that are shared between two biconnected components. Nodes D and H in Fig. 6.9 are articulation points. The identification of articulation points and the determination of biconnected components are related.

We could identify the articulation points in a brute force manner by removing one node at a time and using one of our traversal methods to see if the remaining nodes are still connected. If they are, the node we removed is not an articulation point, but if they are not, it is an articulation point. This means that we would have to do N traversals of a graph with N nodes. This process would be $O(N^2)$. By keeping a little additional information while we are traversing, we can identify the articulation points and the biconnected components on one traversal.

Think about paths in the graph in Fig. 6.9 that begin at node F. You should see that no matter what order the nodes are visited in, the paths from node F to nodes A, B, and C must go through node D. This means that node D is an articulation point and the subgraph containing nodes A, B, C, and D is a biconnected component.

We base our algorithm on depth-first search. You will recall from Section 6.3.1 that we said a depth-first search will follow edges into a graph until a dead end is reached where there are no unvisited nodes adjacent to the current node. When we reach a dead end, we will back up, but now our algorithm will return information about how high up in the depth-first search tree we could have gone at the dead end. These back edges in the search tree indicate a cycle back in the graph. All the nodes in a cycle must be part of the same biconnected component. The back edge location indicates how far we have to back up in our tree before worrying about finding an articulation point.

To accomplish this algorithm, we will keep a count of how many nodes of the graph we have visited. Each node will be assigned an index number indicating when is it visited. In other words, the first node visited will be numbered 1, the second will be numbered 2, and so on. When we reach a dead end, we will look at all of the adjacent nodes (except for the node we just came from) and will use the smallest index number as our back index. If there is just one adjacent node (the one we just came from), we will return the dead end node's index as our back index. When we return to a node that is not the root of the search tree, we will compare the back index value that was returned. If that value is greater than or equal to the current node's index value, the subtree just visited (minus any previously found biconnected components) is a biconnected component. Each internal node of the depth-first search tree will return the smallest value from among the indices of adjacent nodes and any back indices returned to it.

How would this process work in our graph of Fig. 6.9? If we begin at node F, it would be assigned an index of 1. We move to node D (index 2), then nodes B (index 3), A (index 4), and C (index 5). Node C is a dead end, and we have back edges to nodes A, B, and D. The index on node D is smallest, so a value of 2 would be returned to node A as the back index. At node A, because the value of 2 is less than node A's index, it is not an articulation point. The value of 2 is the smallest so far, and it is also returned to node B. This continues until we get back to node D, where we find that the back index returned is the same as node D's index, and so the nodes A, B, C, and D make up a biconnected component. We return to the root of the search tree at node F and then move off to node E (index 6), followed by node G (index 7), and node H (index 8). We next traverse down to node I (index 9), and because it is a dead end with no adjacent nodes other than H, we return its index as the back index. When node H receives a value of 9 from node I, which is greater than the index of node H, we find another biconnected component with nodes H and I. Node H now considers the values of 1 (the back edge to F), 9 (returned from node I), and 8 (node H's index), returning the smallest of these to node G and then to node E. This value is then returned by node E to the root node, and because all nodes have been visited, those that remain (nodes D, E, F, G, and H) comprise the final biconnected component. In Fig. 6.10 we see the result of this process, and from this we can see that the articulation points in the original graph are nodes D and H, which are the only nodes that appear in two separate components.

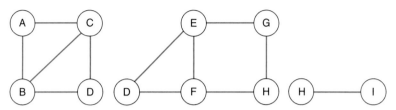

FIGURE 6.10
The biconnected
components of the
graph in Fig. 6.9

■ 6.6.1 EXERCISES

1. Determine the biconnected components of the following graphs:

a.
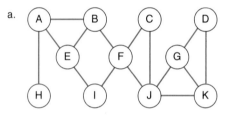

b.
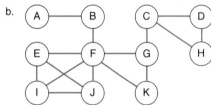

c.
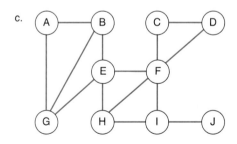

d.
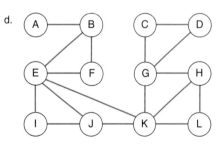

2. Write an algorithm that determines the biconnected components of a graph using an adjacency matrix.

3. Write an algorithm that determines the biconnected components of a graph using an adjacency list.

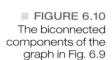

6.7 PARTITIONING SETS

A number of algorithms need to maintain a set of values as a collection of disjoint sets, with the ability to combine them. The inherent set capability of modern programming languages could be used, but there is nothing in their implementation that guarantees that disjoint sets will occur. Additionally, not all programming languages have set capabilities. This section will look at a method for implementing this set partitioning using arrays. We have seen a use for this capability in our algorithm for Kruskal's minimum spanning tree algorithm.

We begin with an array called `Parent`, which has one location for each element of the set we are working with. We initialize all of the elements to −1, which represents that each is the root of a partition (the negative) and that the partition has one element in it (the 1). As things progress, if some element is the root of a partition with seven elements, its value in the array `Parent` will be −7. As elements are added to a partition, their value in the array `Parent` will be set to the root of the partition they are added to. For example, if element 5 is added to the partition rooted by element 8, the fifth location of `Parent` will have 8 stored in it, and the eight location will have its negative value "increased" to indicate that there is one more value in the partition. The elements of the `Parent` array will only have their immediate parent in the partition as their value, because when two partitions are combined, only the root entries of the array will be changed.

Consider the partitioning in Fig. 6.11. We see that there are three partitions with roots of 5, 6, and 11. These array locations have negative values indicating the number of elements in those partitions. Each of the other locations has the value of the immediate parent. If we now joined together the partitions rooted at 6 and 11, we would change `Parent[11]` to have the value 6, its new root, and we would change `Parent[6]` to be −5, representing the fact that this partition has five elements.

The algorithms to accomplish this partition structure follow.

```
InitializePartition( N )
N  the number of elements in the set

For i = 1 to N do
   Parent[i] = -1
end do
```

Index	1	2	3	4	5	6	7	8	9	10	11	12
Parent	5	8	5	11	−7	−3	1	6	1	3	−2	1

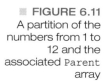

■ FIGURE 6.11
A partition of the
numbers from 1 to
12 and the
associated `Parent`
array

As was discussed, the initialize routine just sets each location of the `Parent` array to −1 to indicate that each value is in its own partition and each partition has a size of 1.

```
Union( i, j )
i, j  the partitions to join together

totalElements = Parent[i] + Parent[j]
if Parent[i] ≥ Parent[j] then
    Parent[i] = j
    Parent[j] = totalElements
else
    Parent[j] = i
    Parent[i] = totalElements
end if
```

The `Union` function is responsible for combining two partitions into one. It begins by calculating the total number of elements that will be in the resulting combined partition. It then adds the smaller partition to the larger one. Remember that the partition sizes are stored as negative numbers, so the `then` clause adds the *i* partition to the larger *j* partition, and the `else` clause adds the *j* partition to the larger *i* partition.

```
FindRoot ( s )
s   the element whose partition root we want

result = s
while Parent[result] > 0 do
   result = Parent[result]
end while
return result
```

The `FindRoot` routine begins at `Parent[s]`, which has the location of the parent of the element s. If this value is negative, it means that s is the root of a partition, so the result of s is returned. If, however, s is not a root, we update result to be the parent of s and check to see if that is the root of the partition. We continue to work our way up this partition until we reach the root. An efficiency improvement not included here would then follow this path again and update all of the entries along it to point to the root directly. This process takes a little more time, but future attempts to find the root for those updated elements will be done faster.

6.8 PROGRAMMING EXERCISES

For these problems, you will be generating complete weighted graphs with N nodes. This is easiest using an adjacency matrix because you just need to fill every entry, except for those along the diagonal, which should be zero. You will work with undirected graphs, so you need to make sure that AdjMat[i, j] has the same value as AdjMat[j, i].

These problems ask you to compare two spanning trees or paths. This will be easier if you make sure that the edges involved are listed with the smaller label first, which is possible because these problems work with undirected graphs. Then you can sort the edges based on their nodes. If two minimum spanning trees or paths are the same, their two sorted lists should match exactly.

1. Generate a complete weighted undirected graph with 50 nodes. Run the Dijkstra–Prim minimum spanning tree algorithm starting at each of the nodes, and determine how many different minimum spanning trees are found. Do this process four times with a maximum random edge weight of 10, 25, 50, and 100. Write a report of your results with an explanation of

what you have found. If you do this for multiple graphs for each maximum, your results will be more reliable.

2. Generate a complete weighted undirected graph with 50 nodes. Run the Kruskal minimum spanning tree algorithm. If faced with two edges of the same weight, randomly choose between them. Generate 10 minimum spanning trees for each graph and see how many are unique. Because you make choices randomly, if there are multiple minimum spanning trees based on these choices, you should find them. Do this process four times with a maximum random edge weight of 10, 25, 50, and 100. Write a report of your results with an explanation of what you have found. If you do this for multiple graphs for each maximum, your results will be more reliable.

3. Generate a complete weighted undirected graph with 50 nodes. For every pair of nodes (A and B), check to see if the shortest path generated from A to B is the same as the shortest path generated from B to A, and note how many times they are different. Do this process four times with a maximum random edge weight of 10, 25, 50, and 100. Write a report of your results with an explanation of what you have found. If you do this for multiple graphs for each maximum, your results will be more reliable.

4. Write a program that will generate a complete weighted undirected graph and then use the Dijkstra–Prim and Kruskal minimum spanning tree algorithms. You should put in counters to keep track of how many times each algorithm looks at any edge. In other words, count every time the adjacency matrix is accessed. Run this for graphs with 10, 25, 50, and 100 nodes, and then write a report comparing the relative efficiencies of these two algorithms. To get more accurate results, you should generate and test multiple random graphs of each size.

CHAPTER 7

Parallel Algorithms

PREREQUISITES

Before beginning this chapter, you should be able to

• Read and create algorithms
• Analyze algorithms like those in Chapters 2 through 6

GOALS

At the end of this chapter, you should be able to

• Explain the PRAM models
• Recognize simple cases when parallelism can be used
• Write simple parallel algorithms

STUDY SUGGESTIONS

As you are working through the chapter, you should rework the examples to make sure you understand them. You might find it helpful to make drawings to trace parallel algorithms with arrows to show how data is read and written in the process. You should also try to answer any questions before reading on. A hint or the answer is in the sentences following the question.

People have recognized for a long time that in most instances two people can accomplish a task faster than one, and three people can accomplish it even faster. The way that this has been implemented in practice has varied. In offices, folders would be refiled faster if they were split among a group of workers. Assembly lines speed up a process, because if one person does the same task over and over, that person can do it more quickly because he or she doesn't need to take time to change tools. Bucket brigades were discovered when people realized that more buckets of water could be moved if, instead of having people running back and forth, they stood in a line and just passed the buckets back and forth.

When we talk about parallel algorithms and programming, we see very similar concepts. There are multitasking systems, where each processor does the same task with different data. There are pipelined systems, where each processor does just one step of the task of decoding and executing a program instruction, passing the results onto another processor, which does the next step. Dataflow systems set up a series of processors to carry out a task or calculation, and then the input data is passed from processor to processor in the calculation of the result.

This chapter is an introduction to the concept of parallel algorithms. Due to the complex nature of parallel algorithms and programming, to cover these ideas completely would at least double the size of this book. We begin with an overview of some of the general concepts related to the structure of parallel computer systems and then look at parallel algorithms for some of the problems we have considered in Chapters 2 through 6. The parallel algorithms presented will not always be the best parallel option but instead will give you an idea of how the problem could be solved in a parallel manner. The amount of detail that would be necessary to always present the most efficient parallel algorithm is well beyond this text.

 7.1 PARALLELISM INTRODUCTION

In this section, we will introduce the basic concepts involved in a study of parallelism. We will begin looking at a way to categorize processing by a computer. We then will look at architectures that are used to implement these categories. This section will conclude with an examination of some of the principles that we will use in our analysis of parallel algorithms.

■ 7.1.1 Computer System Categories

Computer systems can be divided into four main categories. To understand these, you need to think of how a program runs in a slightly different way. From the perspective of the main processor in a computer, the program arrives in a stream of instructions that have to be decoded and then executed. The data can also be seen as arriving in a stream. Our four categories are then based on whether there is one or multiple streams of instructions and data.

Single Instruction Single Data

Single instruction single data (SISD) is the classic single processor model that includes all early computers and many modern computers. In this case, there is one processor that can carry out one program instruction at a time. This processor can work with only one set of data at a time as well. These sequential systems exhibit no parallelism, as will be seen in comparison with the other three categories.

Single Instruction Multiple Data

In single instruction multiple data (SIMD) machines, there is some number of processors all doing the exact same operation but on different data. SIMD machines are sometimes referred to as vector processors because their operation is well suited to doing vector operations, where each processor gets a different element of the vector and after one instruction cycle, the entire vector has been handled. For example, adding two vectors together requires that each of the elements be added. The first element of the resulting vector is the sum of the first elements of the two input vectors, and the second element of the result is the sum of the second elements of the input vectors. In our SIMD machine, the instruction given to each processor would be an add, and each processor would be given one pair of values from the two input vectors. After this one instruction cycle, the entire result would be available. Notice that if the vector has N elements, a SISD machine would take N cycles doing one add per cycle, where a SIMD machine with at least N processors can do the addition in one instruction cycle.

Multiple Instruction Single Data

The option of having different operations all applied to the same data may seem strange, because there are not many programs where you need the results of taking a single data value and squaring it, multiplying it by 2, subtracting 10 from it, and so on. But if we begin to think of this process from a different perspective, we see that finding if a number is prime can be improved with this type of machine. [1] If we have N processors, in one cycle we can determine if a number between 1 and N^2 is prime with a multiple instruction single data (MISD) machine, because if X is not prime, it will have a factor that is less than or equal to $\sqrt{X}$. To find out if $X \leq N^2$ is prime, we have the first processor divide by 2, the second divide by 3, the third divide by 4, and so on up to processor $K - 1$, which divides by K, where $K = \lceil \sqrt{X} \rceil$. If any of these processors finds that it can divide evenly by the number it is given, X is not prime. So in one operation, each of the processors does its division and we have the result. On a sequential machine, you should see that a simple solution to this problem would take at least $\lceil \sqrt{X} \rceil$ passes through a loop doing a division each time.

Multiple Instruction Multiple Data

Our final category is the most flexible of the options. In this case, we have multiple processors, each of which is capable of carrying out a different instruction. We also have multiple data streams, so that each processor can work on independent data sets. In practice, this means that a multiple instruction multiple data (MIMD) system could be running different programs on each processor or different parts of the same program or the vector operations we saw for the SIMD configuration. This category includes most of the modern attempts at parallelism, including clusters of computers and multiprocessor systems.

■ 7.1.2 Parallel Architectures

There are two main issues in the architecture of parallel computer systems: How are memory and processors connected, and how do the processors communicate? These issues will be used when we discuss algorithms because some parallel options are best suited to one or another of these configurations.

Loosely versus Tightly Coupled Machines

In a loosely coupled machine, each of the processors has its own memory, and communication between processors occurs across "network" cables. This is the architecture of computer clusters, where each element of the cluster is a com-

---

[1] Recall that a prime number is one that is only evenly divisible by itself and the number 1. So, for example, 17 is a prime number because the only numbers between 1 and 17 that divide it evenly are 1 and 17.

plete computer system that could function on its own. Parallelism is achieved by the way that tasks are assigned to each of the computers in the cluster by a central controlling computer.

In a tightly coupled machine, each of the processors shares a centralized memory. Communication between the processors is done by one processor writing information into memory and then one or more processors reading that information back out. An example of this communication will be given in Section 7.3.

Processor Communication

In a loosely coupled machine, we said that the processors communicate over cables or wires. We now look at some of the possible configurations that are possible for these processors and wires. At one extreme is a fully connected network, where each processor has a connection to every other processor. At the other extreme is a linear network, where the processors are laid out in a line, and each processor is connected to the two immediately adjacent (except for the two ends, which have only one adjacent processor). In a fully connected network, information can flow quickly between processors, but at the high cost for the extensive amount of wiring that is necessary. In a linear network, information travels more slowly because it must be passed from processor to processor until it reaches its destination, and single point failure disrupts the information flow. This is not surprising if you recall our discussion of biconnected components in Chapter 6.

An alternative to a linear network that improves reliability is a ring network, which is like a linear network, except that the first and last nodes in the line are also connected. Information can now travel more quickly because it will only need to be passed through at most one-half of the processors. Notice in Fig. 7.1 that a message from node 1 to node 5 would have to pass through three

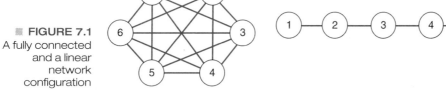

■ FIGURE 7.1
A fully connected and a linear network configuration

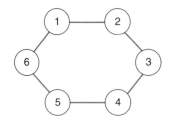

FIGURE 7.2
A ring network
configuration

intermediate nodes, whereas in the ring network of Fig. 7.2, that message could now get there by passing through just node 6.

In a mesh network (see Fig. 7.3), the processors are laid out in a two-dimensional grid, and connections are made to those nodes that are adjacent either horizontally or vertically. Information now has even more ways to travel through the network, and the network is more reliable, but this is achieved at the cost of more complicated wiring.

There are other possible configurations that are not important to our discussion. Those include a tree network, where the processors are connected like a binary tree, and a hypercube, which is an expansion of a mesh network to three or more dimensions.

■ 7.1.3 Principles for Parallelism Analysis

There are two new concepts that we encounter when dealing with the analysis of a parallel algorithm: speed up and cost. The speed up of a parallel algorithm is the factor by which it is faster than an equivalent optimal sequential algorithm. For example, we saw that the optimal time for a sorting algorithm was $O(N \lg N)$. If we have a parallel sorting algorithm that is of order $O(N)$, we have achieved a speed up of $O(\lg N)$.

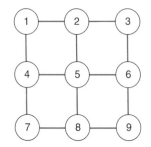

FIGURE 7.3
A mesh network

The second issue that we must consider is the cost of the parallel algorithm, which we will define as the time of the algorithm multiplied by the number of processors used. In our example, if the parallel sorting algorithm of $O(N)$ required that the number of processors be the same as the number of data values, the cost would be $O(N^2)$. This means that the parallel sorting algorithm would be more expensive because the cost of a one-processor sequential sorting algorithm is the same as its run time of $O(N \lg N)$.

A related issue is the scalability of the problem. If our only option for a parallel sort requires that we have the same number of processors as input values, we will find that this algorithm is not usable for a list of any significant size. This would be a problem, because our sequential sort algorithm has no such size restrictions. In general, we will be interested in parallel solutions where the number of processors is significantly less than the potential size of the input and where the algorithm can handle an increase in the size of the input without an increase in the number of processors.

■ 7.1.4 EXERCISES

1. A problem you are working on needs the series of numbers that are the summations of numbers from a set. More specifically, for the set $\{s_1, s_2, s_3, \ldots, s_N\}$ you need the sums $s_1 + s_2, s_1 + s_2 + s_3, s_1 + s_2 + s_3 + s_4, \ldots, s_1 + s_2 + s_3 + \cdots + s_N$. Design a method that you could use to solve this problem using parallelism.

2. Another network configuration is a star network, where there is one central processor, and every other processor is just connected to this central one. Draw a picture of a star network that has seven processors. This section discussed some advantages and disadvantages of a linear network. Using that discussion as the basis, what do you see as some of the advantages and disadvantages of a star network?

7.2   THE PRAM MODEL

In constructing parallel algorithms, we consider a set of four models of the actual computer system on which our design will run. These models deal with the issue of reading from and writing to memory, which can be a problem in parallel systems. For example, what if two of our processors want to write a value to the same memory location at the same time—which one will succeed?

If we consider that the general model for the algorithms presented in Chapters 2 through 6 is a machine that can randomly access any location of memory, we can call that a random access machine (RAM). The base model that we will use for this chapter is a parallel version of this machine called a parallel random access machine (PRAM). Our PRAM will be a tightly coupled machine with all of the processors sharing one block of memory. Each processor may have a small number of registers so that some data can be kept with the processor, but in general we will assume that the data is kept in the shared memory.

In addition to having a tightly coupled machine, we will also require that all of our processors follow the same processing cycle of a read from memory, doing an operation, and then writing a result back to memory. This means that all of the processors will read at the same time, process at the same time, and write at the same time. There are two times when we may have contention for a memory location: when reading and when writing. By enforcing this three-step cycle, we don't need to worry about the additional problem of processor X reading a value from memory, and while it is working with it, processor Y changes the value in that memory location. We also don't need to worry about contention between a processor reading from a memory location while another one is trying to write to that location.

We can handle the contention times by allowing access to be either concurrent or exclusive. In concurrent access, more than one processor can have access to a memory location at one time. In exclusive access, only one processor can have access to a memory location and an attempt by more than one to gain access is signaled as an error.

In the case of reading, concurrent access will not be a problem. We will, however, look at some algorithms that can operate under exclusive read access. If we are operating under an exclusive read, and more than one processor tries to read from one memory location, an error will occur.

When we write, we also have the choice of exclusive or concurrent. If we have exclusive write, only one processor will be allowed to write into one location of memory, and an error will occur if more than one tries. With exclusive write, two processors are, however, allowed to write to different memory locations at the same time. With concurrent access, we have a more involved situation because we must decide how the conflict will be resolved. In a priority model, each processor has an assigned priority and the highest priority processor attempting to write into a location will succeed. In a simple version of this, the processor's number is its priority, and the lower the number, the higher the priority. For example, if processor 4 and processor 7 are both trying to write to one location, processor 4 would succeed. In an arbitrary model, one of the processors will succeed in writing to memory, but it is not known which will succeed. In the common model, multiple writes are allowed but only if all processors are attempting to write the same value. In the combining model, the system will perform some sort of combination on all of the values written. So, the system may sum the values, take their product, store only the largest or smallest of the values, or perform a logical operation (and, or, or exclusive or) on the values. Each of these options may be useful in various circumstances.

We then have four combinations of these read and write options: Concurrent Read Concurrent Write (CRCW), Concurrent Read Exclusive Write (CREW), Exclusive Read Concurrent Write (ERCW), and Exclusive Read Exclusive Write (EREW).

■ 7.2.1 EXERCISES

1. Write an algorithm to compute the sum of N numbers using the CREW PRAM model. How efficient is your algorithm in terms of both run time and cost?
2. Write an algorithm to find the largest and second largest values in a set of numbers using the CRCW PRAM model, being specific about your write conflict resolution mechanism. How efficient is your algorithm in terms of both run time and cost?

7.3 SIMPLE PARALLEL OPERATIONS

We now investigate two simple operations: broadcasting a data value to all processors and finding the minimum or maximum value in a list. In the algorithms in the rest of this chapter, we will use P_i to refer to the ith processor, p to refer to the number of processors, N to refer to the number of input data items, and M_j to refer to the jth memory location. Operations to be done in parallel will be nested between `Parallel Start` and `Parallel End` keywords. If there is one set of operations that are to be done in parallel and on their completion another set is to be performed, this will be expressed by placing these into two separate parallel blocks.

■ 7.3.1 Broadcasting Data in a CREW PRAM Model

You will recall that in a CREW model we have the ability for more than one processor to read from a single memory location at one time. This allows for a very rapid transfer of the data value to the other processors:

```
P₁ writes the data value into M₁
Parallel Start
   for k = 2 to p do
      Pₖ reads the data value from M₁
   end for
Parallel End
```

This broadcast operation takes two cycles. The first writes the data into memory and the second has all of the processors read the value. This speed is only possible because of the concurrent read capability. Now we consider how the process must differ for a model with exclusive read.

■ 7.3.2 Broadcasting Data in an EREW PRAM Model

In an exclusive read model, only one processor can read the data that was written by P_1. If we were to just loop through the rest of the processors, we would have a sequential algorithm and would lose all of the power that we added with parallelism. If we use the read/process/write cycle of the second processor to write the data value into a second memory location, on the next pass two more processors can read the data value. If they then write the data value into new locations, four processors can read on the next pass. This gives us the following algorithm:

```
P₁ writes the data value into M₁
procLoc = 1
for j = 1 to lg p do
   Parallel Start
      for k = procLoc + 1 to 2 * procLoc do
         Pₖ reads Mₖ₋procLoc
         Pₖ writes to Mₖ
      end for k
   Parallel End
   procLoc = procLoc * 2
end for j
```

This algorithm will first write the data value to location M_1. On the first pass of the outer loop, P_2 will read the data value and write it to M_2, and procLoc becomes 2. The second pass has P_3 and P_4 read from locations M_1 and M_2 and then write to locations M_3 and M_4, and procLoc becomes 4. The third pass has P_5 through P_8 read from locations M_1 through M_4 and then write to locations M_5 through M_8. You should see that (assuming p is a power of 2) on the second to last pass, half of the processors will now have the data value and will have written it to M_1 through $M_{p/2}$, which allows the second half of the processors to read in the data value. Because the read and write can be done in one instruction cycle as we defined it at the beginning of Section 7.2, the parallel block does one instruction cycle, and the outer loop executes that block $\lg p$ times. Therefore, this parallel broadcast algorithm does $O(\lg p)$ operations.

■ 7.3.3 Finding the Maximum Value in a List

For this and our other operations on lists, we assume that the list has been loaded into memory locations M_1 through M_N. We assume that we have $p = N / 2$ processors. (The case where $p < N / 2$ will be discussed after the algorithm.)

On the first pass, processor P_i will compare the values in locations M_{2i} and M_{2i+1} and will write the larger of the two into location M_i. On the second pass, only half of the processors are needed to compare pairs of elements in memory locations M_1 through $M_{N/2}$ and then write the larger of each pair into locations M_1 through $M_{N/4}$. This gives the following algorithm:

```
count = N / 2
for i = 1 to (lg count) + 1 do
    Parallel Start
        for j = 1 to count do
            Pj reads M2j into X and M2j+1 into Y
            if X > Y
                Pj writes X into Mj
            else
                Pj writes Y into Mj
            end if
        end for j
    Parallel End
    count = count / 2
end for i
```

We see that each of the passes of this algorithm cuts in half the number of values that have the potential for being the largest until eventually we are left with just one value. This is very much like the tournament method used with a single processor. If we have $p < N / 2$, we can perform a "preprocessing" step that reduces the number of values to $2 * p$, and then this algorithm can continue as shown above.

You should see that there are lg N passes of this algorithm, putting the time at $O(\lg N)$. You may recall that we talked about the cost of an algorithm in Section 7.1.3. We said that the cost was the time multiplied by the number of processors, so the cost for this algorithm is $N / 2 * O(\lg N)$, or more simply $O(N \lg N)$. The simple sequential algorithm we considered in Chapter 1 took only $O(N)$, so this parallel version is more costly, although it does run much faster.

If parallel computing is really beneficial, there must be a faster alternative method that will cost no more than the sequential version. If we look closely, we see that the problem with the cost is the number of processors. We need to consider how we can reduce this number. If we want the total cost at the optimal level of $O(N)$ and the run time of the parallel algorithm is $O(\lg N)$, it must be the case that we can only use $N / \lg N$ processors. This also means that the first pass must have each processor handle $N / (N / \lg N)$ values, which is lg N. This results in the following alternative parallel algorithm:

```
Parallel Start
    for j = 1 to N/lg N do
        Pⱼ finds the maximum of M₁₊₍ⱼ₋₁₎*lg N through Mⱼ*lg N
            using the sequential algorithm
        Pⱼ writes the maximum to Mⱼ
    end for
Parallel End

count = (N / lg N) / 2
for i = 1 to (lg count) + 1 do
    Parallel Start
        for j = 1 to count do
            Pⱼ reads M₂ⱼ into X and M₂ⱼ₊₁ into Y
            if X > Y
                Pⱼ writes X into Mⱼ
            else
                Pⱼ writes Y into Mⱼ
            end if
        end for j
    Parallel End
    count = count / 2
end for i
```

In this version, we have a preprocessing step that has each processor do a sequential algorithm on a list of lg N elements, which you will recall will take $O(\lg N)$ operations. The next part of this algorithm is our original attempt with the number of processors now reduced to $(N / \lg N) / 2$ (but the preprocessing step still requires $N / \lg N$ processors). So, the total cost of this algorithm is

Step	Cost	Time
Preprocessing	$(N / \lg N) * O(\lg N) = O(N)$	$O(\lg N)$
Main Loop	$[(N / \lg N) / 2] * O(\lg N) = O(N)$	$O(\lg N)$
Total	$O(N)$	$O(\lg N)$

This last parallel version has the same cost as the sequential version, but it runs in a fraction of the time.

7.3.4 EXERCISES

1. The median of a set of numbers is the value for which half of the numbers in the set are larger and half of the numbers are smaller. In other words, if the numbers were sorted, the median value would be in the exact center of this sorted list. Design a parallel algorithm to determine the median of a set of numbers using the CREW PRAM model. How efficient is your algorithm in terms of both run time and cost?
2. Design a parallel algorithm to determine the median of a set of numbers using the CRCW PRAM model, being very specific about your write conflict resolution mechanism. (The median is described in question 1.) How efficient is your algorithm in terms of both run time and cost?

7.4 PARALLEL SEARCHING

In investigating a parallel method for searching, we will begin with a naive attempt with as many processors as elements of the list we are searching. Our analysis will indicate to us how far away from optimal this solution's cost is. We will then attempt to reduce the costs by reducing the processors, like we did in the case of finding the maximum value. We will assume that the list has no duplicate elements.

If we have the same number of processors as elements in the list ($p = N$), we can have each processor compare the target to one of the list items. If there is a match, we can have the processor that found the match write its location to some place special in memory. The following algorithm expects that the list will be in locations M_1 through M_N, the target will be in location M_{N+1}, and the place where it is found will be written into location M_{N+2}.

```
Parallel Start
    for j = 1 to N do
        P_j reads X from M_j and target from M_{N+1}
        if X = target then
            write j to M_{N+2}
        end if
    end for
Parallel End
```

Because we assume that the empty memory cells are all zero at the start of the algorithm, if there is no match, M_{N+2} will have a value of zero indicating that the search failed. If the search succeeded, the one processor that found the match will write its location into M_{N+2}.

This algorithm does one read/process/write cycle for each of the N processors, giving a run time of $O(1)$ and a cost of $O(N)$. You should recall from Chapter 2 that our optimal sequential search was a binary search that had a cost of $O(\lg N)$.

Our alternative search provides us with a scalable algorithm that can vary in cost and speed based on the number of processors that we can make available to it. This gives us a clear illustration of the scalability issue discussed in Section 7.1.3.

```
Using p ≤ N processors
Parallel Start
    for j = 1 to p do
        P_j performs a sequential binary search on M_{(j-1)*(N/p)+1} through M_{j*(N/p)}
            writing the location where X is found to M_{N+2}
    end for
Parallel End
```

If we use one processor, notice that the range of memory cells considered is from M_1 through M_N, which is the entire list. So, with one processor we have a sequential binary search. We, therefore, have a cost of $O(\lg N)$ and a run time of $O(\lg N)$. If we use N processors, we are back at the previous case where we had a cost of $O(N)$ and a run time of $O(1)$. At points in between, we will have p lists that each have N / p elements. This gives a run time of $O(\lg(N / p))$ and a cost of $O(p \lg(N / p))$. A special case to note is when $p = \lg N$, which means that $\lg(N / \lg N) = \lg N - \lg(\lg N) \approx \lg N$. This gives a run time of $O(\lg N)$, and a cost of $O[(\lg N) * (\lg N)] = O(\lg^2 N)$. Even though the run time is of the same order as that of a sequential binary search, the parallel version will have a smaller constant multiplier than that for the sequential version, so even though it is not of a smaller order, it will run faster. The cost of $O(\lg^2 N)$ is higher than the optimal sequential cost of $O(\lg N)$, but not so much higher as to be unreasonable.

■ 7.4.1 EXERCISES

1. The two searches discussed in this chapter implicitly assumed that each element in the list was unique. If there are duplicate keys for the target, it is typical for a search to return the location of the first matching key. Given the restrictions of a CREW PRAM model, what changes would need to be made to both searches if there could be duplicates in the list?

2. Give a parallel search algorithm for a list with duplicates using the CRCW PRAM model. If there are duplicate keys for the target, it is typical for a search to return the location of the first matching key. Make sure to specify your write conflict resolution method. How efficient is your algorithm in terms of both run time and cost?

7.5 PARALLEL SORTING

There are a number of ways to do a parallel sort. In this section, we will look at two ways in detail and discuss in general other techniques that can be used that are beyond the scope of this text.

■ 7.5.1 Linear Network Sort

We begin by considering a sorting method based on a linear network configuration. If we have the same number of processors as we have data values, we can sort by passing one data value into the network at each cycle. The first processor will read this value, compare it to the current value it holds, and then pass on the larger of these two values to the next processor. As this continues, each of the processors will keep the smaller value and then pass on the larger of the values to the next processor in line. This is expressed more formally in the following algorithm:

```
for j = 1 to N-1 do
   put next value into M₁
   Parallel Start
      Pⱼ reads Mⱼ into Current
      for k = 1 to j-1 do
         Pₖ reads Mₖ into New
         if Current > New then
            Pₖ writes Current to Mₖ₊₁
            Current = New
         else
            Pₖ writes New to Mₖ₊₁
         end if
      end for k
   Parallel End
   put next value into M₁
   Parallel Start
      for k = 1 to j do
         Pₖ reads Mₖ into New
         if Current > New then
            Pₖ writes Current to Mₖ₊₁
            Current = New
         else
            Pₖ writes New to Mₖ₊₁
         end if
      end for k
   Parallel End
end for j
Parallel Start
   for j = 1 to N-1 do
      Pⱼ writes Current to Mⱼ
   end for j
Parallel End
```

Before each parallel step, the next value of the list, if there is another, is placed into the first memory location. At the very start, this value is just read into the first processor. On succeeding steps, this first processor will then read the next value into its New variable, compare it to the processor's Current value, and then write the larger of the two to the second memory location.

The outer `for` loop has the two parallel blocks nested inside it because at each pass of this loop, a new processor joins the sort, and the first block primes this processor with the read of its first value, while the second loop involves it in the comparing process. At the very end, the values are all written back into memory.

Figure 7.4(a), (b), and (c) show this process in action for the input list of 15, 18, 13, 12, 17, 11, 19, 16, and 14. We see in Step A that the first value has been put into memory and will be read into the first processor. In Step B, the second value has been put into memory, it is compared with P_1's current value, and the larger is written to M_2. In Step C, the third value has been put into M_1 so that it can be compared to P_1's current value, while P_2 is reading its first value out of M_2. In Step D, both P_1 and P_2 can now do a comparison. If you look at the "odd" steps, you will notice that in each one, a new processor is about to read its first value. If you look at the "even" steps, you will notice that all of the processors that are active are making comparisons.

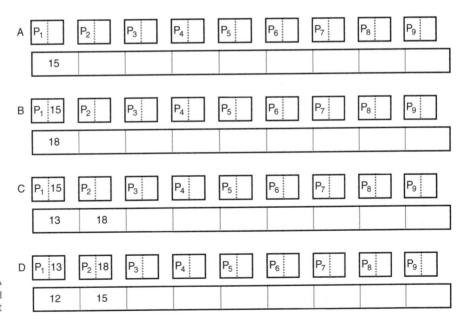

FIGURE 7.4A
A linear parallel
network sort

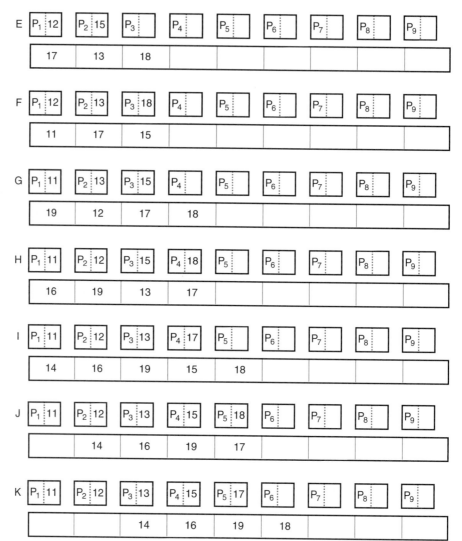

FIGURE 7.4B
A linear parallel network sort

You can see in Fig. 7.4 that this process takes 16 parallel steps to sort these numbers and 1 step to write the results. In general, this process will take $2 * (N - 1) + 1$, or $O(N)$, run time. Because there are N processors the cost of this sort is $O(N^2)$, which is the same as our slower sorts.

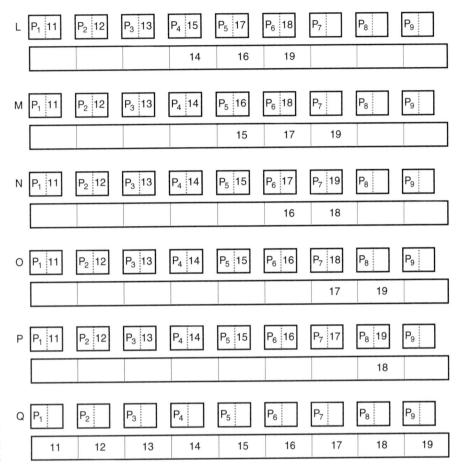

■ 7.5.2 Odd-Even Swap Sort

In previous sections, we were able to reduce costs by reducing the number of processors. We can cut the number of processors needed in half with the following sorting method, which compares adjacent values and swaps them if they are out of order.

```
for j = 1 to N/2 do
    Parallel Start
        for k = 1 to N/2 do
            P_k compares M_{2k-1} and M_{2k}
```

```
            if they are out of order then
                swap them
            end if
        end for k
    Parallel End
    Parallel Start
        for k = 1 to N/2-1 do
            P_k compares M_2k and M_2k+1
            if they are out of order then
                swap them
            end if
        end for k
    Parallel End
end for j
```

On each pass, this algorithm will first compare M_1 and M_2, M_3 and M_4, . . ., M_{N-1} and M_N and then compare M_2 and M_3, M_4 and M_5, . . ., M_{N-2} and M_{N-1}, swapping those that are out of order. So, imagine that the smallest value is in the last position. The first comparison will move it into the second to last position, and then the second comparison will move it into the third to last position. Each pass of the algorithm moved this element two positions closer to where it should be. The fact that the algorithm loops $N / 2$ times will move this element $N - 1$ positions forward and into the correct position.

Figure 7.5 shows this sorting process on our list of 15, 18, 13, 12, 17, 11, 19, 16, and 14. Each of the rows shows the result of either an odd (labeled with O) or and even (labeled with E) pass through the list.

Because the comparisons are done in parallel, each pass of the loop does two comparisons, so the overall run time of this algorithm is $O(N)$. The cost will be $N / 2 * O(N)$, which is smaller than our linear network attempt but is still $O(N^2)$.

■ 7.5.3 Other Parallel Sorts

We can also sort a list of values that are unique by a counting method. If we compare each value with the entire list and count how many numbers are less than this value, we will get the number of list elements that must occur before this one in the sorted list. We can then use this count plus 1 as the location in the list for this value. If we use the CREW PRAM model, with one processor for each data value, we can identify the location for each value in $O(N)$ comparisons. Because we need N processors, the cost of this technique is $O(N^2)$.

15	18	13	12	17	11	19	16	14

O1	15	18	12	13	11	17	16	19	14
E1	15	12	18	11	13	16	17	14	19
O2	12	15	11	18	13	16	14	17	19
E2	12	11	15	13	18	14	16	17	19
O3	11	12	13	15	14	18	16	17	19
E3	11	12	13	14	15	16	18	17	19
O4	11	12	13	14	15	16	17	18	19
E4	11	12	13	14	15	16	17	18	19

FIGURE 7.5
The odd-even parallel sort

There are parallel merge techniques that are beyond the level of this text that can merge two lists with an optimal cost of $O(N)$ using no more than $N / \lg N$ processors. If we divide the list into $N / \lg N$ pieces and then sort these using an efficient sequential sort, like quicksort, we can use a parallel merge technique to recombine the pieces into one list. We could also use a parallel merge algorithm to construct a parallel version of merge sort.

■ 7.5.4 EXERCISES

1. Write a formal parallel algorithm for the counting sort as described in Section 7.5.3. Analyze your algorithm for both its speed and its cost.

2. Write an algorithm for merge sort as described in Section 3.6, using the call ParallelMergeLists(i, j, k, 1) to represent the invocation of the parallel merge that combines the sublist in locations M_i through M_j and the sublist in locations M_k through M_l. Analyze your algorithm for both its speed and its cost. You can assume that ParallelMergeLists takes $\lg N + 1$ steps using N processors, where N is the number of elements in the resulting list ($N = j - i + l - k + 2$).

3. Write a formal parallel algorithm that will divide a list into $N / \lg N$ pieces that are sorted using `Quicksort` and then merged. In your algorithm, use the call `Quicksort(M, j, k)` to invoke `Quicksort` on the sublist in locations M_j through M_k. You should also use the call to `ParallelMerge-Lists` as described in question 2.

7.6 PARALLEL NUMERICAL ALGORITHMS

In this section, we will explore parallel algorithms to solve numerical problems. We will begin with two varieties of parallel matrix multiplication algorithms and then we will look at the problem of finding the solution to a system of linear equations.

7.6.1 Matrix Multiplication on a Parallel Mesh

One method to achieve parallelism in matrix multiplication is to use a mesh network related to the size of the matrices. To multiply an $I \times J$ matrix and a $J \times K$ matrix, you would use an $I \times K$ mesh of processors, with a row of processors for each row of the first matrix and a column of processors for each column of the second matrix.

The numbers of the first matrix would be passed into the rows of the mesh one per cycle. The first row would begin on the first cycle, the second row on the second cycle, and so on. A similar process would be followed with the numbers in the second matrix and the mesh columns, starting with the numbers in the first column. The delay in the later rows and columns is so that the numbers that need to be multiplied by each processor arrive at the same time. Each processor will then multiply the two numbers that arrive at it during each cycle and add the result to its current total. At the end, each processor will hold one value of the result. Figure 7.6(a) through (i) shows the steps to multiply

$$\begin{bmatrix} 2 & 3 & 5 \\ 4 & 1 & 7 \end{bmatrix} \text{ by } \begin{bmatrix} 3 & 5 & 8 & 4 \\ 1 & 4 & 7 & 3 \\ 9 & 6 & 2 & 1 \end{bmatrix}$$

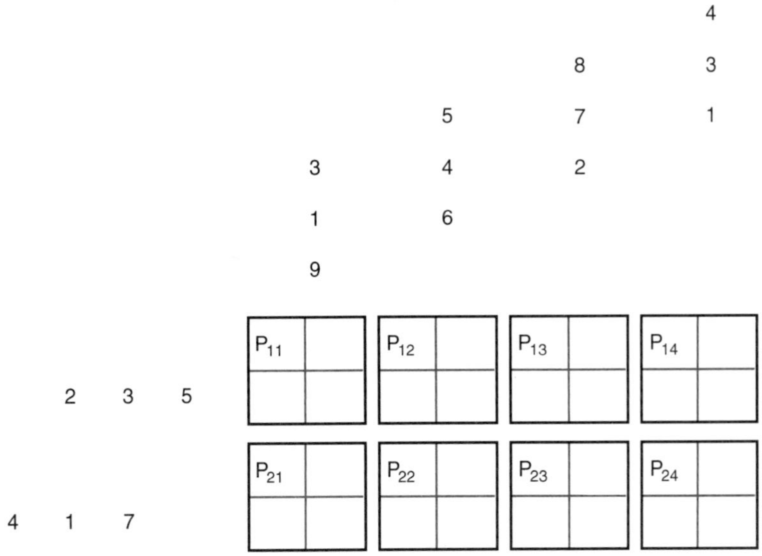

```
                                              4
                                    8         3
                          5         7         1
                3         4         2
                1         6
                9
```

P_{11}	

P_{12}	

P_{13}	

P_{14}	

2   3   5

P_{21}	

P_{22}	

P_{23}	

P_{24}	

4   1   7

FIGURE 7.6A
The initial mesh network setup

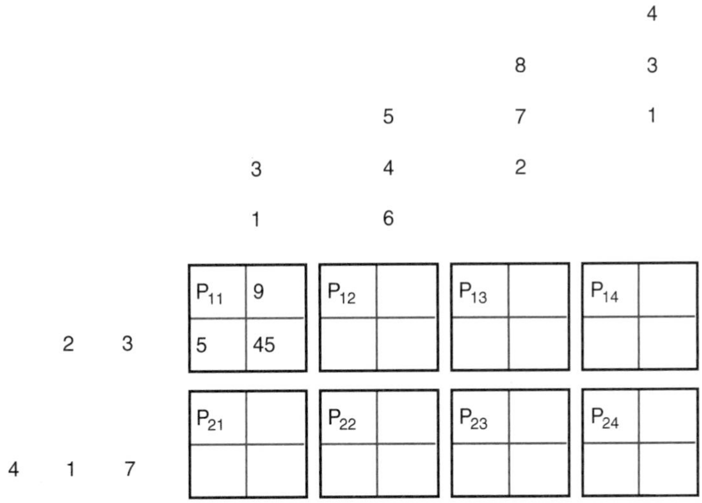

```
                                              4
                                    8         3
                          5         7         1
                3         4         2
                1         6
```

P_{11}	9
5	45

P_{12}	

P_{13}	

P_{14}	

2   3

P_{21}	

P_{22}	

P_{23}	

P_{24}	

4   1   7

FIGURE 7.6B
The first two values are multiplied by P_{11} and stored in its register

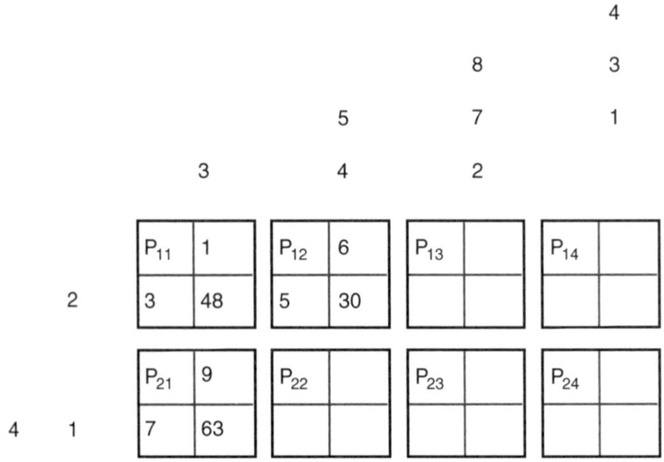

4

8   3

5   7   1

3   4   2

FIGURE 7.6C
P_{11} multiplies the
next two values
and adds the result
to its register and
P_{12} and P_{21} multiply
their first two
numbers

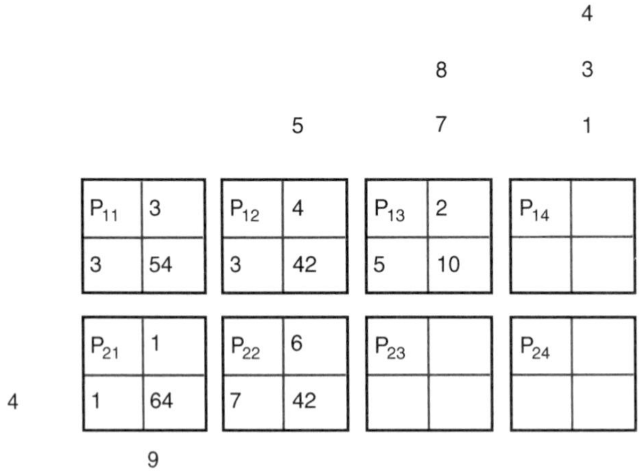

2

P_{11}	1		P_{12}	6		P_{13}			P_{14}	
3	48		5	30						

P_{21}	9		P_{22}			P_{23}			P_{24}	
7	63									

4   1

4

8   3

5   7   1

FIGURE 7.6D
P_{11}, P_{12}, and P_{21}
handle their next
two numbers, and
P_{13} and P_{22} join the
process

4

P_{11}	3		P_{12}	4		P_{13}	2		P_{14}	
3	54		3	42		5	10			

P_{21}	1		P_{22}	6		P_{23}			P_{24}	
1	64		7	42						

9

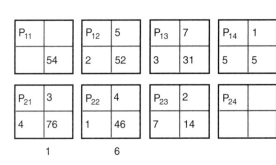

FIGURE 7.6E

P_{11} is now finished and the result for row 1 column 1 is in its register; P_{12}, P_{21}, P_{13}, and P_{22} work on their next two values; and P_{14} and P_{23} get started

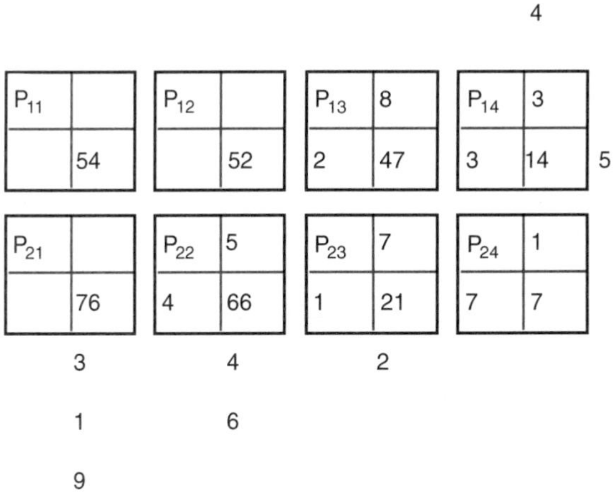

FIGURE 7.6F

P_{12} and P_{21} are now done, P_{24} gets its first two numbers, and P_{13}, P_{22}, P_{14}, and P_{23} work on their next values

P_{11}		P_{12}		P_{13}		P_{14}	4		
	54		52		47	2	22	3	5

P_{21}		P_{22}		P_{23}	8	P_{24}	3		
	76		66	4	53	1	10	7	

```
   3        5        7        1
   1        4        2
   9        6
```

■ FIGURE 7.6G
P_{13} and P_{22} are now done, and P_{14}, P_{23}, and P_{24} work on their next values

P_{11}		P_{12}		P_{13}		P_{14}				
	54		52		47		22	2	3	5

P_{21}		P_{22}		P_{23}		P_{24}	4		
	76		66		53	4	26	1	7

```
   3        5        8        3
   1        4        7        1
   9        6        2
```

■ FIGURE 7.6H
P_{14} and P_{23} finish, and P_{24} works on its last two values

P_{11}		P_{12}		P_{13}		P_{14}				
	54		52		47		22	2	3	5

P_{21}		P_{22}		P_{23}		P_{24}				
	76		66		53		26	4	1	7

```
   3        5        8        4
   1        4        7        3
   9        6        2        1
```

■ FIGURE 7.6I
The multiplication is done and the processors hold the result of

$$\begin{bmatrix} 54 & 52 & 47 & 22 \\ 76 & 66 & 53 & 26 \end{bmatrix}$$

Analysis

This process took seven cycles to multiply a 2×3 matrix by a 3×4 matrix. There is a general formula that we can develop to determine the number of cycles that we need to complete this process. We first need to consider the process involved. Counting how many cycles are necessary to get the last value in the last row of the first matrix out of the mesh is one way to determine how long this process takes. We could also do this analysis based on the columns because for the process to finish, the last element of the final row of the first matrix and the last element of the final column of the second matrix must leave the mesh, which happens at the same time.

The rows of the first matrix shift by one column each cycle of the process. If our first matrix has I rows and J columns ($I \times J$), how many cycles will it take before the last number of the first row is inside the mesh? Because each cycle adds one number to the mesh and the first number enters the mesh on the first cycle, it will take $J - 1$ more cycles for the last value in the first row to be in the mesh. How many additional cycles will it take for this number to leave the mesh when we are done with it? Because this number needs to be multiplied by a value in each column of the second matrix ($J \times K$), it will take K cycles for this number to leave the matrix. Because we delay each of the successive rows and columns, we need to consider what happens with the last row to see what really goes on overall now that we understand how the first row works.

As was said, each row of the first matrix starts one cycle later than the row above it. So, the second row starts on cycle 2, the third row starts on cycle 3, and the last row starts on cycle I. We said that it takes $J - 1$ more cycles for the last value in a row to enter the mesh and K cycles for it to leave the mesh. This means that the entire process will, in general, take $I + J + K - 1$ cycles to complete. The run time of our mesh matrix multiplication is $O(N)$, where N = maximum(I, J, K). The number of processors we need is $O(N^2)$, and so the cost of our parallel version is $O(N^3)$, which is the same as the standard matrix multiplication algorithm. The real value of this mesh algorithm is that it has a much shorter run time than any of the sequential matrix multiplication methods we considered in Chapter 4. Any algorithm that relies on a large number of matrix multiplications can see a dramatic improvement by implementation on a mesh network. For example, in the introduction to Chapter 4, we discussed a convolution that multiplies a 5×5 matrix by every 5×5 patch of a 512×512 image. Using the standard sequential matrix multiplication algorithm, we would do 32,258,000 multiplications, each one in a separate processor cycle for 32,258,000 cycles. Using a 5 × 5 processor mesh (25 processors), we would do the same number of multiplications, but it would only take 3,612,896 cycles, almost a 90% time savings.

■ 7.6.2 Matrix Multiplication in a CRCW PRAM Model

Parallel matrix multiplication in a combining CRCW PRAM model that adds concurrent writes to one memory location can be done in constant time with sufficient processors. To multiply an $I \times J$ matrix A by a $J \times K$ matrix B will require $I * J * K$ processors. Each of these processors will be responsible for exactly one of the $O(N^3)$ multiplications necessary to calculate the overall result. This gives the following algorithm:

```
Parallel Start
   for x = 1 to I do
      for y = 1 to J do
         for z = 1 to K do
            P_xyz calculates A_xy * B_yz and stores it in M_xz
         end for z
      end for y
   end for x
Parallel End
```

Analysis

As was mentioned, each of the processors does one multiplication and then stores its result in the proper memory location. This takes one cycle. There will be J processors that write concurrently to each of the memory locations that are part of the result. We indicated that this concurrent write model will combine all concurrent writes by adding the values together, so the write process handles the additions that are the other component of the standard sequential matrix multiplication algorithm.

The run time of this algorithm is $O(1)$, when using $O(N^3)$ processors where $N = \text{maximum}(I, J, K)$. This gives a total cost of $O(N^3)$, which is the same as our standard sequential algorithm. The run time reduction is even more dramatic than with our mesh-based algorithm. Returning again to our convolution example, we see that with 125 processors, we can do the matrix multiplication for one location in one processor cycle. This means that the convolution with the entire image could be done in just 258,064 cycles, 125 times faster than the sequential version.

■ 7.6.3 Solving Systems of Linear Equations with an SIMD Algorithm

In Section 4.3, we looked at a sequential algorithm to solve a system of N linear equations with N unknowns using the Gauss-Jordan method. For that algorithm, we represented the linear equations as a matrix with N rows and $N + 1$ columns and got our solution by doing operations on rows and between rows until we were left with an identity matrix in the first N rows and columns. The values of the unknowns then appeared in the last column of this matrix. We now present an SIMD algorithm for the CREW PRAM model to accomplish the same thing. Our discussion below will use the notation of M_{ij} to represent the memory location for the coefficient of the jth unknown (columN) in the ith equation (row).

Before presenting the parallel algorithm, let's review the sequential algorithm presented in Section 4.3. We said that the process would begin by dividing the first row by the value in the first column of that row. So, if the first value in the first row was 5, each value in that row would be divided by 5. Next, the sequential algorithm would subtract from every other row the first row multiplied by the first value of that other row. For example, if the second row had a value of 12 in the first column, the second row would have the first row times 12 subtracted from it.

The following CREW PRAM model algorithm requires $N * (N + 1)$ processors, each handling the update of just one element in our matrix. As with our sequential algorithm for the Gauss-Jordan method, this parallel algorithm does not handle problems with round-off error or matrix singularity.

```
for x = 1 to N do
   Parallel Start
      for y = x to N+1 do
         Pxy reads Mxx into factor and Mxy into value
         Pxy calculates value/factor and writes it to Mxy
      end for y
   Parallel End
   Parallel Start
      for y = x to N+1 do
         for z = 1 to N do
            if x ≠ z
               Pzy reads Mzy into current, Mzx into factor,
                  and Mxy into value
               Pzy calculates current - factor * value and
                  writes it to Mzy
```

```
              end if
           end for z
        end for y
     Parallel End
  end for x
```

In this algorithm, the outer loop steps through each of the unknowns. The first parallel block will divide the current row by the appropriate element. The second parallel block then subtracts the proper multiple of this row from every other. In this second block, the outer loop handles the remaining columns that still need adjustment and the inner loop does this for all of the equations.

■ 7.6.4. EXERCISES

1. Trace the mesh network matrix multiplication as in Fig. 7.6 for the multiplication of the matrices

$$\begin{bmatrix} 2 & 3 \\ 7 & 4 \end{bmatrix} \quad \text{and} \quad \begin{bmatrix} 5 & 1 \\ 2 & 9 \end{bmatrix}$$

2. Trace the mesh network matrix multiplication as in Fig. 7.6 for the multiplication of the matrices

$$\begin{bmatrix} 8 & 2 \\ 3 & 5 \end{bmatrix} \quad \text{and} \quad \begin{bmatrix} 3 & 2 \\ 7 & 4 \end{bmatrix}$$

3. Trace the mesh network matrix multiplication as in Fig. 7.6 for the multiplication of the matrices

$$\begin{bmatrix} 1 & 5 \\ 4 & 6 \\ 7 & 2 \end{bmatrix} \quad \text{and} \quad \begin{bmatrix} 8 & 2 & 3 \\ 5 & 1 & 9 \end{bmatrix}$$

4. Do an analysis of the run time and cost of the parallel Gauss–Jordan method for solving a system of linear equations. Your analysis should determine the number of multiplication or division operations and the number of addition or subtraction operations. How does this compare to the sequential algorithm for the Gauss–Jordan method?

7.7 PARALLEL GRAPH ALGORITHMS

To explore parallel graph algorithms, we will use the representation of graphs in an adjacency matrix form. We will explore some fascinating relationships between matrix operations on adjacency matrices and what this means about the related graph.

■ 7.7.1 Shortest-Path Parallel Algorithm

We said that the values of the adjacency matrix for a weighted graph would be defined as follows:

$$\text{AdjMat}[i, j] = \begin{cases} w_{ij} & \text{if } v_i v_j \in E \\ 0 & \text{if } i = j \\ \infty & \text{if } v_i v_j \notin E \end{cases} \quad \text{for all } i \text{ and } j \text{ in the range 1 to } N$$

Figure 7.7 shows a weighted graph and its corresponding adjacency matrix. The adjacency matrix shows the direct paths between nodes of the graph, which could be seen as the shortest paths with lengths of just one edge. Because we are interested in knowing the shortest paths through the graph with any number of edges, perhaps we can build up from the adjacency matrix. If we use A^1 to represent the matrix showing the shortest paths with 1 or 0 edges (the original adjacency matrix), we can then use A^j to represent the shortest paths with j or fewer edges. You should see that A^{N-1} would be the

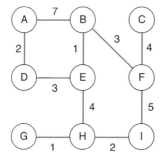

$$\begin{bmatrix} 0 & 7 & \infty & 2 & \infty & \infty & \infty & \infty & \infty \\ 7 & 0 & \infty & \infty & 1 & 3 & \infty & \infty & \infty \\ \infty & \infty & 0 & \infty & \infty & 4 & \infty & \infty & \infty \\ 2 & \infty & \infty & 0 & 3 & \infty & \infty & \infty & \infty \\ \infty & 1 & \infty & 3 & 0 & \infty & \infty & 4 & \infty \\ \infty & 3 & 4 & \infty & \infty & 0 & \infty & \infty & 5 \\ \infty & \infty & \infty & \infty & \infty & \infty & 0 & 1 & \infty \\ \infty & \infty & \infty & \infty & 4 & \infty & 1 & 0 & 2 \\ \infty & \infty & \infty & \infty & \infty & 5 & \infty & 2 & 0 \end{bmatrix}$$

■ FIGURE 7.7
A weighted graph and its adjacency matrix

matrix with the shortest paths through the entire graph because any path with N or more edges must include a cycle, and so a path without the cycle would have fewer than N edges.

We begin by thinking about how we might construct A^2 from A^1. The shortest path with two edges between any nodes x and y will go through exactly one of the other nodes. For example, the paths of length two between nodes A and E go through either nodes B or D. If we look at the sum of the weights of the edges AB and BE verses the sum of the weights of the edges AD and DE, we see that the path through node D is shorter than the path through node B. In general, if we looked at the sum of A⋆ and ⋆E, where ⋆ takes on the value of every node from A through I (except A and E), the minimum of these sums will be the shortest path with two edges. If we allow A and E to also be included for the ⋆, we would get the shortest path with two or fewer edges as our result. This then gives the general form

$$A_{ij}^{2} = \text{minimum}_{k \in V}(A_{ik}^{1} + A_{kj}^{1})$$

If we apply this to the adjacency matrix of Fig. 7.7, the result is shown in Fig. 7.8.

We could construct A^3 from A^1 and A^2 by noticing that the shortest path with three edges or less would be a shortest path with two edges or less to some node followed by a shortest path of length one edge or less from that node to the destination, or vice versa. We could construct A^4 either from A^1 and A^3 or from just A^2. Because of this, we can get to our result more quickly by just calculating $A^2, A^4, A^8, \ldots, A^{N'}$, where N' is the power of 2 just greater

$$\begin{bmatrix}
0 & 7 & \infty & 2 & 5 & 10 & \infty & \infty & \infty \\
7 & 0 & 7 & 4 & 1 & 3 & \infty & 5 & 8 \\
\infty & 7 & 0 & \infty & \infty & 4 & \infty & \infty & 9 \\
2 & 4 & \infty & 0 & 3 & \infty & \infty & 7 & \infty \\
5 & 1 & \infty & 3 & 0 & 4 & 5 & 4 & 6 \\
10 & 3 & 4 & \infty & 4 & 0 & \infty & 7 & 5 \\
\infty & \infty & \infty & \infty & 5 & \infty & 0 & 1 & 3 \\
\infty & 5 & \infty & 7 & 4 & 7 & 1 & 0 & 2 \\
\infty & 8 & 9 & \infty & 6 & 5 & 3 & 2 & 0
\end{bmatrix}$$

■ FIGURE 7.8
A^2 for the weighted graph of Fig. 7.7

than the number of nodes minus 1. For the graph in Fig. 7.6, we would have all of the shortest-weight paths when we calculated A^8.

The parallel computation of the shortest path in a graph can be based on this adjacency matrix manipulation. If we modify the matrix multiplication algorithm so that addition is replaced by taking the minimum and multiplication is replaced by addition, the resulting algorithm will calculate the matrices discussed above. Using this modified matrix multiplication algorithm with A^1 and A^1 will produce A^2 as its result, and "multiplying" A^2 and A^2 gives A^4. Our parallel shortest-path algorithm becomes nothing more than the parallel matrix multiplication algorithm, and, so, its analysis also applies here.

■ 7.7.2 Minimum Spanning Tree Parallel Algorithm

You will recall that the Dijkstra-Prim minimum spanning tree (MST) algorithm slowly builds the tree by adding the node connected to the current tree by the edge with the smallest weight. The algorithm did this task from the perspective of the MST looking at those nodes that were connected to it and placing those in the "fringe." With the power of multiple processors, we can instead look at the tree from the perspective of all of the nodes and see which is closest at each pass.

Our algorithm will be designed with p processors. Because p will be less than the number of nodes in the graph, each processor will be responsible for N / p nodes. We will choose one node to start the MST, and it will be the closest tree node for all of the others, because it is the one and only tree node. On each pass, each processor will examine each of its nodes and select the one that is closest to a node in the tree. That information will be passed by each processor to a central processor, which will choose the one with the smallest distance overall. This node will be added to the tree and will also be broadcast to the processors so that they can update their nodes. This process will be repeated $N - 1$ times as the other nodes are added to the tree.

In the following algorithm, V_j will represent the set of nodes that are the responsibility of processor P_j, and v_k will represent a single node of the graph. We will use two arrays locally in each of the processors. The first will be closest(v), which will hold the name of the MST node that this closest to node v, and distance(v_i, v_j), which gives the shortest distance between nodes v_i and v_j. Formally, this algorithm for the CREW PRAM model is

```
v₀ is labeled as the first tree node
Parallel Start
   for j = 1 to p do
      for each node in Vⱼ do
         set closest to v₀
      end for each
   end for j
Parallel End

for j = 1 to N-1 do
   Parallel Start
      for k = 1 to p do
         Pₖ finds the smallest distance among its nodes
         Pₖ reports distance(v, closest(v)), v, and closest(v)
            (where v ∈ Vₖ)
      end for k
   Parallel End
   Pcontrol finds the smallest reported distance and adds the
      node vₛ and its edge to the MST
   Pcontrol broadcasts the new MST node to P₁ through Pₚ
   Parallel Start
      for k = 1 to p do
         if vₛ ∈ Vₖ then
            Pₖ marks it as now in the tree
         end if
         Pₖ updates closest and distance based on vₛ being in
            the tree for each of its nodes that are not yet in the tree
      end for k
   Parallel End
end for j
```

Analysis

The first loop is the initialization loop, and it will execute in N / p time, because each processor has to initialize the data for the number of nodes that are its responsibility. The first parallel block in the main for loop will do $N / p - 1$ comparisons each time, because sequentially finding the minimum or maximum was shown in Chapter 1 to take this many comparisons. The next step is to find the minimum distance of those reported by the p processors, which will take another $p - 1$ comparisons. The broadcast step in a CREW model was shown to take two cycles. The last parallel block takes one comparison to see if the new node is in the processors set and then N / p updates of closest and distance. In summary, the main processing loop has $2(N / p) + p + 1$ instructions and is executed $N - 1$ times, giving $(N - 1) * (2(N / p) + p + 1)$. This works out to an $O(N^2 / p)$ run time and a cost of $p * O(N^2 / p)$, or $O(N^2)$. As we saw in the other cases, to achieve optimality, the number of processors should be about $N / \lg N$.

■ 7.7.3 EXERCISES

1. Give the weighted adjacency matrix for the following four graphs, and calculate $A^2, A^4,$ and A^8.

a.
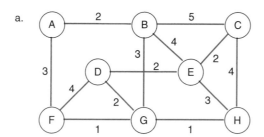

b.
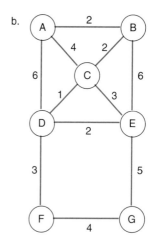

c.
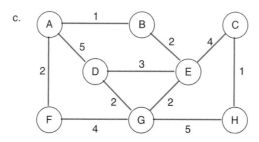

d.
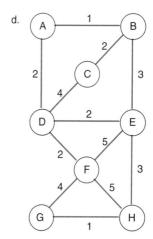

2. Formally rewrite the standard sequential matrix multiplication to calculate the shortest path as described at the end of Section 7.7.1. Use the graph in Fig. 7.7 to verify your algorithm.

3. Give the details of the analysis of the shortest-path algorithm that uses parallel matrix multiplication. Your analysis should be based on the matrix multiplication taking an $O(N)$ run time and a cost of $O(N^3)$. Your complete answer will depend on your determination of how many times this will be called and for what size of array.

4. Using three processors, trace the execution of the parallel minimum spanning tree algorithm on the graphs in question 1, starting at node A. Your trace should show the nodes each processor is responsible for, as well as the values that each processor returns for each pass. If you have also worked problem 1 from Section 6.4.2, compare your answers from that sequential algorithm and this parallel one.

CHAPTER 8

Nondeterministic Algorithms

PREREQUISITES

Before beginning this chapter, you should be able to

- Write and explain an algorithm
- Describe growth rates and order

GOALS

At the end of this chapter, you should be able to

- Define class P, class NP, and NP-complete
- Explain the difference between decision and optimization problems
- Describe the classic NP problems and why they are important
- Describe what puts a problem into class NP
- Describe why P ⊆ NP
- Explain why "P = NP?" is still an open question
- Write an algorithm to check a potential solution to an NP problem

STUDY SUGGESTIONS

As you are working through the chapter, you should rework the examples to make sure you understand them. You should specifically trace through the algorithms and input data presented to try to recreate the "results" given. You should also try to answer any questions before reading on. A hint or the answer is in the sentences following the question.

U p to now, all of the algorithms we have considered have solved their problems in a reasonable amount of time. These problems all have an order that can be expressed by some polynomial equation. In some cases, we have seen algorithms that had linear time, like sequential search, where if the list size doubled, the amount of time the algorithm would take also doubled. We have seen algorithms that had $O(N^2)$ time, like some of the sort algorithms, where if the list size doubled, the amount of time the algorithm would take would go up by a factor of 4. And we have seen algorithms that had $O(N^3)$ time, like matrix multiplication, where if the size of the matrix doubled, the amount of time the algorithm would take would go up by a factor of 8. Even though these increases can be significant, they are still relatively controlled. The difference this makes can be seen in Figs. 1.1 and 1.2.

In this chapter, we will look at a set of problems that have run times that are factorial $O(N!)$ and exponential $O(x^N)$ $(x \geq 2)$. In other words, these are problems for which there is no known algorithm to solve the problem in a reasonable amount of time. We will see that the only way to find a correct or optimal solution will be to guess at the answer and check to see if it is correct.

Even though these problems take a long time to solve, we can't just dismiss them because they have important applications. These problems are needed to decide on an efficient route for delivery trucks, to develop reasonable exam schedules, and to schedule tasks so that as many deadlines are met as possible. Because the problems are important but we don't have a way to quickly get the correct answer, we will look at approximations of the correct answer in the next chapter.

This class of problems is called NP. We begin this chapter with an examination of the class NP. We then look at a set of classic problems that are in the class NP. The next section looks at the elements of these problems that put them into the class NP. We finish with a section that looks at the process of testing our guess solutions.

8.1   WHAT IS NP?

The algorithms that we worked with in Chapters 1 through 7 have all had a complexity that was expressible as a polynomial. In fact, all of the algorithms that we have considered had complexity in $O(N^3)$.[1] In fact, the most time-complex algorithm we examined was matrix multiplication. The bottom line, however, is that we can get an exact solution to those problems within some reasonable amount of time. This group of problems is said to be in the class P, where P stands for polynomial time complexity. Problems for which there is a polynomial time algorithm are called tractable.

There is another class of problems that are intractable, for which we currently have no algorithm that will solve the problems in any reasonable amount of time. These problems are in the class NP, which stands for nondeterministic polynomial time complexity. The meaning of the phrase "nondeterministic polynomial time" will become clearer through the rest of this section. The thing to note is that the only deterministic algorithms that are known to solve these problems have a complexity that is of exponential or factorial order. For some problems, the complexity is given by 2^N, where N is the number of input values. In this case, each time we add one additional input value, the amount of time the algorithm needs to solve the problem would double. If it takes 1024 operations to solve the problem with an input of 10 elements, it would take 2048 operations to solve the problem with an input of 11 elements. This is a significant increase in time for a small increase in the input.

The name *nondeterministic polynomial* for problems of the class NP comes from a two-step process to solve them. In the first step, there is a nondeterministic process that generates a possible solution to the problem. You can see this as a random guess at the solution that will sometimes be good (the solution or close to it) and at other times be bad (a far from optimal answer). The second step will look at the output of the first step and determine if it is a true solution. Individually, we will see that both of these steps work in polynomial time. The problem is that we don't know how many times this process will need to be repeated before a solution is generated. Even though the individual steps are polynomial, we may need to call them an exponential or factorial number of times.

One of the problems in the class NP is the traveling salesperson problem. In this problem, we are given a set of cities and a "cost" to travel between each of

---

[1] Remember that to say a function $g(x)$ is in $O(f(x))$ means that $g(x)$ grows no faster than $f(x)$. So, x^2 is in $O(x^3)$.

these cities. The goal is to determine the order we should visit all of the cities (once), returning to the starting city at the end, while minimizing the total cost. This problem can be applied to the order streets should be visited to collect garbage efficiently, deciding on the route a truck should take to make deliveries in the shortest time possible, or choosing the routing of a packet so that information is transmitted quickly between all nodes in a network. When we have 8 cities, there are 40,320 possible orderings of the cities, and when that number increases to 10 cities, there are now 3,628,800 possible orderings of the cities. To find the most efficient route, we would have to examine all of the possibilities. Let's say that we have an algorithm that can calculate the cost of traveling between a set of 15 cities in a given order. If this algorithm can do 100 of these calculations per second, it would still take *over four centuries* to look at all of the possible orderings of those 15 cities to find the quickest possible trip. Even if we had 400 computers work on this problem, it would still take over a year, and there are only 15 cities. If we have 20 cities, it would take *one billion computers* working in parallel about nine months to find the most efficient route. Clearly, it is faster and cheaper to travel to all of them via any path than to wait for the algorithm to find the shortest path.

Is it possible that we might be able to construct the shortest path without looking at all of the possible paths? At this point, no one has been able to devise a construction algorithm that doesn't effectively just check all of the potential paths. The situation where the number of cities is small could be solved quickly, but one instance of the problem (with a restricted input) that can be done quickly doesn't mean that there is an algorithm that can do all instances of the problem quickly. We are interested in the general solution to this problem.

If you think about the traveling salesperson problem, you should see it's similarity to the graphs and graph algorithms that were discussed in Chapter 6. Each city can be represented by a node in the graph, the ability to travel between two cities can be represented in the edges of the graph, and the cost to travel between those cities can be the weight attached to the edge. From this, you might be tempted to think that the shortest-path algorithm we discussed in Section 6.5 would also solve this problem, but it won't. What are the two requirements of the traveling salesperson problem that make it different from the shortest-path problem? The first is that we must visit all of the nodes and the shortest-path algorithm only tells us the quickest way to get between two nodes. If you try to use multiple pieces that the shortest-path algorithm produces, you might find that the paths you put together take you to a node more than once. The second difference is that we are expected to return to the starting point in the traveling salesperson problem, whereas the shortest-path algorithm has no such expectation.

Our brief discussion of the extremely large number of possible orderings of the nodes should convince you that a deterministic algorithm that examines all of the different orders of nodes would take an extremely long time to complete. To show that this algorithm is in the class NP, we need to show how a two-step process as described above would solve it. For the traveling salesperson problem, the first step would be to nondeterministically generate a list of the cities. Because this process is nondeterministic, each time it is run, a different order of the cities will be generated. Obviously this generation process can be done in polynomial time, because we can keep a list of city names, generate a random number, output the corresponding city name, and then remove that name from the list to prevent it from appearing twice. This process would run in order $O(N)$ where N is the number of cities. The second step would be to determine the cost of traveling to the cities in the order specified. To determine this, we would simply have to look at the cost for each successive pair of cities in the list, which would have complexity $O(N^2)$ in the worst case. Because both of these steps are of polynomial complexity, the traveling salesperson problem is in the class NP. Notice that it is the potential number of times that this would have to be done that makes this problem so time consuming.

At this point, you might notice that we could use this two-step process for any of our previous algorithms. For example, we could have sorted a list by outputting a random order of the original list and then checking to see if the elements are in increasing order. Doesn't this make sorting a member of the class NP? Yes it does. The difference between a problem in class P and one just in class NP is that, in the former case, we also have a deterministic algorithm that runs in polynomial time, whereas in the later we don't. We will discuss this issue again in Section 8.3.

■ 8.1.1 Problem Reductions

One way that we can get a solution to a problem is through the concept of a reduction. If we can reduce one problem to another, we could use an algorithm for the second problem to get a solution and then transform this answer into a solution for the first problem. If we can do the transformations in polynomial time and the second problem can be solved in polynomial time, we know that our new problem also has a polynomial time solution.

Let's look at an example of this that will make the process clearer. Our first problem will be to return "yes" if any of a group of Boolean variables has a value of true and return "no" if all are false. The second problem is to find the largest value in a list of integers. You should be able to see a very clear and easy solution for each of these problems, but for the sake of this example, let's say that we have a solution to the largest integer problem but not for the Boolean variable problem. We can solve the Boolean variable problem by reducing it to the largest-integer problem. We begin by taking an instance of the Boolean variable problem and writing a conversion algorithm that will, for each Boolean variable, assign the next list entry the value of 0 if the Boolean variable is false, and a value of 1 if the Boolean variable is true. We now use our algorithm to find the largest value in the list. You should see that the answer will be either 0 or 1 because of how we set up the list. We now convert this answer back into a solution to the Boolean variable problem by returning yes if the largest value is 1 and returning no if the largest value is 0.

In Chapter 1, we saw that finding the largest value in a list can be done in linear time, and we see that our reduction can also be done in linear time; therefore, the Boolean variable problem must also be solvable in linear time.

In the next section, we will use this technique to learn some thing about NP problems. We will see, however, that the reductions of NP problems can be much more involved that this.

■ 8.1.2 NP-Complete Problems

When discussing the class NP, we must remember that we might think these problems take a long time to solve because we just haven't found a faster algorithm to solve them. If we thought about the traveling salesperson problem differently, perhaps we could develop a deterministic algorithm that could solve it in polynomial time. The same could be said about any of the problems that we will consider in the next section.

The term *NP-complete* is used to describe the hardest of the problems in the class NP. These problems are singled out because if at any point we find a deterministic polynomial time algorithm for one of them, all of the problems in NP must have deterministic polynomial time algorithms.

We show that a problem is NP-complete by showing that every other problem in the class NP can be transformed into it. This is not as daunting of a task as it sounds because we don't have to do this for every NP problem. Instead, if we have an NP problem A, we can show that it is NP-complete by reducing an NP-complete problem B into it. Because B is NP-complete, every problem in NP can be transformed into problem B. So, by reducing B to A, we effectively show that all NP problems can be transformed into A by a two-step process that first transforms them to B. Therefore, our NP problem A is now known to be NP-complete.

In the last section we did a reduction of a polynomial time algorithm; now we do one for an NP problem. We need a process that will modify all of the components of one problem so that they become an equivalent component in another problem. This transformation must preserve the information so that every time the first problem gives a positive result so does the transformed problem, and every time the first problem gives a negative result so does the second problem.

In a graph, a Hamilton path is one that visits every node of the graph exactly once. If the path returns to the starting node, it is called a Hamilton circuit. A graph doesn't need to be complete for it to have a Hamilton path or circuit. We can reduce the Hamilton circuit problem to the traveling salesperson problem in the following way. Each node in the graph becomes a city. For each edge in the graph, we assign the cost of traveling between the two equivalent cities a value of 1. For each pair of nodes that have no edge connecting them, we assign the cost of traveling between the two equivalent cities a value of 2. This converts the graph into a set of cities. We now solve the related traveling salesperson problem. If there is a Hamilton circuit in the graph, the traveling salesperson problem will be able to find a solution traveling between cities that just have costs of 1. If there is no Hamilton circuit, the solution the traveling salesperson problem finds will travel between at least one pair of cities with a cost of 2. If there are N nodes in the graph, there is a Hamilton circuit if the traveling salesperson path is of length N, and there is no Hamilton circuit if the path is of length greater than N.

In 1971, Cook showed that the CNF-satisfiability problem described in the next section was NP-complete. A large number of additional problems have been shown to be NP-complete by reducing the satisfiability problem, or another NP-complete problem, to them. A 1979 book by Garey and Johnson lists hundreds of problems that have been shown to be NP-complete.

The power of the reduction process is that if any NP-complete problem can be reduced to a class P problem, all of the NP problems must have polynomial time solutions. So far, all attempts at reductions of this type have failed.

8.2 TYPICAL NP PROBLEMS

Each of the problems that we will discuss can be viewed as either an optimization problem or a decision problem. Optimization problems look for a specific result that is usually a minimum or maximum value. Decision problems look at a limit and ask if there is a solution that has a value above (for maximization problems) or below (for minimization problems) the limit provided. Optimization problems will supply as their result an answer to the problem, whereas decision problems will reply with just a yes or no answer.

In Section 8.1, we discussed the traveling salesperson problem. In that section, we discussed the optimization version of this problem. This is a minimization problem and so we were interested in finding the path that has the lowest cost. This problem can also be presented as a decision problem. For the traveling salesperson decision problem, we would ask if there is a path that has a cost below some limit C. Obviously, decision problem answers will vary based on the limit provided. In cases where the limit is very large (perhaps larger than the total of all the costs), an answer of yes might be easy to provide. In cases where the limit is very small (perhaps smaller than the costs to travel between any two cities), an answer of no might be easy to provide. For most other possibilities, the time to determine an answer is very long and related to the time needed to solve the optimization version. For this reason, we will talk about the optimization and decision versions interchangeably and at different times will use the one that is most appropriate for the discussion.

In the next few sections, a set of six additional NP problems will be described in both their optimization and decision form.

■ 8.2.1 Graph Coloring

As was discussed in Chapter 6, a graph $G = (V, E)$ is a set of vertices or nodes (V) and a set of edges (E) that connect pairs of nodes. For this problem, we will only be concerned with undirected graphs. We can color a graph by associating with each node of the graph a different color, usually represented by some integer. The complexity of the problem comes from the requirement that for every edge of the graph, the nodes at the two ends must have different colors. It should be obvious that if there are N nodes in the graph, we can color the graph with N different colors, but can we do any better? As an optimization problem, we ask what is the smallest number of colors that are needed to color a given graph. As a decision problem, we ask if a graph can be colored with C colors or less.

Graph coloring can have practical applications. If we assign every course offered at a college to a node and add edges between every pair of nodes for the courses each student is taking, we have a rather complex graph. Given that most students take 5 courses, there would be 10 edges added for each student. Let's say that there are 500 different courses offered and about 3500 students. That means the final graph would have 500 nodes and 35,000 edges. We can now associate each exam week slot with a different color. If there are 20 slots, we try to produce a coloring of the graph with 20 different colors. Assigning different colors or exam slots to the nodes at the opposite ends of an edge means that those two courses cannot have exams at the same time, and so the student cannot have a conflict between these two exams.

Creating an exam schedule with no conflicts is the equivalent of the graph coloring problem. But because graph coloring is an NP problem, it is not possible to produce a conflict-free exam schedule in any reasonable amount of time. Additionally, exam scheduling typically tries to limit students to no more than two exams in one day and to schedule multiple sections of a course at the same time. This would place further limits on the color options at each node. Obviously, because creating the "perfect" exam schedule is impossible, there must be another technique used to get exam schedules that are as good as they are. Approximation algorithms will be discussed in Chapter 9.

■ 8.2.2 Bin Packing

We have a number of bins each with a capacity of 1, and we have a set of objects all with different sizes, $s_1, s_2, \ldots, s_N$ between 0 and 1. The optimization problem asks what is the fewest number of bins that would be needed to store all of these objects, and the decision problem would ask if it is possible to store all of the objects in B bins or less.

This problem can be related to storing information on disks or in fragmented computer memory banks, to shipping companies who would like to pack materials as efficiently as possible, and to the production of custom-ordered pieces of some material that has to be cut from larger stock. For example, if we have large sheets of metal and we have a bunch of orders for smaller pieces of metal, we would obviously want to cut things as tightly as possible to reduce waste and increase profits.

■ 8.2.3 Backpack Problem[2]

We have a set of objects that have different sizes, $s_1, s_2, \ldots, s_N$, and each of these objects has a worth associated with it, $w_1, w_2, \ldots, w_N$. If we have a backpack of size K, the optimization problem determines the objects that we should put in the backpack to maximize the total worth. As a decision problem, we would ask if there is a set of objects that will fit in the backpack and have a total worth that is at least W.

This problem is related to investment strategies where the size of the objects is the cost of various investments, the worths are the potential returns of those investments, and the backpack size is the amount of capital available to invest.

■ 8.2.4 Subset Sum Problem

We have a set of objects that have different sizes, $s_1, s_2, \ldots, s_N$, and we have some positive upper limit L. The optimization version determines the subset of the objects that produces the largest sum of sizes that is no greater than L. The decision version would ask if there is a subset of the objects that has a total size of L. This is a simplified version of the backpack problem.

■ 8.2.5 CNF-Satisfiability Problem

Conjunctive normal form (CNF) is a series of Boolean expressions that are all combined by the AND operator ($\wedge$). Each of the individual expressions is a series of Boolean variables combined with the OR operator ($\vee$). A sample CNF expression is (where $\bar{x}$ represents "not x")

$$(a \vee b) \wedge (\bar{a} \vee c) \wedge (a \vee b \vee \bar{c} \vee d) \wedge (b \vee \bar{c} \vee \bar{d}) \wedge (a \vee \bar{b} \vee c \vee \bar{d} \vee e)$$

The CNF-satisfiability problem only has a decision version that asks if there is some combination of true and false values for the variables so that the entire equation is true. Because there is no limit on the number of variables or the

---

[2] The classic name for this problem is the Knapsack Problem.

number of terms, the possible combination of trues and falses that would have to be checked can get very large.

8.2.6 Job Scheduling Problem

We have a set of jobs with the amount of time they need to complete, $t_1, t_2, \ldots, t_N$, the deadline they need to be completed by, $d_1, d_2, \ldots, d_N$, and a penalty incurred if the job is not completed by the deadline, $p_1, p_2, \ldots, p_N$. The optimization problem attempts to order the jobs so as to incur the smallest penalty. The decision problem asks if there is a schedule that has a penalty less than P.

8.2.7 EXERCISES

1. In Section 8.1, a two-step nondeterministic process was described for solving problems in the class NP. Give the process that could be used for the following problems. Your answer should describe the format of the output of the nondeterministic step. This output should have all of the elements that are part of the solution to the whole problem. For example, for the traveling salesperson problem, this was a list of cities in the order of the visits. Then your answer should describe a process that would be used to check to see if this generated "solution" satisfies the problem.

   a. Graph coloring problem
   b. Bin packing problem
   c. Backpack problem
   d. Subset sum problem
   e. CNF-satisfiability problem
   f. Job scheduling problem

2. In Section 8.1, a process to transform one problem into another was discussed as a way to identify problems that are NP-complete. All of the problems in Section 8.1 and 8.2 are NP-complete, so any of these problems can be transformed into any other problem. For the following sets of problems, describe how you would transform the first into the second:

   a. Backpack problem, bin packing
   b. Bin packing, job scheduling
   c. Job scheduling, subset sum
   d. Subset sum, traveling salesperson
   e. Traveling salesperson, job scheduling

8.3 WHAT MAKES SOMETHING NP?

We have looked at a lot of problems that are in the class P and a handful that are in the class NP. We described the class NP as those problems that are solvable in polynomial time by a nondeterministic algorithm. As was mentioned, we could describe the process of sorting as follows:

1. Nondeterministically output the elements of a list.
2. Check to see if $s_i < s_{i+1}$ for $i = 1$ through $N - 1$.

This describes a two-step nondeterministic process. The first step takes no comparisons and will be completed in N steps, each outputting one element. The second step is also polynomial time because it only does $N - 1$ comparisons. This process fits our definition of the class NP, so it would seem that sorting is in the class NP as well as the class P. Because we can do this with any algorithm, all algorithms in the class P are also in the class NP. In the case of problems just in class NP, there is, however, no known deterministic polynomial time algorithms. This makes P a subset of NP, but at present there are problems in NP that are not known to be in P.

The heart of this difference is really the large number of combinations that we must necessarily examine for these NP problems. But it's a little more complex than just the number of combinations of input values. We can have a list of 30 distinct elements or a list of 30 distinct cities. In the both cases, there are 30! combinations of these 30 elements or cities and only one of these can be correctly sorted or can be a shortest path. The difference is that we have polynomial time algorithms that will create the correctly sorted list, some in as few as 150 comparisons. For bubble sort, the first pass through the list will at minimum put the last element into the correct place in the list, eliminating with 29 comparisons at least 1 / 30 of the possible combinations. On the second pass, 28 comparisons will eliminate at least 1 / 29 of the combinations that are still left. When we look at the process closer, we see that even more of the possibilities might get eliminated, because each pass of the algorithm might not only move the next largest element to the end of the list but also fix other elements that are out of order.

The best we can do to find the shortest path is to examine all of the possible paths to see which has the shortest length. We don't have an algorithm that, with a few operations, can successfully eliminate a significant number of the combinations from consideration.[3] So instead, we need to look at all of them. If we could examine the path length of 1,000,000,000 of the 30! combinations in 1 second, this would still take more than 840 billion centuries to check all of the paths. In Chapter 9, we will look at algorithms that will come up with answers for these problems that approximate the optimal answer. We have no way of knowing how good an approximation we produce because we don't know what the optimal value is. Instead, these algorithms can be run for as much time as we have available, and the longer they run, the better the answer they will produce. They may stumble on the optimal answer, but that is not guaranteed.

So, the thing that puts problems in the class NP is that there are an extremely large number of possibilities for the optimal answer, and we don't have an efficient deterministic algorithm to sift through them to find the correct one.

■ 8.3.1 Is P = NP?

After the discussion of the previous section, it might seem ridiculous to even ask if the set of problems in the class P is the same as the set of problems in the class NP. The discussion showing that there is both a polynomial and nondeterministic polynomial time algorithm for sorting should demonstrate the basis for the fact that P is a subset of NP. Our discussion of the difference between sorting and shortest path might lead you to believe that we know that there are problems in the class NP that are not in the class P. That, however, is not the correct idea to take away from the last section. All we know at this point is that we have not been able to find a deterministic polynomial time algorithm that will solve any of the problems in the class NP. That doesn't mean that there is no such algorithm, and researchers are still working to resolve this point. It is believed that there is no polynomial time solution for the class NP problems, but how do you prove that a polynomial time algorithm doesn't exist to solve a problem? Our best option is to examine the problem and attempt to determine the lower bound on the work that must be done. At this point, however, no

---

[3] It might appear that we could try, for example, to eliminate a path between two cities that costs a lot. But that simple attempt might not work because it could make us take a couple of paths that are overall more expensive, so we would not really be better off. To check to see if eliminating an expensive edge will cause this to happen puts us back at a high-complexity algorithm.

one has been able to prove that the smallest lower bound for these problems must be larger than polynomial time. The question Is P = NP? is still open and being studied by researchers around the world.

■ 8.3.2 EXERCISES

1. For each of the following problems, indicate which are in P and which are in NP. For those you think are in P, give an outline of the algorithm to solve them. For those you think are in NP, explain why you think they are not solvable in polynomial time. (*Hint:* Think about an algorithm to solve these problems, and then determine if it is polynomial.)

a. The Smarandache function, $S(k)$, gives the smallest integer m, so that $m!$ can be evenly divided by k. For example, $S(9) = 6$ because $6! = 720$ and 9 doesn't divide any smaller factorial. Calculate the Smarandache function for any number.

b. You have to seat N children in the smallest number of rows in an auditorium. For each child, you have a list of who that child dislikes. Past experience shows that if a child is in the same row or any row behind a child that he or she dislikes, he or she will throw things at the other child. Given this list, determine the smallest number of rows needed for these children, or determine that they can't be seated.

c. Ackermann's function is defined as

$$A(0, y) = y + 1$$
$$A(x + 1, 0) = A(x, 1)$$
$$A(x + 1, y + 1) = A(x, A(x + 1, y))$$

Calculate Ackermann's function.

d. You are in front of a wall that stretches infinitely in both directions. You know that there is a door in the wall, but it is dark, and you only have only a dim flashlight that allows you to see no more than one step in either direction. Find the door.

8.4   TESTING POSSIBLE SOLUTIONS

The description of the class NP stated that these problems had a solution that included a nondeterministic first step that generated a potential solution and a deterministic second step that checked that solution. Both of these steps operate in polynomial time. This section will look at algorithms that check proposed solutions for the job scheduling and graph coloring problems.

■ 8.4.1 Job Scheduling

You will recall that the job scheduling problem gives a set of jobs that need to be done. Each job has a time it takes to complete, a deadline by which it must be completed, and a penalty if that job is not completed in time. Jobs are done one at a time, and the deadlines are measured from the start of the first job. The jobs are specified as a 4-tuple (n, t, d, p) where n is the job number, t is the amount of time it will take, d is the deadline, and p is the penalty. For example, a set of five jobs could be $\{(1, 3, 5, 2), (2, 5, 7, 4), (3, 1, 5, 3), (4, 6, 9, 1), (5, 2, 7, 4)\}$.

The decision problem specifies some value P and wants to know if there is an ordering of the jobs that can be done with penalty less than or equal to P. The optimization problem wants to know the smallest penalty for any ordering of the jobs. We will consider the decision problem, because calling the decision problem with a series of values until it answers yes can solve the optimization problem. In other words, we ask if there is an order with penalty 0 and if it answers no, we try a penalty of 1. We keep increasing the penalty until we get an answer of yes. The following algorithm will test one potential solution for the decision version of the problem:

```
PenaltyLess( list, N, limit )
list   the ordering of the jobs
N      the number of jobs
limit the maximum penalty

currentTime = 0
currentPenalty = 0
currentJob = 1
while (currentJob ≤ N) and (currentPenalty ≤ limit) do
    currentTime = currentTime + list[currentJob].time
    if (list[currentJob].deadline < currentTime) then
        currentPenalty = currentPenalty +
            list[currentJob].penalty
    end if
    currentJob = currentJob + 1
end while

if currentPenalty ≤ limit then
```

```
      return yes
else
      return no
end if
```

The requirement of the class NP is that we are able to check the proposed solution in polynomial time. You should see that this algorithm properly checks the penalties for the list of jobs provided. If we analyze the time complexity of this algorithm, we see that the while loop will do at most N passes if the currentPenalty is never increased. If we count all of the work, there will be $3N + 1$ comparisons and at most $3N$ additions. This means that this algorithm is in $O(N)$, which is clearly polynomial and meets our requirements.

■ 8.4.2 Graph Coloring

The graph coloring problem attempts to determine how to assign colors (represented as integers) to the nodes of the graph so that no two nodes that are connected by a single edge have the same color. You will recall that the decision version of this problem tries to determine if the graph can be colored in C colors or less, whereas the optimization version tries to determine the smallest number of colors needed.

Our nondeterministic step will produce a proposed solution that will be a list of the nodes and the colors assigned to them. The nondeterministic step will be responsible for deciding how many colors to use, so that's not something we need to check. For the decision problem, the nondeterministic step will try to assign at most C colors. For the optimization problem, it might start with a large number of colors and keep decreasing it as long as a valid coloring is still possible. Then when it determines that the graph can't be colored with X colors, it knows that $X + 1$ is the minimal number of colors required.

The following algorithm will check to see if the colors proposed are a valid way to color the graph. This algorithm uses an adjacency list to hold the graph, so that graph[j] represents the jth node of the graph, graph[j].edge-Count represents the number of edges leaving node j, and graph[j].edge is an array with the nodes that are adjacent to node j.

```
boolean
ValidColoring( graph, N, colors )
graph  the adjacency list
N      the number of nodes in the graph
colors the array of colors assigned to each node
```

```
for j = 1 to N do
    for k = 1 to graph[j].edgeCount do
        if (colors[j] = colors[ graph[j].edge[k] ]) then
            return no
        end if
    end for k
end for j
return yes
```

You should see that this algorithm properly checks the colors for the graph provided. It goes through each node and if that node is directly connected to another node that has the same color, it stops and returns no. If all are different, it returns yes. If we analyze the time complexity of this algorithm, we see that the outer for loop will do N passes. The inner loop looks at each edge connected to the current node. The overall process, therefore, does a comparison for each node's edges. This means that this algorithm is in $O(edges)$, which is clearly polynomial because the number of edges is less than N^2. This, therefore, meets our requirements.

■ 8.4.3 EXERCISES

1. Develop an algorithm to check a proposed decision solution for the following problems:

   a. Bin packing problem
   b. Traveling salesperson problem
   c. Backpack problem
   d. Subset sum problem
   e. CNF-satisfiability problem

CHAPTER 9

Other Algorithmic Techniques

PREREQUISITES

Before beginning this chapter, you should be able to

- Write and explain an algorithm
- Describe the class NP
- Describe growth rates and order
- Use random number tables and generators (Appendices A and B)
- Write a recursive algorithm

GOALS

At the end of this chapter, you should be able to

- Explain the approximation algorithm concept
- Explain approximation algorithms for some class NP problems
- Explain the four types of probabilistic algorithms
- Use arrays to improve algorithm efficiency

STUDY SUGGESTIONS

As you are working through the chapter, you should rework the examples to make sure you understand them. You should specifically trace through the algorithms and input data presented to try to recreate the results given. You should also try to answer any questions before reading on. A hint or the answer is in the sentences following the question.

A s was discussed in Chapter 8, problems in the class NP are important to a number of applications, and so their solution is of interest. Because these problems do not have polynomial time algorithms that can produce an exact solution, we must consider alternative algorithms that can only produce reasonably good answers. In some cases, these algorithms will find the optimal answer, but that is luck and cannot be guaranteed. We will explore a number of approximation algorithms for the problems we looked at in Chapter 8.

The basic idea of probabilistic algorithms is that it is sometimes better to guess than to figure out which option is correct. There are four classifications of probabilistic algorithms—numerical, Monte Carlo, Las Vegas, and Sherwood—although some analysis texts will refer to all probabilistic algorithms as "Monte Carlo." The common theme throughout these categories is that probabilistic algorithms will produce better results the longer that they are run.

This chapter ends with the application of dynamic programming algorithms to improve the efficiency of recursive algorithms and to select an order to multiply a series of matrices to reduce the computational complexity.

9.1 GREEDY APPROXIMATION ALGORITHMS

In Chapter 6, we saw two greedy algorithms that identified the minimum spanning tree of a graph and one that determined the shortest path between two nodes of a graph. In this section, we look at a number of greedy algorithms that approximate the optimal solution for problems in the class NP.

As we have discussed, the difficulty of finding an exact solution for problems in the class NP is the number of combinations of the input values that must be checked. For each collection of input values I, we can create a set of possible solutions PS_I. An optimal solution would be $S_{optimal} \in PS_I$, such that Value $(S_{optimal}) \leq Value(S')$ for all $S' \in PS_I$ if the problem is a minimization problem and $\text{Value}(S_{\text{optimal}}) \geq \text{Value}(S')$ for all $S' \in \text{PS}_I$ if the problem is a maximization problem.

Approximation algorithms for class NP problems will not necessarily find an optimal solution because they will only look at a portion of the set PS_I or will construct potential solutions from just a small subset of PS_I. We can determine how good an approximation algorithm is by looking at the solution that the algorithm produces relative to this optimal value. In some cases, we can determine the optimal value even if we cannot find a solution that will produce that value. The quality of an approximation algorithm is then given by the equation

$$Q_A(I) = \begin{cases} \dfrac{\text{Value}(A(I))}{\text{Value}(S_{\text{optimal}})} & \text{for minimization problems} \\[2em] \dfrac{\text{Value}(S_{\text{optimal}})}{\text{Value}(A(I))} & \text{for maximization problems} \end{cases}$$

In some cases, it will matter whether we are considering cases that have a fixed number of input values or cases that all have the same optimal solution. In other words, do we look at how good an approximation algorithm is for cases of 10 input values or different-sized input cases that all have an optimal solution of 50? These two views can result in two different quality ratings.

The following subsections look at a few of the approximation algorithms for the problems we have discussed. The algorithms given are not the only possibilities but rather give you a feel for the range of techniques. All of these approximations are polynomial time algorithms.

■ 9.1.1 Traveling Salesperson Approximations

There is a whole set of algorithms for various problems (including those in the class P) that are classified as greedy algorithms. These algorithms always look at the current situation and make the best choice based on the information available. Recall that the minimum spanning tree and shortest-path algorithms are examples of greedy algorithms.

It would seem that we could just apply the shortest-path algorithm to solve this problem, but it's not quite as easy as that. Dijkstra's algorithm is actually interested in the shortest path between two nodes but does not necessarily go through every node in the graph. We can, however, use this general greedy

From	To	2	3	4	5	6	7
1		16	12	13	6	7	11
2			21	18	8	19	5
3				20	1	3	15
4					14	10	4
5						2	17
6							9

■ FIGURE 9.1
The adjacency matrix for a fully connected weighted graph

technique to find an approximate algorithm. The cost of traveling between cities could be represented by an adjacency matrix like the one in Fig. 9.1. [1]

Our algorithm will go through the set of edges, picking them in order of increasing weight. It will not be concerned about forming the path, but instead it will make sure that edges added to the path meet two criteria:

1. They do not form a cycle with the other edges chosen unless all the nodes are in the cycle (in other words, we are done).
2. They are not the third edge connected to some node.

For the example in Fig. 9.1, we would first choose the edge (3,5) because it has the smallest weight. We would then choose edge (5,6). The next edge to consider would be (3,6), but it would be rejected because it forms the cycle [3, 5, 6, 3], which is not complete. Instead we would add the edges (4,7) and (2,7). The next edge to consider is (1,5), but it would be rejected because it is the third edge containing the node 5. We would then add the edge (1,6), and after that (1,4). The last edge to be added would be (2,3). This would give us the path of [1, 4, 7, 2, 3, 5, 6, 1] with a total length of 53. This is a good approximation but is clearly not the optimal solution because there is at least one path, [1, 4, 7, 2, 5, 3, 6, 1], which has a total length of 41.

---

[1] This matrix is upper triangular because the cost of going from city i to city j is the same as going in the other direction. If we were to store all of these values, we would find the bottom half just a repetition of the top half. Using an upper triangular matrix makes it easier to trace this algorithm.

9.1.2 Bin Packing Approximations

One technique to approximate the bin packing problem is to use the first fit strategy. This strategy will, for each item, look at the bins in order until one is found that has enough space to hold the item. If we have a set of items with sizes of (0.5, 0.7, 0.3, 0.9, 0.6, 0.8, 0.1, 0.4, 0.2, 0.5), how would the bins be packed using this strategy? You should have found that the bins would be packed so that bin 1 would have [0.5, 0.3, 0.1], bin 2 would have [0.7, 0.2], bin 3 would have [0.9], bin 4 would have [0.6, 0.4], bin 5 would have [0.8], and bin 6 would have [0.5]. You should see that this is not optimal because we could have five bins with [0.9, 0.1], [0.8, 0.2], [0.7, 0.3], [0.6, 0.4], and [0.5, 0.5]. The algorithm for first fit would be

```
FirstFit( size, N, bin )
size   the list of item sizes
N      the number of items
bin    the location for each item

for i = 1 to N do
   binUsed[i] = 0
end do
for item = 1 to N do
   binLoc = 1
   while used[binLoc]+size[item] > 1 do
      binLoc = binLoc + 1
   end while
   bin[ item ] = binLoc
   used[ binLoc ] = used[ binLoc ] + size[ item ]
end for
```

Another version of this would be a decreasing first fit, where the items are first sorted in decreasing order and then we begin the first fit process.[2] The reader should be able to show that this would give the optimal answer for the previous set of items. This will not, however, always do better than regular first fit. Consider the set of items (0.2, 0.6, 0.5, 0.2, 0.8, 0.3, 0.2). With the regular

---

[2] This is really nonincreasing, because we do not require that the sizes of the objects be distinct. The analysis literature is split between whether to call this decreasing first fit or nonincreasing first fit.

first fit, we will use the optimal three bins. If we sort first, we get the list (0.8, 0.6, 0.5, 0.3, 0.2, 0.2, 0.2, 0.2). When we do the first fit algorithm with this new list, we get bins of [0.8, 0.2], [0.6, 0.3], [0.5, 0.2, 0.2], and [0.2], which is 1 more than optimal.

Analysis has shown that this decreasing first fit technique will require approximately 50% more than the optimal number of bins. This means that if some set of input requires 10 bins in the optimal case, this algorithm will produce a result that will likely need 15 bins. First fit without sorting has been shown to need about 70% more than the optimal number of bins, or about 17 bins if optimal is 10 bins.

■ 9.1.3 Backpack Approximation

The backpack approximation algorithm is a simple greedy algorithm that is based on the worth ratio of the items. We create a sorted list of the items based on the ratio of the worth to the item size. We represent each item as a pair [size, worth]. If we had the list of items of ([25, 50], [20, 80], [20, 50], [15, 45], [30, 105], [35, 35], [20, 10], [10, 45]), they would have worth ratios of (2, 4, 2.5, 3, 3.5, 1, 0.5, 4.5). Sorting by the worth ratios would put our items in the order ([10, 45], [20, 80], [30, 105], [15, 45], [20, 50], [25, 50], [35, 35], [20, 10]). We now begin filling the backpack using the items in the order of this list. If the next item will not fit, we skip it and continue down the list until the backpack is full or we have passed through the entire list. So, if we have a backpack of size 80, we would be able to put in the first four items for a total size of 75 and a total worth of 275. This is not, however, optimal, because using the first three items and the fifth item would give a total size of 80 and a total worth of 280.

■ 9.1.4 Subset Sum Approximation

In the backpack problem, if you set the worth of each item to be the same as its size, the resulting problem is the same as the subset sum problem. This means that the greedy algorithm described there could also be used here. In each case, the worth ratio would be 1, so the sorting method could put the items in order of decreasing size.

There is an alternative algorithm for the subset sum approximation that has some of the flavor of a greedy algorithm. In this alternative, we have an algorithm that will be able to do better the longer it is run and will be optimal if, for a set of N numbers, we can run it for all $N + 1$ passes. This is because each pass of this algorithm considers additional cases. The first pass begins with the empty set and adds items in decreasing order until the limit is reached or all of the items have been tried. The second pass begins with all of the possible sets of one item from the list and adds more items from there. The third pass begins with all of the possible sets of two items. The more time that is available, the more passes that the algorithm can do. If there are 10 items in the input and 11 passes can be done, the optimal solution will be found. You should see that, for 10 items, on the first pass there is 1 empty set, on the second pass there are 10 sets of one element, and on the third pass there are 45 sets of two elements. The sixth pass will be the worst with 252 sets of five elements. So, even though this process might sound simple, it can still take a significant amount of time. The algorithm for one pass of this process is

```
SubsetSum(sizes, N, limit, pass, result, sum)
sizes   the list of item sizes
N       the number of items in the list
limit   the maximum sum for the subset
pass    used to set the number of items in the starting set
result  the items in the best subset found
sum     the sum of the items in result

sum = 0
for each subset T of {1,..,n} with pass items do
    tempSum = 0
    for i = 1 to N do
        if i ∈ T then
            tempSum = tempSum + sizes[i]
        end if
    end for
    if tempSum ≤ limit then
        for j = 1 to N do
            if j ∉ T and tempSum + sizes[j] ≤ limit then
                tempSum = tempSum + sizes[j]
                T = T ∪ {j}
            end if
        end for
    end if
    if sum < tempSum then
        sum = tempSum
        result = T
    end if
end for
```

Pass	Subsets of size pass	Item added	Sum
0	∅	27,22,1	50
1	27	22,1	50
	22	27,1	50
	14	27,11,1	53
	11	27,14,1	53
	7	27,14,1	49
	1	27,22	50
2	27, 22	1	50
	27, 14	11,1	53
	27, 11	14,1	53
	27, 7	14,1	49
	27, 1	22	50
	22, 14	11, 7, 1	55
	22, 11	14, 7, 1	55
	22, 7	14, 11, 1	55
	22, 1	27	50
	14, 11	27,1	53
	14, 7	27,1	49
	14, 1	27,11	53
	11, 7	27,1	46
	11, 1	27,14	53
	7, 1	27,14	49

FIGURE 9.2
Results of first three passes of subset sum approximation algorithm

For example, with a set of items of sizes {27, 22, 14, 11, 7, 1} and an upper limit on the size of the subset sum of 55, the process would have the series of passes as given in the table in Fig. 9.2. We see that this algorithm has found an optimal solution of 55 on the third pass.

■ 9.1.5 Graph Coloring Approximation

Graph coloring is an unusual problem because, as opposed to the previous cases, it has been shown that getting an approximate coloring that is even close to the optimal coloring is as complex as getting the optimal coloring. The best of the approximation algorithms that run in polynomial time will use more than twice as many colors as optimal. Research has also shown that if there was a polynomial algorithm that could color any graph with no more than twice as many colors as optimal, there would be a polynomial algorithm that could color any graph optimally. This would mean that P = NP. There are some restrictions that can be placed on the complexity of graphs that make it easier for them to be colored. For example, if a graph is planar, in other words, when drawn in one plane none of its edges cross, there are algorithms that can color it within polynomial time.

A simple algorithm to color any graph with N nodes uses a sequential coloring method. An algorithm for this is

```
ColorGraph( G )
G   the graph to be colored

for i = 1 to N do
   c = 1
   while there is a node in G adjacent to node_i that is colored c do
      c = c + 1
   end while
   color node_i with c
end for
```

The degree of a graph is the largest number of edges leaving one node. This coloring algorithm will use C colors where C is 1 greater than the degree of the graph. It is possible to do better than this, but the algorithm is beyond the scope of this book.

■ 9.1.6 EXERCISES

1. What path would the greedy traveling salesperson algorithm find if the city matrix is

From	To	2	3	4	5	6	7
1			5	1	2	16	17	21
2				10	7	18	8	15
3					9	11	13	4
4						3	20	14
5							12	6
6								19

Is the path it finds optimal?

2. Another technique for bin packing is best fit, where each item is placed in the bin so that the least amount of space is left over. New bins are started

only when an object will not fit in any of the current bins. Write an algorithm for best fit. Show how best fit would have handled the two unsorted examples in the text.

3. Another technique for bin packing is next fit, where we keep putting items into a bin as long as they will fit. The first object that doesn't fit in a bin causes the algorithm to start a new bin. The algorithm never backs up to a previous bin. Write an algorithm for next fit. Show how next fit would have handled the two unsorted examples in the text.

4. Another technique for bin packing is worst fit, where each item is placed in the bin so that the most amount of space is left. New bins are started only when an object will not fit in any of the current bins. Write an algorithm for worst fit. Show how worst fit would have handled the two unsorted examples in the text.

5. What will be the best worth found by the backpack approximation algorithm with a limit of 55 and the items ([5, 20], [10, 25], [15, 30], [20, 70], [25, 75], [30, 15], [35, 35], [40, 60])? Is the result found optimal?

6. What will be the best result found by the subset sum approximation algorithm if it was run for pass values of 0, 1, and 2 and for the set of values {29, 21, 16, 11, 3} with a limit of 52? Is this result optimal?

9.2 PROBABILISTIC ALGORITHMS

Probabilistic algorithms take a radically different approach from the deterministic algorithms that were explored in Chapters 1 through 7. In some applications, these probabilistic algorithms provide results that cannot be achieved through deterministic means. The examples and applications presented here are not meant to be exhaustive. They are intended to illustrate the range of possibilities.

■ 9.2.1 Numerical Probabilistic Algorithms

Numerical probabilistic algorithms calculate an approximate result for some mathematical problem. The longer these algorithms are given to generate a result, the greater precision that result will have.

Buffon's Needle

Let's say that you have a set of 355 sticks and the lengths of these sticks are one-half the widths of the boards in a hardwood floor. If we dump these sticks on the floor, how many will fall across the cracks between two boards? The number will have to be between 0 and 355, but Georges Louis Leclerc showed the average number to be almost exactly 113. Each stick has a 1 in π chance of landing on a crack. This is because of the relationship of the rotation of a stick to the spacing of the boards. If the stick falls perpendicular to the cracks there is a one-half chance it will fall on a crack (the ratio of its length to the width of the boards). But if it falls parallel to the crack, the chance it will cross a crack is extremely small (the ratio of its width to the width of the boards). So this technique could be used to calculate π by randomly dropping sticks and counting how many fall across the cracks. The ratio of the total number of sticks to the number that cross a crack gives an approximation of π.

A similar technique can be used by simulating throwing darts at a board that has a circle inscribed within a square (Fig. 9.3). We randomly choose points in the square and count how many fall into the circle. If r is the radius of the circle, the area of the circle is πr^2, and the area of the square is $(2r)^2$, or $4r^2$. The ratio of the area of the circle to the area of the square is $\pi / 4$. If our numbers are truly random, the darts will be spread relatively evenly across the square. If we randomly "throw" darts at the square, π can be estimated by $4 * c / s$, where c is the number of darts that fall in the circle and s is the number of darts thrown. The more darts we throw, the more accurate our calculation of π.

This technique could also be used to approximate the area of any irregular shape for which we can determine if a point (x, y) is inside or outside the

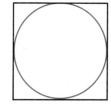

■ FIGURE 9.3
A circle inscribed within a square

shape. We would just generate random points in a surrounding square and determine the ratio that fall inside the shape. The ratio of

$$\frac{\text{darts inside the shape}}{\text{total darts thrown}}$$

is the same as the ratio of

$$\frac{\text{area of the shape}}{\text{area of the square}}$$

Monte Carlo Integration[3]

You may recall that for a continuous function f, the area under the curve for f is the integral of the function. For some functions, it is difficult or impossible to determine this integral, but we can get it through our dart technique. For the purposes of illustration, we will restrict ourselves to that portion of f bounded by the x and y axes and the lines $x = 1$ and $y = 1$ (see Fig. 9.4). You should be able to generalize this to any size bounding box.

We randomly throw darts at the square and count how many wind up below the curve. The number below the curve divided by the number thrown will give us an approximation of the area under the curve. As in past cases, the more darts that are thrown, the more accurate the approximation. The following algorithm achieves this:

```
Integrate ( f, dartCount )
f          is the function to be integrated
dartCount  is the number of darts to throw
```

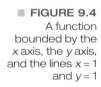

y = 1

x = 1

■ FIGURE 9.4
A function
bounded by the
x axis, the y axis,
and the lines $x = 1$
and $y = 1$

---

[3] It is unfortunate that this is the traditional name for this technique because it is unrelated to the Monte Carlo techniques to be discussed later.

```
hits = 0
for i=1 to dartCount do
   x = uniform(0, 1)
   y = uniform(0, 1)
   if y ≤ f(x) then
      hits = hits + 1
   end if
end for
return hits/dartCount
```

Probabilistic Counting

A classic problem is to bet that in a room of 25 randomly chosen people at least two of them will have the same birthday. Although this would seem a foolish bet, in reality the odds are greater than 56% that this will happen. In general, there are $N! / (N - k)!$ ways to choose k distinct objects from a set of N objects if order matters. There are N^k different ways of choosing k objects if repetitions are allowed. Putting all of this together means that the chance of winning the bet is $1 - 365! / (340! * 365^{25})$. In reality, the chances are even better because this equation does not account for the fact that births are not uniformly distributed through the year. This number is not easy to calculate, nor it is easy for us to figure out the reverse problem: Given a set of N elements, how many choices must you make before you will pick an element for the second time? In other words, given 365 days in the year, how many different people must you have for there to be a good chance that at least two people have the same birthday. Because it's difficult to calculate, the following algorithm will approximate the number:

```
ProbabilityCount( N )

k = 0
s = {}
a = uniform( 1, N )
repeat
   k = k + 1
   s = s ∪ {a}
   a = uniform( 1, N )
until a ∈ s
return k
```

The function will randomly generate numbers from 1 to N until it generates a number for the second time. To get more accurate results, this function could be called a number of times, averaging the answers it returns. For our birthday example ($N = 365$), this function would give us an answer of about 25.

■ 9.2.2 Monte Carlo Algorithms

Monte Carlo algorithms will always give an answer, but the probability that the answer is correct increases the longer the algorithms run. These algorithms can occasionally return an incorrect answer. Monte Carlo algorithms are called *p*-correct when they return a correct answer with probability of *p* ($1/2 < p < 1$). If there is more than one correct answer for a given input, a Monte Carlo algorithm is called consistent if it returns the same correct answer each time.

There are two ways to improve the results of a Monte Carlo algorithm. The first is to increase the amount of time it runs, and the second is to call it multiple times. The second option can only be used if the Monte Carlo algorithm is consistent. In this case, we would make several calls to it and choose the answer that appears most frequently. An algorithm to do this would be something like the following:

```
Monte3( x )

one = Monte(x)
two = Monte(x)
three = Monte(x)
if one  = two or one = three then
   return one
else
   return two
end if
```

In this algorithm, the first solution will be returned if it appears at least twice. If, however, it doesn't, we can just return the second answer because it either matches the third answer, or all three are different and so it doesn't matter. Because Monte Carlo algorithms have a greater than 50% chance of returning the correct answer, it is unlikely that all three will be different. The process in Monte3 will improve a consistent 80% Monte Carlo algorithm to about 90%.

This is not always the best way to approach the problem of improving probability. Consider a Monte Carlo decision algorithm that is biased in that it is 100% correct if it returns the answer false, and it only makes mistakes if it returns true. In other words, if the algorithm returns false, the answer is always correct, but if it returns true, the answer may be true or false. This means that any answer of false should be returned immediately, and repeated calls to the function would be looking for a series of repeated true answers to increase the chance that true is really correct. The algorithm for this would be

```
MultipleMonte( x )

if not Monte( x ) then
    return false
end if
if not Monte( x ) then
    return false
end if
return Monte( x )
```

The only way for this algorithm to return true is if we get three true answers in a row. In this situation, if the original Monte Carlo algorithm was correct overall 55% of the time, calling this function improves its accuracy to 90%. This is also possible for "numeric" algorithms that will be biased toward some number for the correct answer.

Majority Element

A problem to which this technique can be applied is finding if there is a majority element in an array. An array has a majority element if there is one element that is stored in more than half of the array locations. If solved by the most obvious means, this process would take $O(N^2)$ comparisons because we would have to potentially compare every element to every other element until we found one that was in more than half of the array locations. Because there is a known linear algorithm to solve this problem that is similar to the selection algorithm discussed in Chapter 2, this version is merely another illustration of the Monte Carlo technique.

A Monte Carlo algorithm for this process would be

```
Majority( list, N )
list   the list of elements
N      the number of elements

choice = uniform( 1, N )
count = 0
for i = 1 to N do
   if list[i] = list[choice] then
      count = count + 1
   end if
end for
return (count > n/2)
```

This function randomly picks an element and checks to see if it appears in a majority of locations. This algorithm is considered to be true-biased because if the algorithm returns true, it means we found the majority element, so true is absolutely correct. But if it returns false, it is possible we picked the wrong element and that there still is a majority element. If there is a majority element, the chance of picking a minority element is less than 50% and gets smaller the more that the majority element appears. This still means that it is possible that this algorithm might be correct only 50% of the time in some cases. If we call `Majority` five times, the algorithm improves to 97% correct, and the complexity would be just $5N$, or $O(N)$.

Monte Carlo Prime Testing

We can check to see if a number N is prime by using a Monte Carlo algorithm. In this case, we generate a random number between 2 and $\sqrt{N}$ and see if it divides evenly into N. If it does, N is not prime; if it doesn't, we can't be sure. This algorithm is not very good because it will return false frequently. For example, if we consider the number 60,329, which is the product of the three prime numbers 23, 43, and 61, the algorithm will generate a random number between 2 and 245, but only three numbers in this range will produce the correct answer. This has a 1.2% chance of being correct.

Although this simple algorithm will not do very well, there are other similar techniques that are beyond the scope of this book that will solve this problem with a higher probability of correct answers.

■ 9.2.3 Las Vegas Algorithms

Las Vegas algorithms will never return the wrong answer but sometimes will return no answer at all. The longer these algorithms run, the higher their probability of success. The basic idea is that a Las Vegas algorithm will randomly make decisions and then check to see if they have resulted in a successful answer. A program that uses a Las Vegas algorithm would repeatedly call it until the algorithm indicated success. If we say that success(x) and failure(x) are the times necessary to calculate a successful or unsuccessful answer, respectively, for input of size x, and we say that $p(x)$ is the probability that the algorithm will be successful, we get the following equation:

$$\text{time}(x) = p(x) * \text{success}(x) + (1 - p(x)) * (\text{failure}(x) + \text{time}(x))$$

This equation is saying that if we succeed, the overall time is the time it takes to get a success. But if we fail, it is the time for the failure plus another call to the function. Solving this equation for time(x), we get

$$\text{time}(x) = p(x) * \text{success}(x) + (1 - p(x)) * \text{failure}(x) + (1 - p(x)) * \text{time}(x)$$

$$\text{time}(x) - (1 - p(x)) * \text{time}(x) = p(x) * \text{success}(x) + (1 - p(x)) * \text{failure}(x)$$

$$\text{time}(x) - \text{time}(x) + p(x) * \text{time}(x) = p(x) * \text{success}(x) + (1 - p(x)) * \text{failure}(x)$$

$$p(x) * \text{time}(x) = p(x) * \text{success}(x) + (1 - p(x)) * \text{failure}(x)$$

$$\text{time}(x) = \text{success}(x) + ((1 - p(x)) / p(x)) * \text{failure}(x)$$

This means that the time is dependent on the execution of success, failure, and the probability of each. The interesting fact is that if the probability of success ($p(x)$) is lowered, the overall time can still be reduced if failures are calculated more quickly. So, we can improve efficiency by solving failures faster even if it slightly lowers the chance of success.

How would this work in practice? Well, consider the eight queens problem, which tries to place a set of eight queens on a chessboard so that they are not attacking each other.[4] One possible solution for this problem is shown in Fig. 9.5. A recursive algorithm to solve this problem would place a queen in the first column of the first row and then call itself to place a queen in the second row. If at any point it can't find a location for a queen on the current row, it will back up and try a different location for the queen on the previous row.

There is a probabilistic alternative to this recursive algorithm. We could place queens on the board so that each new queen gets placed randomly on one of the spaces on the next row that is not attacked. The difference between a Las Vegas and the standard recursive algorithm is that when the Las Vegas version can't place a queen on a row, it just gives up and signals a failure. The recursive version backs up to try to fix things so as to force an answer. An algorithm for Las Vegas eight queens would be

```
Queens( result )
result   holds the column positions of the queens for each row
returns 1 if this succeeded and 0 if it failed
```

----

[4] In chess, the queen can attack any other piece that is in the same row, column, or along a diagonal.

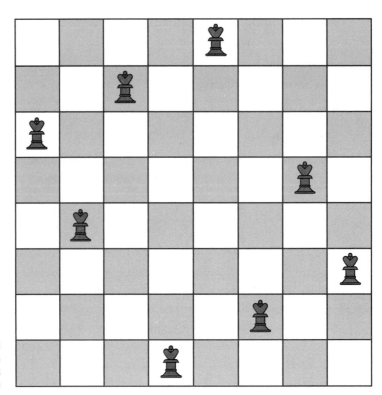

```
row = 1
repeat
    // at this point we have placed queens in rows 1...row - 1
    spotsPossible = 0
    for i = 1 to 8 do
        if location row, i is not attacked then
            spotsPossible = spotsPossible + 1
            if uniform(1, spotsPossible) = 1 then
                try = i
            end if
        end if
    end for
    if spotsPossible > 0 then
        result[row] = try
        row = row + 1
    end if
until spotsPossible = 0 or row = 9
return (spotsPossible > 0)
```

Let's look at what this algorithm is doing. The repeat loop will take us through each of the eight rows on the board. For each of these rows, we look at each column location, and if it isn't attacked, we increment `spotsPossible`. The next `if` statement looks a little strange, but watch what happens when we move down the first row in which no spaces are attacked. For the first column, `uniform` generates a number between 1 and 1, which must be 1, so `try` gets set to the first column. For the second column, `uniform` generates a number between 1 and 2, which has a 50% chance of being 1, so there is a 50% chance that `try` will be changed to 2. For the third column, `uniform` generates a number between 1 and 3, which has a 33% chance of being 1, so there is a 33% chance that `try` will be changed to 3. For the fourth column, `uniform` generates a number between 1 and 4, which has a 25% chance of being 1, so there is a 25% chance that `try` will be changed to 4. The end result is that each of the free columns will have the chance of 1 / `spotsPossible` of being the one tried on this pass. We do this again for the rest of the rows. This repeats until either `spotsPossible` is zero because there are no unattacked locations or `rows` is nine because we filled all of the rows. In the first case, this algorithm stops and indicates failure. In the second case, we solved the eight queens problem and return true.

A full statistical analysis discovers that the probability of success is about 0.1293, and the number of passes for a failure is about 6.971. Using the equation above, we find that this algorithm will take about 55 passes. If we looked at an analysis of the recursive version of the eight queens problem, you would see that it takes more than twice as many passes.

■ 9.2.4 Sherwood Algorithms

Sherwood algorithms always give an answer, and the answer is always correct. These algorithms are applied to situations where the best, average, and worst cases for a deterministic algorithm differ significantly. Sherwood algorithms introduce randomness to help move the complexity of the deterministic algorithm from the extremes of its worst and best cases.

An example of this would be the choice of the pivot element for quicksort. In the analysis of that algorithm, we pointed out that the worst case would be if the list was already sorted because each time we would pick the smallest element for the pivot. If instead, we randomly picked the pivot element between first and last, we would lessen the chance of the worst case occurring. We would not eliminate that chance, because we could randomly pick the smallest element each time, but the chances of that happening are very small. The down side of this is that if our list happened to have the median element of each of the subdivided pieces in the first location of that piece (the best case), our randomness would not be likely to choose that element. So, the chance of the worst or best cases occurring are both diminished.

We could apply this technique to searching as well. With a binary search, there are some locations that require a number of failures before we check them. A Sherwood version of "binary" search would randomly pick a location to check between `start` and `end`. Sometimes we would wind up with a part that is smaller than what it would be in a true binary search and sometimes with a part that is larger. For example, with a list of 400 elements, instead of choosing the 200th element for our comparison, we perhaps choose the 100th element. If what we are looking for is smaller than the 100th element, our Sherwood version will discard 75% of the elements instead of 50% for the standard algorithm. But if what we are looking for is larger than the 100th element, we would only discard 25% of the elements. Again, our Sherwood algorithm will sometimes do better and sometimes worse.

The basic idea is that a Sherwood algorithm reduces the time of the worst case and increases the time of the best case. Just like Robin Hood in Sherwood Forest, this technique robs from the rich (the best case) and gives to the poor (the worst case).

■ 9.2.5 Probabilistic Algorithm Comparison

Let's summarize the algorithms covered in this section. We saw that numerical probabilistic algorithms will always supply an answer but that the longer the algorithm runs, the more accurate the answer becomes. Monte Carlo algorithms will always give an answer, but sometimes that answer will be wrong. The longer that a Monte Carlo algorithm runs, the higher the probability the answer will be correct. Multiple calls to a Monte Carlo algorithm can also improve the results. Las Vegas algorithms never return a wrong answer but might not return an answer if they are unable to find a correct one. Sherwood techniques can be applied to any deterministic algorithm. They do not influence the correctness of the algorithm but rather reduce the chance of the worst-case behavior. In doing so, however, they reduce the chance of the best-case behavior as well.

■ 9.2.6 EXERCISES

1. On a recent outing in the woods, you found a cave that had a map, a large computer, and a magic button in the wall. The map indicates the location of two islands that are each five days travel away from where you are now and are also five days travel apart. (You can imagine that you and the two islands are at the corners of an equilateral triangle.) A gnome appeared and told you that when you press the button, a treasure consisting of 15 bars of pure gold encrusted with diamonds, emeralds, rubies, and other priceless gems will appear randomly on one of the two islands. The computer will begin to calculate the location of the bars, but it will take four days to get the answer. The computer is not portable and so you would have to wait four days for its answer before you could start out. The problem is that there is a dragon that takes one of these bars away every night to a place that is completely inaccessible. The gnome has offered to tell you the correct location of the gold bars in exchange for three of the bars. The gnome also tells you that each time you return from your journey, you can press the button again, and another treasure will randomly appear on one of the two islands.

   Consider *all* of your possible choices and their potential return, and decide what choice gives you the best possible return in the long run (in other words, if you go treasure hunting a number of times). Your answer should list all of the possibilities you have considered along with the amount you would expect to get for each. You should assume that you will repeat the treasure hunt at least 10 times. Because there is no limit on the number of times you can go on the treasure hunt, you should not include the time of your return to the cave in your analysis.

   For problems 2 through 4, use the table of random numbers in Appendix A. For each question, begin at the start of the table and work through until you reach either the end of the problem or the end of the table. If you reach the end of the table, just continue from the first number of the table.

2. The function x^3 can be integrated directly, and the result is 0.25 in the range 0 to 1. Use the function `Integrate` from Section 9.2 with 20 darts. Compare the answers you get after 5, 10, 15, and 20 darts with the correct answer of 0.25. (Show all work.)

3. Run the Monte Carlo prime testing process for the number 182 (2 * 7 * 13) and for 255 (3 * 5 * 17) showing the numbers chosen and the result

returned. How many times do you have to call this function before you get the correct answer? (Start at the beginning of the list of random numbers for each case.)

4. Show the first three boards that the Queens algorithm would generate in its attempt at solving the eight queens problem.

5. Modify PivotList so that it is a Sherwood-based algorithm.

6. Write the Sherwood search, based on binary search, that is described in Section 9.2.4.

9.3 DYNAMIC PROGRAMMING

Richard Bellman first used the term *dynamic programming* to describe a type of problem in which the most efficient solution depended on choices that may change with time instead of being predetermined. The key value of his ideas was the use of a polynomial time computation in place of an exponential time one. There are two applications of dynamic programming algorithms that we will now consider: a method to improve the calculation efficiency of some recursive algorithms and a method to decide the order in which to multiply a series of matrices to reduce the calculation time. Another dynamic programming application was discussed in Chapter 5, namely, the approximate string matching algorithm.

■ 9.3.1 Array-Based Methods

Array-based methods replace traditional recursive algorithms that may calculate results multiple times. The classic example of a recursive function is the calculation of numbers in the Fibonacci sequence described in question 1 in Section 1.5.3. If you trace this calculation for the tenth Fibonacci number, you will see that you need to calculate the ninth and eighth Fibonacci numbers and add them together. The traditional method will wind up calculating the eighth Fibonacci number as part of determining the ninth, but it then throws this information away and calculates it again. The algorithm from Chapter 1 is reproduced here:

```
Fibonacci( N )
N        the Nth Fibonacci number should be returned
```

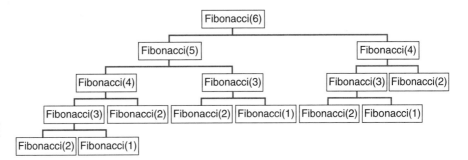

FIGURE 9.6
The calling
sequence for
Fibonacci(6)

```
if (N = 1) or (N = 2) then
   return 1
else
   return Fibonacci( N-1 ) + Fibonacci( N-2 )
end if
```

If we use this algorithm to find the sixth Fibonacci number, we would wind up making the series of calls to this function represented in the tree in Fig. 9.6. In examining this tree, you will see that Fibonacci(4) gets calculated twice and Fibonacci(3) gets calculated three times. For even larger Fibonacci numbers, these values could be calculated even more times. For the tenth Fibonacci number, the third would be calculated 21 times. We could improve the efficiency of this algorithm if, instead of calculating from the top down, we calculated from the bottom up. An alternative algorithm follows that uses an array of previous values:

```
Fibonacci2( N )
N   the Nth Fibonacci number should be returned

if (N = 1) or (N = 2) then
   return 1
else
   val[1] = 1
   val[2] = 1
   for i = 3 to N do
      val[i] = val[i-1] + val[i-2]
   end for
   return val[N]
end if
```

This example is not very complicated, and you should see that it would even be possible to accomplish this with just two variables for the last two values instead of an entire array.

A more involved example is the calculation of the binomial coefficient, which tells us the number of different ways that we could pick k objects from a set of N objects if the order we pick them doesn't matter.[5] The binomial coefficient is given by the equation

$$\begin{bmatrix} N \\ k \end{bmatrix} = \frac{N!}{k!(N-k)!}$$

This equation cannot be calculated directly, as we discussed in the last section, because the factorial value gets very large very quickly. An alternative and equivalent formula for the binomial coefficient is

$$\begin{bmatrix} N \\ k \end{bmatrix} = \begin{cases} \begin{bmatrix} N-1 \\ k-1 \end{bmatrix} + \begin{bmatrix} N-1 \\ k \end{bmatrix} & 0 < k < N \\ 1 & k = 0 \\ 1 & k = N \end{cases}$$

You should easily be able to write a recursive algorithm from this equation, but it will have the same recalculation problem that we saw with the Fibonacci numbers. Instead, we can use this equation to begin calculating at the bottom and moving up until we reach the answer we are looking for. This process will be familiar to anyone who has written out the values in Pascal's Triangle.

For our algorithm, we will need an array called BiCoeff with $N + 1$ rows and $k + 1$ columns that we will number starting at zero. In this array, location BiCoeff[i, j] stores the value of

$$\begin{bmatrix} i \\ j \end{bmatrix}$$

We initialize locations BiCoeff[0, 0], BiCoeff[1, 0], and BiCoeff[1, 1] all to a value of 1, and then loop through values until we reach

---

[5] The formula given in Section 9.2 under "Probabilistic Counting" is different because in that application the order mattered.

BiCoeff[N, k]. The following algorithm gives the dynamic programming solution to this problem:

```
for i = 0 to N do
   for j = 0 to minimum( i, k ) do
      if j = 1 or j = i then
         BiCoeff[ i, j ] = 1
      else
         BiCoeff[ i, j ] = BiCoeff[ i-1, j-1 ] + BiCoeff[ i-1, j ]
      end if
   end for j
end for i
```

Here the recursive algorithm would calculate

$$2 * \begin{bmatrix} N \\ k \end{bmatrix} - 1$$

terms, and the dynamic programming version would only calculate $O(N * k)$ terms.

■ 9.3.2 Dynamic Matrix Multiplication

If you have a series of matrices, each having a different dimension, which need to be multiplied together, the order in which the multiplication is done can have a dramatic impact on how quickly this is accomplished. For example, if we have four matrices that we will call M_1, M_2, M_3, and M_4, and they have sizes of 20 × 5, 5 × 35, 35 × 4, and 4 × 25, respectively, there are five different ways that they can be multiplied together that will take from 3100 to 24,500 multiplications. The full details are given in Fig. 9.7. This figure shows various ways in which these can first be paired, then the ways in which three of the matrices can be multiplied, and finally the ways that all four can be multiplied together. The final column shows the number of multiplications necessary to achieve the multiplication order of the first column. You should recall that to multiply a matrix of size A × B by a matrix of size B × C will take $A * B * C$ multiplications.

The following algorithm will build an upper triangular matrix with the minimum costs from Fig. 9.7. The size of matrix M_j is given as s_j × s_{j+1}. The minimum cost will be in location $cost_{1,N}$ (in other words the upper right location) at the completion of this algorithm. This algorithm will also calculate

Multiplication Order	Resulting Matrix Size	Total Cost in Multiplications
$M_1 * M_2$	20×35	3500
$M_2 * M_3$	5×4	700
$M_3 * M_4$	35×25	3500
$(M_1 * M_2) * M_3$	20×4	3500 + 2800 = 6300
$M_1 * (M_2 * M_3)$	20×4	700 + 400 = 1100
$(M_2 * M_3) * M_4$	5×25	700 + 500 = 1200
$M_2 * (M_3 * M_4)$	5×25	3500 + 4375 = 7875
$((M_1 * M_2) * M_3) * M_4$	20×25	6300 + 2000 = 8300
$(M_1 * (M_2 * M_3)) * M_4$	20×25	1100 + 2000 = 3100
$M_1 * ((M_2 * M_3) * M_4)$	20×25	1200 + 2500 = 3700
$M_1 * (M_2 * (M_3 * M_4))$	20×25	7875 + 2500 = 10,375
$(M_1 * M_2) * (M_3 * M_4)$	20×25	3500 + 3500 + 17,500 = 24,500

■ FIGURE 9.7
The amount of work needed to multiply four matrices in different orders

a matrix called trace that is used by the next algorithm to actually determine the order of the multiplication that will produce this minimum cost.

```
for i = 1 to N do
    cost_i,i = 0
end for
for i = 1 to N-1 do
    for j = 1 to N-i do
        loc = i + j
        tempCost = ∞
        for k = i to loc-1 do
            if tempCost > cost_i,k + cost_k+1,loc + s_i*s_k*s_loc then
                tempCost = cost_i,k + cost_k+1,loc + s_i*s_k*s_loc
                tempTrace = k
```

```
        end if
      end for k
      cost_{i,loc} = tempCost
      trace_{i,loc} = tempTrace
   end for j
end for i
```

Once the trace array has been calculated, the following recursive algorithm will use it to determine the actual order for the multiplication. This algorithm uses a global variable called position that is initialized to 1 and will keep its value as it is being changed during the recursive calls.

```
GetOrder( first, last, order )
first the starting matrix location
last  the ending matrix location
order the order of matrix multiplication

if first < last then
   middle = trace_{first,last}
   GetOrder( first, middle, order )
   GetOrder( middle, last, order )
   order_{position} = middle
   position = position + 1
end if
```

If you use these two algorithms with the matrix sizes of the last example, you will get a multiplication order of 2, 1, and 3, which represents doing the second multiplication first, followed by the first multiplication, and finishing with the third multiplication. This is the same result shown in Fig. 9.7.

■ 9.3.3 EXERCISES

1. Use the matrix multiplication algorithms in Section 9.3.2 to determine the most efficient order to multiply the matrices in each of the four following cases:

 a. M_1 is 3×5, M_2 is 5×2, M_3 is 2×1, and M_4 is 1×10.
 b. M_1 is 2×7, M_2 is 7×3, M_3 is 3×6, and M_4 is 6×10.
 c. M_1 is 10×3, M_2 is 3×15, M_3 is 15×12, M_4 is 12×7, and M_5 is 7×2.
 d. M_1 is 7×2, M_2 is 2×4, M_3 is 4×15, M_4 is 15×20, and M_5 is 20×5.

9.4 PROGRAMMING EXERCISES

1. Write a program for the traveling salesperson approximation algorithm. Run your program for a set of 10 cities by randomly placing distance values between 1 and 45 into the adjacency matrix. Print out the adjacency matrix and the path found. Check them to see if the result is optimal.

2. Write a program for the bin packing approximations. Your program should implement the four methods mentioned in the text and exercises: first fit, best fit, next fit, and worst fit. Generate a random set of objects and pass the same set into each of the four methods to see how many bins each would use. Write a report on your results. You should test these methods with the number of objects being 50, 100, 200, and 500. To get more accurate results, you should generate and test multiple sets of sizes for each of these four cases.

3. Write a program to do Monte Carlo integration of the function x^3 in the range between 0 and 1. Because we know that the answer is 0.25, you should write your program to test how many darts need to be thrown for the answer to be within various levels of accuracy. You should run this to test the number of darts needed to be within ± 0.0001, ± 0.000001, and ± 0.00000001 of the correct answer.

4. Write a program to use random numbers to calculate the value of π as described in the text. How many darts are needed for the fifth digit after the decimal point to be correct? How many darts are needed for the seventh and tenth digits after the decimal point to be correct?

5. Create a program that will sort a list using a standard `Quicksort` and a `Quicksort` with a Sherwood-based `PivotList`. Generate a number of random lists of 500 values and count the number of comparisons done by each of these sorts. Report the maximum, minimum, and average number of comparisons done. Write a report describing your findings. (Additional details on how to do this are given in the programming exercises in Chapter 3.)

6. Write a Sherwood-based binary search. Create an ordered list with the numbers from 1 to 10,000. Generate a series of values between 1 and 10,000 and pass them to both the standard and Sherwood binary searches. Write a report comparing the maximum, minimum, and average number of comparisons done by these two methods. The more values you test, the better your results will be.

APPENDIX A

Random Number Table

This table has random numbers between 0 and 1. If you need a random number between 0 and N, just multiply the value in the table by N. If you need a number between "low" and "high," multiply the value in the table by (high − low) and then add low to this result.

0	0.21132	20	0.92500	40	0.28029
1	0.26215	21	0.46777	41	0.73297
2	0.79253	22	0.33873	42	0.00309
3	0.28952	23	0.30228	43	0.31992
4	0.93648	24	0.27223	44	0.76521
5	0.93726	25	0.57355	45	0.47253
6	0.35606	26	0.96965	46	0.84203
7	0.16043	27	0.14291	47	0.45840
8	0.40480	28	0.56575	48	0.64955
9	0.74225	29	0.94983	49	0.87323
10	0.70183	30	0.71092	50	0.74374
11	0.41904	31	0.13687	51	0.21248
12	0.75691	32	0.19618	52	0.47449
13	0.00524	33	0.17474	53	0.30492
14	0.59544	34	0.57817	54	0.16348
15	0.51846	35	0.98727	55	0.75307
16	0.38344	36	0.80415	56	0.40643
17	0.30438	37	0.07641	57	0.73857
18	0.05253	38	0.83702	58	0.25217
19	0.16183	39	0.64725	59	0.83369

60	0.32764	100	0.47643	140	0.90770
61	0.62633	101	0.93607	141	0.27310
62	0.96292	102	0.48024	142	0.98280
63	0.34499	103	0.87140	143	0.10394
64	0.31622	104	0.56047	144	0.29839
65	0.48381	105	0.16733	145	0.17819
66	0.49887	106	0.35188	146	0.55171
67	0.42757	107	0.26331	147	0.74780
68	0.70032	108	0.00486	148	0.45567
69	0.07664	109	0.80191	149	0.76785
70	0.31314	110	0.81044	150	0.36943
71	0.47206	111	0.75385	151	0.88635
72	0.05804	112	0.82524	152	0.36378
73	0.42046	113	0.54294	153	0.76584
74	0.10886	114	0.49654	154	0.66698
75	0.11909	115	0.17114	155	0.02154
76	0.21753	116	0.28722		
77	0.78087	117	0.34354		
78	0.83914	118	0.30080		
79	0.25929	119	0.59332		
80	0.25690	120	0.90642		
81	0.67351	121	0.40683		
82	0.70712	122	0.36385		
83	0.03327	123	0.34851		
84	0.50427	124	0.44847		
85	0.86400	125	0.18594		
86	0.16592	126	0.07630		
87	0.83168	127	0.01483		
88	0.53778	128	0.92900		
89	0.36797	129	0.38400		
90	0.91867	130	0.07881		
91	0.29512	131	0.42041		
92	0.18555	132	0.61363		
93	0.45103	133	0.95413		
94	0.91849	134	0.26198		
95	0.31422	135	0.64337		
96	0.52570	136	0.01799		
97	0.62883	137	0.09945		
98	0.36850	138	0.76643		
99	0.02961	139	0.01184		

Pseudorandom Number Generation

Random numbers are useful in a number of computer applications. Any algorithmic process we may develop, however, will not produce truly random numbers because each time we use that same process, we will get the same set of numbers. This is not random but can be typically made to appear random by using a different starting point each time the program is run. This starting point will usually depend on the computer's system clock, which adds randomness based on when the program is started.

One benefit to this is that the program can be tested using a consistent starting point. This will generate the same sequence of numbers, making it easier to test the program. Once the program is believed to be error free, the change to randomize these numbers can be added.

There are a few techniques that can be used, but we will only describe one here. The mixed congruential method has a seed value that is updated each time a new number is needed. The new seed value is the basis for the next pseudorandom number. The function for this is as follows:

```
function RanNum() returns float
    seed = (seed * p + i) mod m
    return seed / m
end RanNum
```

Because of the mod operation, the seed value will always be between zero and $m - 1$. The division of the seed by m means that this process will always return a number in the range $0 \leq N < 1$.

If the three constants of p, i, and m are relatively prime, meaning that they have no factors in common, the resulting sequence will produce m different values before it repeats. For example, if p is 25,173, i is 13,849, and m is 65,536, this function will generate a series of 65,536 different values before it repeats. For testing purposes, the initial seed value can be set to zero, producing the same sequence each time. After testing, the initial seed value could be set to the seconds or milliseconds portion of the system clock to give a more random appearance to the sequence.

B.1   GENERATING NUMBERS IN A DIFFERENT RANGE

Frequently, an application of random numbers will need values in a range different from that generated by `RanNum( )`. If we need a value in the range Low $\leq N <$ High, the following equation will create them:

```
(High - Low) * RanNum( ) + Low
```

B.2   EXAMPLE APPLICATION

Suppose that we need a list of the numbers between 1 and N in a random order. There are a few ways that we could create this list.

■ B.2.1 Method 1

If we initialize the list locations to zero, as we place values in the list, "empty" locations will still be zero. In this first method, we will place the numbers from 1 to N into random places in the list. If the random location we choose is zero, it is available for the next number. If not, we just generate another random location. This gives the algorithm

```
for i = 1 to N do
   list[i] = 0
end for
for i = 1 to N do
```

```
repeat
   location = ⌊ N * RanNum() + 1 ⌋
until list[location] = 0
list[location] = i
end for
```

Even though the first bunch of values will be placed quickly, the problem with this method is that as the list fills up, it will be harder and harder to find a free location. This method, therefore, could take a long time to accomplish this simple task.

▦ B.2.2 Method 2

We saw in Method 1 that a problem occurred when the random location we chose was "full." In this alternative, if the location is full, we will just try successive locations until we find one that is free. This gives the algorithm

```
for i = 1 to N do
   list[i] = 0
end for
for i = 1 to N do
   location = ⌊ N * RanNum() + 1 ⌋
   while list[location] ≠ 0 do
      location = (location mod N) + 1
   end while
   list[location] = i
end for
```

This method will work relatively quickly, but if we have a block of filled locations, it is possible we may have a lot of values in relatively sequential order. In other words, let's say that in a list with 100 locations those from 1 to 25 are filled first in some random order. There is now a 25% chance that our next choice will be in the range of the first 25 locations, in which case, the value will be stored in location 26. If it happens again, the next value will go into location 27, then 28, and so on. This could happen anywhere in the list and has the potential of creating a block of locations that have numbers that are sequential or almost sequential.

▦ B.2.3 Method 3

In this last method, we will use the random number we generate as a counter for how many empty locations to skip in deciding on where to place the next value. This eliminates the problem of Method 1 by placing a value for each random number generated. This reduces the chance of two locations having sequential numbers, because that will only happen when the adjacent location is free and the number generated mod the number of spaces still free results in 1.

The algorithm to accomplish this is

```
for i = 1 to N do
   theList[i] = 0
end for
location = 1
freeCount = N
for i = 1 to N do
   skip = ⌊freeCount*RanNum() + 1⌋
   while skip > 0 do
      location = (location mod N) + 1
      if theList[location] = 0 then
         skip = skip - 1
      end if
   end while
   theList[location] = i
   freeCount = freeCount - 1
end for
```

In this algorithm, we use how many cells are free, and generate a random number up to that value. This is done so that we don't have to loop though the list more than one time. You should see that the while loop will always end, because even in the last case, there will be at least one empty location.

B.3 SUMMARY

This appendix gives one technique that can be used in a program to generate pseudorandom numbers and then shows how that can be used to create a random list of values. These methods could be used to create lists that can then be searched or sorted to measure the complexity of various algorithms from Chapters 2 and 3.

Results of Chapter Study Suggestions

This appendix gives the output that should be produced from a hand execution of the algorithms in this book, when using the suggested input in each chapter.

Chapter 3

Insertion Sort

The Original List:	6	2	4	7	1	3	8	5
Pass 1:	2	6	4	7	1	3	8	5
Pass 2:	2	4	6	7	1	3	8	5
Pass 3:	2	4	6	7	1	3	8	5
Pass 4:	1	2	4	6	7	3	8	5
Pass 5:	1	2	3	4	6	7	8	5
Pass 6:	1	2	3	4	6	7	8	5
Pass 7:	1	2	3	4	5	6	7	8

The Original List:	15	4	10	8	6	9	16	1	7	3	11	14	2	5	12	13
Pass 1:	4	15	10	8	6	9	16	1	7	3	11	14	2	5	12	13
Pass 2:	4	10	15	8	6	9	16	1	7	3	11	14	2	5	12	13
Pass 3:	4	8	10	15	6	9	16	1	7	3	11	14	2	5	12	13
Pass 4:	4	6	8	10	15	9	16	1	7	3	11	14	2	5	12	13
Pass 5:	4	6	8	9	10	15	16	1	7	3	11	14	2	5	12	13

Pass 6:	4	6	8	9	10	15	16	1	7	3	11	14	2	5	12	13
Pass 7:	1	4	6	8	9	10	15	16	7	3	11	14	2	5	12	13
Pass 8:	1	4	6	7	8	9	10	15	16	3	11	14	2	5	12	13
Pass 9:	1	3	4	6	7	8	9	10	15	16	11	14	2	5	12	13
Pass 10:	1	3	4	6	7	8	9	10	11	15	16	14	2	5	12	13
Pass 11:	1	3	4	6	7	8	9	10	11	14	15	16	2	5	12	13
Pass 12:	1	2	3	4	6	7	8	9	10	11	14	15	16	5	12	13
Pass 13:	1	2	3	4	5	6	7	8	9	10	11	14	15	16	12	13
Pass 14:	1	2	3	4	5	6	7	8	9	10	11	12	14	15	16	13
Pass 15:	1	2	3	4	5	6	7	8	9	10	11	12	13	14	15	16

Bubble Sort

The Original List:	6	2	4	7	1	3	8	5
Pass 1:	2	4	6	1	3	7	5	8
Pass 2:	2	4	1	3	6	5	7	8
Pass 3:	2	1	3	4	5	6	7	8
Pass 4:	1	2	3	4	5	6	7	8
Pass 5:	1	2	3	4	5	6	7	8

The Original List:	15	4	10	8	6	9	16	1	7	3	11	14	2	5	12	13
Pass 1:	4	10	8	6	9	15	1	7	3	11	14	2	5	12	13	16
Pass 2:	4	8	6	9	10	1	7	3	11	14	2	5	12	13	15	16
Pass 3:	4	6	8	9	1	7	3	10	11	2	5	12	13	14	15	16
Pass 4:	4	6	8	1	7	3	9	10	2	5	11	12	13	14	15	16
Pass 5:	4	6	1	7	3	8	9	2	5	10	11	12	13	14	15	16
Pass 6:	4	1	6	3	7	8	2	5	9	10	11	12	13	14	15	16
Pass 7:	1	4	3	6	7	2	5	8	9	10	11	12	13	14	15	16
Pass 8:	1	3	4	6	2	5	7	8	9	10	11	12	13	14	15	16
Pass 9:	1	3	4	2	5	6	7	8	9	10	11	12	13	14	15	16
Pass 10:	1	3	2	4	5	6	7	8	9	10	11	12	13	14	15	16
Pass 11:	1	2	3	4	5	6	7	8	9	10	11	12	13	14	15	16
Pass 12:	1	2	3	4	5	6	7	8	9	10	11	12	13	14	15	16

Shellsort

The Original List:	6	2	4	7	1	3	8	5
After using increment of 7:	5	2	4	7	1	3	8	6
After using increment of 3:	5	1	3	7	2	4	8	6
After using increment of 1:	1	2	3	4	5	6	7	8

The Original List:	15	4	10	8	6	9	16	1	7	3	11	14	2	5	12	13
After using increment of 15:	13	4	10	8	6	9	16	1	7	3	11	14	2	5	12	15
After using increment of 7:	1	4	3	8	6	2	5	12	7	10	11	14	9	16	13	15
After using increment of 3:	1	4	2	5	6	3	8	11	7	9	12	13	10	16	14	15
After using increment of 1:	1	2	3	4	5	6	7	8	9	10	11	12	13	14	15	16

Heapsort

The Original List:	6	2	4	7	1	3	8	5
After heap construction:	8	7	6	5	1	3	4	2
Pass 1:	7	5	6	2	1	3	4	8
Pass 2:	6	5	4	2	1	3	7	8
Pass 3:	5	3	4	2	1	6	7	8
Pass 4:	4	3	1	2	5	6	7	8
Pass 5:	3	2	1	4	5	6	7	8
Pass 6:	2	1	3	4	5	6	7	8
Pass 7:	1	2	3	4	5	6	7	8

The Original List:	15	4	10	8	6	9	16	1	7	3	11	14	2	5	12	13
After heap construction:	16	13	15	8	11	14	12	4	7	3	6	9	2	5	10	1
Pass 1:	15	13	14	8	11	9	12	4	7	3	6	1	2	5	10	16
Pass 2:	14	13	12	8	11	9	10	4	7	3	6	1	2	5	15	16
Pass 3:	13	11	12	8	6	9	10	4	7	3	5	1	2	14	15	16
Pass 4:	12	11	10	8	6	9	2	4	7	3	5	1	13	14	15	16
Pass 5:	11	8	10	7	6	9	2	4	1	3	5	12	13	14	15	16

```
Pass 6:  10  8  9  7  6  5  2  4  1   3  11  12  13  14  15  16
Pass 7:   9  8  5  7  6  3  2  4  1  10  11  12  13  14  15  16
Pass 8:   8  7  5  4  6  3  2  1  9  10  11  12  13  14  15  16
Pass 9:   7  6  5  4  1  3  2  8  9  10  11  12  13  14  15  16
Pass 10:  6  4  5  2  1  3  7  8  9  10  11  12  13  14  15  16
Pass 11:  5  4  3  2  1  6  7  8  9  10  11  12  13  14  15  16
Pass 12:  4  2  3  1  5  6  7  8  9  10  11  12  13  14  15  16
Pass 13:  3  2  1  4  5  6  7  8  9  10  11  12  13  14  15  16
Pass 14:  2  1  3  4  5  6  7  8  9  10  11  12  13  14  15  16
Pass 15:  1  2  3  4  5  6  7  8  9  10  11  12  13  14  15  16
```

Merge Sort

```
                      The Original List:  6  2  4  7  1  3  8  5
After merging location 1 to location 2:  2  6  4  7  1  3  8  5
After merging location 3 to location 4:  2  6  4  7  1  3  8  5
After merging location 1 to location 4:  2  4  6  7  1  3  8  5
After merging location 5 to location 6:  2  4  6  7  1  3  8  5
After merging location 7 to location 8:  2  4  6  7  1  3  5  8
After merging location 5 to location 8:  2  4  6  7  1  3  5  8
After merging location 1 to location 8:  1  2  3  4  5  6  7  8
```

```
        The Original List:  15   4  10   8   6   9  16   1   7   3  11  14   2   5  12  13
After merging loca-
tion 1 to location 2:        4  15  10   8   6   9  16   1   7   3  11  14   2   5  12  13
After merging loca-
tion 3 to location 4:        4  15   8  10   6   9  16   1   7   3  11  14   2   5  12  13
After merging loca-
tion 1 to location 4:        4   8  10  15   6   9  16   1   7   3  11  14   2   5  12  13
After merging loca-
tion 5 to location 6:        4   8  10  15   6   9  16   1   7   3  11  14   2   5  12  13
After merging loca-
tion 7 to location 8:        4   8  10  15   6   9   1  16   7   3  11  14   2   5  12  13
After merging loca-
tion 5 to location 8:        4   8  10  15   1   6   9  16   7   3  11  14   2   5  12  13
After merging loca-
tion 1 to location 8:        1   4   6   8   9  10  15  16   7   3  11  14   2   5  12  13
```

After merging location 9 to location 10:	1	4	6	8	9	10	15	16	3	7	11	14	2	5	12	13
After merging location 11 to location 12:	1	4	6	8	9	10	15	16	3	7	11	14	2	5	12	13
After merging location 9 to location 12:	1	4	6	8	9	10	15	16	3	7	11	14	2	5	12	13
After merging location 13 to location 14:	1	4	6	8	9	10	15	16	3	7	11	14	2	5	12	13
After merging location 15 to location 16:	1	4	6	8	9	10	15	16	3	7	11	14	2	5	12	13
After merging location 13 to location 16:	1	4	6	8	9	10	15	16	3	7	11	14	2	5	12	13
After merging location 9 to location 16:	1	4	6	8	9	10	15	16	2	3	5	7	11	12	13	14
After merging location 1 to location 16:	1	2	3	4	5	6	7	8	9	10	11	12	13	14	15	16

Quicksort

The Original List:	6	2	4	7	1	3	8	5
Pivot location 6:	5	2	4	1	3	6	8	7
Pivot location 5:	3	2	4	1	5	6	8	7
Pivot location 3:	1	2	3	4	5	6	8	7
Pivot location 1:	1	2	3	4	5	6	8	7
Pivot location 8:	1	2	3	4	5	6	7	8

The Original List:	15	4	10	8	6	9	16	1	7	3	11	14	2	5	12	13
Pivot location 15:	13	4	10	8	6	9	1	7	3	11	14	2	5	12	15	16
Pivot location 13:	12	4	10	8	6	9	1	7	3	11	2	5	13	14	15	16
Pivot location 12:	5	4	10	8	6	9	1	7	3	11	2	12	13	14	15	16
Pivot location 5:	2	4	1	3	5	9	10	7	8	11	6	12	13	14	15	16
Pivot location 2:	1	2	4	3	5	9	10	7	8	11	6	12	13	14	15	16
Pivot location 4:	1	2	3	4	5	9	10	7	8	11	6	12	13	14	15	16
Pivot location 9:	1	2	3	4	5	6	7	8	9	11	10	12	13	14	15	16
Pivot location 6:	1	2	3	4	5	6	7	8	9	11	10	12	13	14	15	16
Pivot location 7:	1	2	3	4	5	6	7	8	9	11	10	12	13	14	15	16
Pivot location 11:	1	2	3	4	5	6	7	8	9	10	11	12	13	14	15	16

Radix Sort

The Original
List: 1113 2231 3232 1211 3133 2123 2321 1312 3223 2332 1121 3312
After pass 1: 2231 1211 2321 1121 3232 1312 2332 3312 1113 3133 2123 3223
After pass 2: 1211 1312 3312 1113 2321 1121 2123 3223 2231 3232 2332 3133
After pass 3: 1113 1121 2123 3133 1211 3223 2231 3232 1312 3312 2321 2332
After pass 4: 1113 1121 1211 1312 2123 2231 2321 2332 3133 3223 3232 3312

Chapter 4

Original Polynomial

$$x^3 + 4x^2 - 3x + 2$$

Horner's Method

$$[(x + 4) * x - 3] * x + 2$$

Preprocessed Coefficients

$$
\begin{array}{r}
x + 4 \\
x - 4 \overline{)\, x^3 + 4x^2 - 3x + 2} \\
-x^3 - 4x^2 + 4x + 16 \\
\hline
x + 18
\end{array}
$$

$$[(x^2 - 4) * (x + 4)] + (x + 18)$$

Original Polynomial

$$x^7 - 8x^6 + 3x^5 + 2x^4 - 4x^3 + 5x - 7$$

Horner's Method

$$\{[(\{[(x - 8) * x + 3] * x + 2\} * x - 4) * x + 0] * x + 5\} * x - 7$$

Preprocessed Coefficients

$$
\begin{array}{r}
x^3 - \ 8x^2 + \ 3x + \ 2 \\
x^4 - 5 \overline{\smash{)}\ x^7 - 8x^6 + 3x^5 + 2x^4 - 4x^3 + \ 0x^2 + \ 5x - \ 7} \\
\underline{-x^7 + 8x^6 - 3x^5 - 2x^4 + 5x^3 - 40x^2 - 15x + 10} \\
x^3 - 40x^2 + 20x + \ 3
\end{array}
$$

$$[(x^4 - 5) * (x^3 - 8x^2 + 3x + 2)] + (x^3 - 40x^2 + 20x + 3)$$

$$
\begin{array}{r}
x - \ 8 \\
x^2 + 2 \overline{\smash{)}\ x^3 - 8x^2 + 3x + \ 2} \\
\underline{-x^3 + 8x^2 - 2x + 16} \\
x + 18
\end{array}
\qquad
\begin{array}{r}
x - \ 40 \\
x^2 + 19 \overline{\smash{)}\ x^3 - 40x^2 + 20x - \ 3} \\
\underline{-x^3 + 40x^2 - 19x + 760} \\
x + 757
\end{array}
$$

$$[(x^4 - 5) * ([(x^2 + 2) * (x - 8)] + (x + 18))] + \{[(x^2 + 19) * (x - 40)] + (x + 757)\}$$

Standard Matrix Multiplication

$$
\begin{bmatrix} 1 & 4 \\ 5 & 8 \end{bmatrix}
\begin{bmatrix} 6 & 7 \\ 3 & 2 \end{bmatrix}
=
\begin{bmatrix} 1*6 + 4*3 & 1*7 + 4*2 \\ 5*6 + 8*3 & 5*7 + 8*2 \end{bmatrix}
=
\begin{bmatrix} 18 & 15 \\ 54 & 51 \end{bmatrix}
$$

Winograd's Matrix Multiplication

Row factors: 4   40
Column factors: 18   14

Strassen's Algorithm

$x_1 = (G_{1,1} + G_{2,2}) * (H_{1,1} + H_{2,2}) = (1 + 8) * (6 + 2) = 9 * 8 = 72$

$x_2 = (G_{2,1} + G_{2,2}) * H_{1,1} = (5 + 8) * 6 = 13 * 6 = 78$

$x_3 = G_{1,1} * (H_{1,2} - H_{2,2}) = 1 * (7 - 2) = 1 * 5 = 5$

$x_4 = G_{2,2} * (H_{2,1} - H_{1,1}) = 8 * (3 - 6) = 8 * -3 = -24$

$x_5 = (G_{1,1} + G_{1,2}) * H_{2,2} = (1 + 4) * 2 = 5 * 2 = 10$

$x_6 = (G_{2,1} - G_{1,1}) * (H_{1,1} + H_{1,2}) = (5 - 1) * (6 + 7) = 4 * 13 = 52$

$x_7 = (G_{1,2} - G_{2,2}) * (H_{2,1} + H_{2,2}) = (4 - 8) * (3 + 2) = -4 * 5 = -20$

$R_{1,1} = x_1 + x_4 - x_5 + x_7 = 72 + -24 - 10 + -20 = 18$

$R_{2,1} = x_2 + x_4 = 78 + -24 = 54$

$R_{1,2} = x_3 + x_5 = 5 + 10 = 15$

$R_{2,2} = x_1 + x_3 - x_2 + x_6 = 72 + 5 - 78 + 52 = 51$

Gauss-Jordan Method

$$\begin{bmatrix} 3 & 9 & 6 & 21 \\ 5 & 3 & 22 & 23 \\ 2 & 5 & 7 & 26 \end{bmatrix}$$

$$\begin{bmatrix} 1 & 3 & 2 & 7 \\ 5 & 3 & 22 & 23 \\ 2 & 5 & 7 & 26 \end{bmatrix}$$

$$\begin{bmatrix} 1 & 3 & 2 & 7 \\ 0 & -12 & 12 & -12 \\ 0 & 2 & 3 & 12 \end{bmatrix}$$

$$\begin{bmatrix} 1 & 3 & 2 & 7 \\ 0 & 1 & -1 & 1 \\ 0 & 2 & 3 & 12 \end{bmatrix}$$

$$\begin{bmatrix} 1 & 0 & 5 & 4 \\ 0 & 1 & -1 & 1 \\ 0 & 0 & 5 & 10 \end{bmatrix}$$

$$\begin{bmatrix} 1 & 0 & 5 & 4 \\ 0 & 1 & -1 & 1 \\ 0 & 0 & 1 & 2 \end{bmatrix}$$

$$\begin{bmatrix} 1 & 0 & 0 & -6 \\ 0 & 1 & 0 & 3 \\ 0 & 0 & 1 & 2 \end{bmatrix}$$

Chapter 5

Knuth-Morris-Pratt

The pattern is

abcabc

The fail array contains

0 1 1 1 2 3

Boyer–Moore

The pattern is

abcbccabc

After the first loop the jump array contains

17   16   15   14   13   12   11   10   9

After the second loop the jump array contains

17   16   15   14   13   12   6   4   1

After the second loop the link array contains

7   8   7   8   8   9   9   9   10

After the third loop the jump array contains

14   13   12   11   10   9   6   4   1

After the fourth loop the jump array contains

14   13   12   11   10   9   6   4   1

Chapter 6

Depth-first traversal from node A

A, B, G, C, D, H, L, K, J, F, I, E

Breadth-first traversal from node A

A, B, E, F, G, I, C, L, D, H, K, J

Dijkstra-Prim minimum spanning tree trace

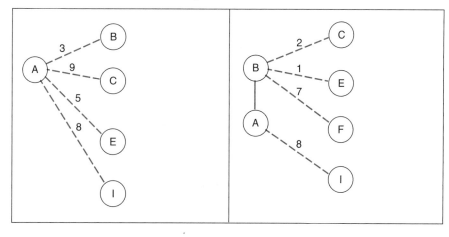

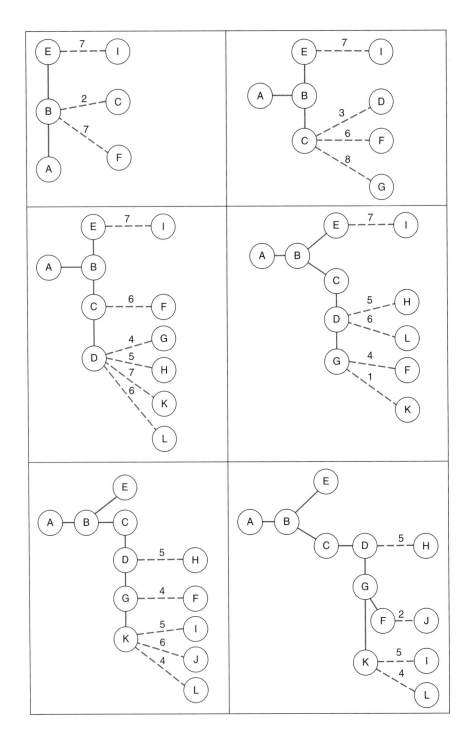

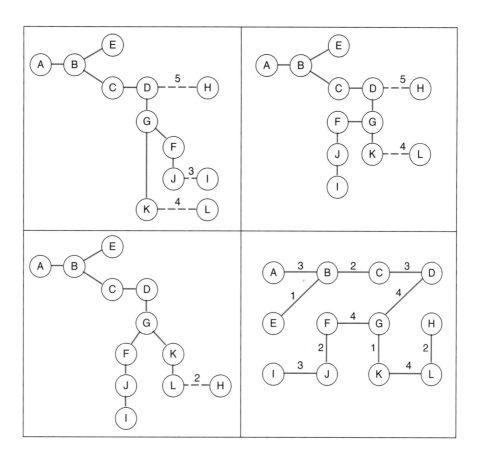

Kruskal's minimum spanning tree trace

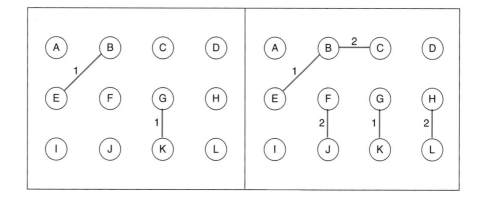

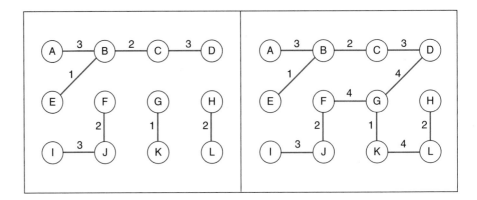

Dijkstra's shortest-path algorithm

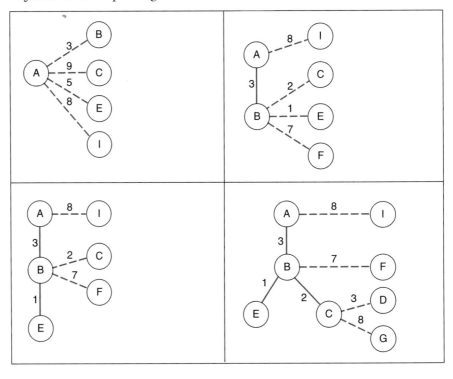

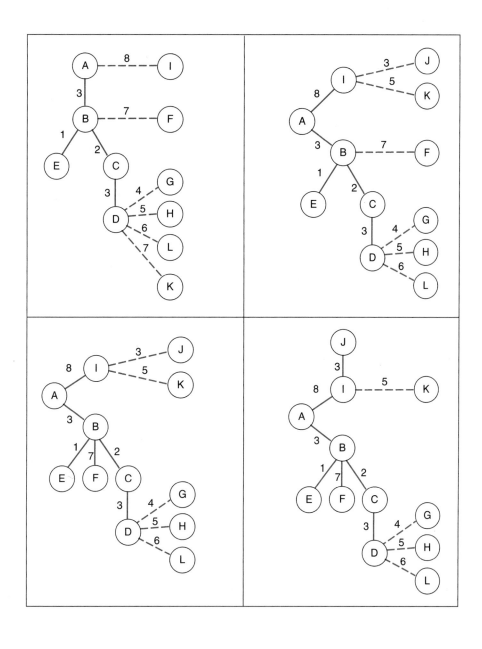

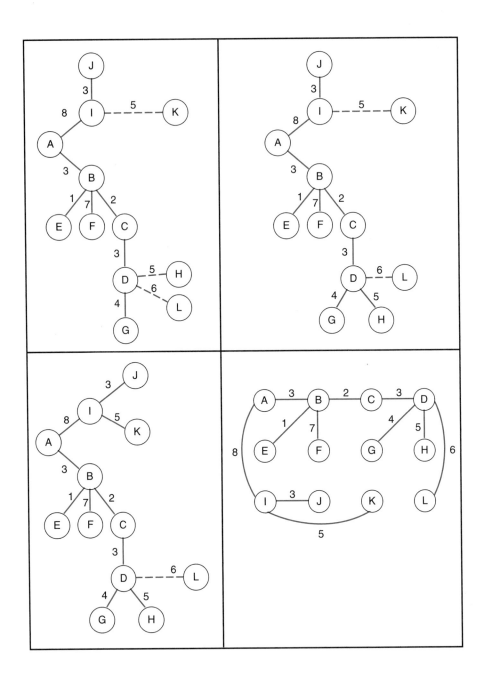

References

Chapter 1. Analysis Basics

Aho, A., Hopcroft, J., and Ullman, J. *The Design and Analysis of Computer Algorithms*. Addison–Wesley, Reading, MA, 1974.

Baase, S. and Van Gelder, A. *Computer Algorithms*. Addison Wesley Longman, Reading, MA, 2000.

Cormen, T., Leiserson, C., and Rivest, R. *Introduction to Algorithms*. McGraw-Hill, New York, 1990.

Knuth, D. "Big Omicron and Big Omega and Big Theta," *SIGACT News*, 8(2), pp. 18–24, 1976.

Parberry, I. *Problems on Algorithms*. Prentice Hall, Englewood Cliffs, NJ, 1995.

Purdom, P. and Brown, C. *The Analysis of Algorithms*. Holt, Rinehart and Winston, New York, 1985.

Sedgewick, R. *Algorithms,* 2d ed. Addison–Wesley, Reading, MA, 1988.

Chapter 2. Searching Algorithms

Knuth, D. E. *The Art of Computer Programming: Volume 3 Sorting and Searching,* 2d ed. Addison–Wesley, Reading, MA, 1998.

Chapter 3. Sorting Algorithms

Hoare, C. A. R. "Quicksort," *Computer Journal*, 5(1), pp. 10–15, 1962.

Knuth, D. E. *The Art of Computer Programming: Volume 3 Sorting and Searching,* 2d ed. Addison–Wesley, Reading, MA, 1998.

Shell, D. L. "A High-Speed Sorting Procedure," *Communications of the ACM*, 2(7), pp. 30– 32, July 1959.

Williams, J. "Algorithm 232: Heapsort," *Communications of the ACM*, 7(6), pp. 347–348, 1964.

Chapter 4. Numeric Algorithms

Strassen, V. "Gaussian Elimination Is Not Optimal," *Numerische Mathematik*, 13, pp. 354– 356, 1969.

Winograd, S. "On the Number of Multiplications Necessary to Compute Certain Functions," *Journal of Pure and Applied Mathematics*, 23, pp. 165–179, 1970.

Chapter 5. Matching Algorithms

Aho, A. and Corasick, M. "Efficient String Matching: An Aid to Bibliographic Search," *Communications of the ACM*, 18(6), pp. 333–340, 1975.

Boyer, R. and Moore, J. "A Fast String Searching Algorithm," *Communications of the ACM*, 20(10), pp. 762–772, 1977.

Crochemore, M. and Rytter, W. *Text Algorithms*. Oxford University Press, New York, 1994.

Hall, P. and Dowling, G. "Approximate String Matching," *Computing Surveys*, 12(4), pp. 381–402, 1980.

Knuth, D., Morris, J., and Pratt, V. "Fast Pattern Matching in Strings," *SIAM Journal on Computing*, 6(2), pp. 323–350, 1977.

Landau, G. and Vishkin, U. "Introducing Efficient Parallelism into Approximate String Matching and a New Serial Algorithm," *Proceedings of the 18th Annual ACM Symposium on Theory of Computing*, pp. 220–230, 1986.

Smit, G. "A Comparison of Three String Matching Algorithms," *Software— Practice and Experience*, 12, pp. 57–66, 1982.

Chapter 6. Graph Algorithms

Dijkstra, E. "A Note on Two Problems in Connexion with Graphs," *Numerische Mathematik*, 1, pp. 269–271, 1959.

Even, S. *Graph Algorithms*. Computer Science Press, Rockville, MD, 1979.

Gibbons, A. *Algorithmic Graph Theory*. Cambridge University Press, Cambridge, England, 1985.

Hopcroft, J. and Tarjan, R. "Dividing a Graph into Triconnected Components," *SIAM Journal on Computing*, 2(3), pp. 135–157, 1973.

Khuller, S. and Raghavachari, B. "Basic Graph Algorithms," in Atallah, M. (ed.), *Algorithms and Theory of Computation Handbook*, pp. 6-1–6-23. CRC Press, New York, 1999.

Prim, R. "Shortest Connection Networks and Some Generalizations," *Bell System Technical Journal*, 36, pp. 1389–1401, 1957.

Tarjan, R. "Depth-First Search and Linear Graph Algorithms," *SIAM Journal on Computing*, 1(2), pp. 146–160, 1972.

Chapter 7. Parallel Algorithms

Akl, S. *Parallel Sorting.* Academic Press, Orlando, FL, 1985.

Akl, S. *The Design and Analysis of Parallel Algorithms.* Prentice Hall, Englewood Cliffs, NJ, 1989.

Fortune, S. and Wyllie, J. "Parallelism in Random Access Machines," *Proceedings of the Tenth Annual ACM Symposium on Theory of Computing*, pp. 114–118, 1978.

Goldschlager, L. "A Unified Approach to Models of Synchronous Parallel Machines," *Proceedings of the Tenth Annual ACM Symposium on Theory of Computing*, pp. 89–94, 1978.

Greenlaw, R., Hoover, H., and Ruzzo, W. *Limits to Parallel Computation: P-Completeness Theory.* Oxford University Press, New York, 1995.

Karp, R. and Ramachandran, V. "A Survey of Parallel Algorithms and Shared Memory Machines," in vanLeeuwen, A. (ed.), *Handbook of Theoretical Computer Science: Algorithms and Complexity*, pp. 869–941. Elsevier, New York, 1990.

Kruskal, C. "Searching, Merging, and Sorting in Parallel Computation," *IEEE Transactions on Computers*, 32(10), pp. 942–946, 1983.

Leighton, F. *Introduction to Parallel Algorithms and Architectures: Arrays, Trees, Hypercubes.* Morgan Kaufmann Publishers, San Mateo, CA, 1992.

Miller, R. and Boxer, L. *A Unified Approach to Sequential and Parallel Algorithms.* Prentice Hall, Inc., Upper Saddle River, NJ, 2000.

Miller, R. and Stout, Q. *Parallel Algorithms for Regular Architectures: Meshes and Pyramids.* The MIT Press, Cambridge, MA, 1996.

Quinn, M. and Deo, N. "Parallel Graph Algorithms," *ACM Computing Surveys*, 16(3), pp. 319–348, 1984.

Shiloach, Y. and Vishkin, U. "Finding the Maximum, Merging, and Sorting in a Parallel Computation Model," *Journal of Algorithms*, 2, pp. 88–102, 1981.

Chapter 8. Nondeterministic Algorithms

Cook, S. "The Complexity of Theorem Proving Procedures," *Proceedings of the Third Annual ACM Symposium on Theory of Computing*, pp. 151–158, 1971.

Garey, M. and Johnson, D. *Computers and Intractability: A Guide to the Theory of NP- Completeness.* W. H. Freeman, San Francisco, CA, 1979.

Karp, R. "Reducibility Among Combinatorial Problems," in Miller, R. and Thatcher, J. (eds.), *Complexity of Computer Computations*, pp. 85–104, Plenum Press, New York, 1972.

Lawler, E., Lenstra, J., Kan, A., and Schmoys, D. (eds.). *The Traveling Salesman Problem*. Wiley, New York, 1985.

Chapter 9. Other Algorithmic Techniques

Bellman, R. *Dynamic Programming*. Princeton University Press, Princeton, NJ, 1957.

Bellman, R. and Dreyfus, S. *Applied Dynamic Programming*. Princeton University Press, Princeton, NJ, 1962.

Bentley, J., Johnson, D., Leighton, F., and McGeoch, C. "An Experimental Study of Bin Packing," *Proceedings of the 21st Annual Allerton Conference on Communication, Control, and Computing*, pp. 51–60, 1983.

Brassard, G. and Bratley, P. *Algorithmics: Theory and Practice*. Prentice Hall, Englewood Cliffs, NJ, 1988.

Garey, M., Graham, R., and Ullman, J. "Worst-Case Analysis of Memory Allocation Algorithms," *Proceedings of the Fourth Annual ACM Symposium on Theory of Computing*, pp. 143–150, 1976.

Garey, M. and Johnson, D. "The Complexity of Near-Optimal Graph Coloring," *Journal of the ACM*, 23(10), pp. 43–49, 1976.

Hall, A. "On an experimental determination of π," *Messenger of Mathematics*, 2, pp. 113– 114, 1973.

Hochbaum, D. (ed.) *Approximation Algorithms for NP-Hard Problems*. PWS Publishing, Boston, MA, 1997.

Johnson, D. "Fast Allocation Algorithms," *Proceedings of the Thirteenth Annual Symposium on Switching and Automata Theory*, pp. 144–154, 1972.

Johnson, D. "Approximation Algorithms for Combinatorial Problems," *Proceedings of the Fifth Annual ACM Symposium on Theory of Computing*, pp. 38–49, 1973.

Johnson, D. "Worst-Case Behavior of Graph Coloring Algorithms," *Proceedings of the Fifth Southeastern Conference on Combinatorics, Graph Theory, and Computing*, pp. 513–528, Utilitas Mathematica Publishing, Winnipeg, Canada, 1974.

Lawler, E., Lenstra, J., Kan, A., and Schmoys, D. (eds.). *The Traveling Salesman Problem*. Wiley, New York, 1985.

Leclerc, G. *Essai d'arithmétique morale*, 1777.

Metropolis, I. and Ulam, S. "The Monte Carlo Method," *Journal of the American Statistical Association*, 44(247), pp. 335–341, 1949.

Sahni, S. "Approximate Algorithms for the 0/1 Knapsack Problem," *Journal of the ACM*, 22(10), pp. 115–124, 1975.

Sahni, S. "Algorithms for Scheduling Independent Tasks," *Journal of the ACM*, 23(1), pp. 116–127, 1976.

Wigderson, A. "Improving the Performance Guarantee for Approximate Graph Coloring," *Journal of the ACM*, 30(4), pp. 729–735, 1983.

Yao, F. "Speed-Up in Dynamic Programming," *SIAM Journal on Algebraic and Discrete Methods*, 3(4), pp. 532–540, 1982.